ARCHITECT'S

JOB

BOOK

Seventh Edition

RIBA Publications

Architect's Job Book
Seventh Edition

© RIBA Enterprises, 2002

Published by RIBA Enterprises Ltd, 1–3 Dufferin Street, London, EC1Y 8NA

ISBN 1 85946 080 1

Product Code: 21008
First published 2000

Editor: Sarah Lupton
Publisher: Geoff Denner
Commissioning Editor: Matthew Thompson
Project Manager: Ramona Lamport
Design and typesetting by Hobbs the Printers, Hampshire
Printed and bound by Hobbs the Printers, Hampshire

Contents

E   Final Proposals   123

Description
Key obligations from SFA/99
Actions

F   Production Information   147

Description
Key obligations from SFA/99
Actions

G   Tender Documentation   169

Description
Key obligations from SFA/99
Actions

H   Tender Action   181

Description
Key obligations from SFA/99
Actions

EDITOR'S NOTES

Seventh edition

This edition of the *Job Book* takes as its basis the revised *Plan of Work*, which first appeared in the 1999 RIBA *Standard Forms of Appointment*, and which is now published in expanded form in *The Architect's Plan of Work for the procurement of feasibility studies, a fully designed building project, employer's requirements and contractor's proposals* (RIBA Publications, 2000).

Each section has been reformatted to combine the 'actions', 'action checks' and 'watchpoints' of previous editions to form a tabular introduction. The watchpoints have been highlighted in purple for ease of reference. The tables form an accessible summary of the key activities that are likely to occur in each Work Stage, and refer to more detailed explanatory sections in other parts of the *Job Book*. The amount of cross-referencing has been increased, and an index introduced, to make it easier to find information quickly. References to 'further reading' are introduced in many sections.

The sixth edition was a major overhaul, addressing new forms of appointment and procurement, the implications of the Latham report and new legislation such as the CDM regulations. In the five years since that edition, there have been considerable further changes, and the text of the *Job Book* has been updated to take account of these changes as appropriate. At the same time care has been taken to retain the straightforward and timeless advice which has made the *Job Book* a popular source of help for architects in the past.

Procurement

The work of the Construction Industry Board in securing 'a culture of cooperation, teamwork and continuous improvement in the industry's performance' with its principal objective 'to implement, monitor and review the recommendations of Sir Michael Latham's report *Constructing the Team*' (CIB, 2000) has had a significant impact on the industry. Included in this work has been the publication of an extensive series of guides prepared by Working Groups, which includes Codes of Practice for many activities such as the selection of main contractors. This work was given further impetus by the Egan report *Rethinking Construction* (DETR 1998), with emphasis on improving efficiency and partnering.

Legislation

There have been several new Acts relating to terms of appointment and building contracts. In particular the Housing Grants, Construction and Regeneration Act 1996, represents a significant government intervention in the terms that may be agreed regarding payment and dispute resolution. The Late Payment of Commercial Debts (Interest) Act 1998 and the Contracts (Rights of Third Parties) Act 1999 also have an impact on contracts within the industry. It is no longer possible to agree ad hoc terms and assume that the obligations set down are the only ones that apply to that agreement, and it is therefore essential that architects understand the significance of these new acts.

In addition to the above, the last few years have seen the introduction of the Party Wall etc Act 1996, the coming into force of the second phase of the Disability Discrimination Act, and numerous changes to secondary legislation and guidance documents such as the Approved Documents to the Building Regulations and the Planning Policy Guidance Notes.

Standard forms   An entirely new suite of RIBA appointment documents was published in 1999, which takes account of the new legislation mentioned above, of changes in practice, and changes to the RIBA and ARB Codes of Conduct. In addition there have been major changes to all the JCT standard forms of contract to both take account of the new legislation and to implement many of the recommendations of the Latham report. Several new forms of contract have been published, and new forms are being generated to accommodate developments in procurement methods.

Terminology   The new *Plan of Work* has adopted the terminology of the CIB Working Group reports, and the *Job Book* in turn reflects the terminology and structure of these documents. The *Plan of Work* now includes a separate section on Design and Build, and the *Job Book* refers to traditional procurement, design and build and management procurement. Although the *Job Book* refers throughout to the Standard Forms of Appointment published by the RIBA and the forms of contract prepared by JCT Ltd, it is intended to be of wider application, and much of the advice would be helpful whatever forms have been adopted.

Sustainability   In parallel with current thinking on exploring new processes with the aim of improving efficiency, other concerns are increasingly apparent — in particular, a growing awareness in the industry concerning environmental and social sustainability. Sandy Halliday's *Green Guide to the Architect's Job Book* was prepared in relation to the sixth edition of the *Job Book*, and would be equally applicable to this publication. Although some of her key points have been absorbed into this text, the *Green Guide* should always be consulted for a more detailed understanding of how sustainability issues can be incorporated in the Work Stages.

Using the *Job Book*   The checklists set out in the *Job Book* for each Work Stage are intended to be generic. Although they are founded in SFA/99, even when using this form of appointment the tasks that may be appropriate or necessary at each stage will vary considerably depending on the context and the nature of the project undertaken. It may well be that many actions listed are not necessary in a given situation, or that additional work may be essential. Furthermore, many architects may amend SFA/99, use a different form, or use entirely different terms of appointment. The actions lists should therefore always be reviewed at the beginning of each specific project and Work Stage.

Quality Management   The *Job Book* is not, of course, intended to constitute a quality management system in itself, and reference should be made to other authoritative publications, for example Tim Jefferies' *Model for a Quality Management System*. Nevertheless some parts of the *Job Book*, for example the checklists, standard forms and charts, may be relevant to an office quality system. It should always be remembered, however, that the *Job Book* checklists are not comprehensive, and though they may form a useful starting point they must be adapted to the specific needs of a particular practice.

The Editor would like to thank Stanley Cox, Tim Jefferies, Roland Phillips, Keith Snook and Manos Stellakis for their helpful comments on drafts of this text.

LIST OF FIGURES

PRE-AGREEMENT

Professional services

Actions

Initial discussions
Bidding for the project
Negotiating terms
Finishing the appointment

Core Material

PRE/CM1	Practice statement
PRE/CM2	Selection processes
PRE/CM3	Outline of possible roles for the architect
PRE/CM4	Current legislation relevant to appointments and fee recovery
PRE/CM5	RIBA Forms of Appointment

PRE-AGREEMENT

Professional services

There is increased potential within the industry for the architect to perform a wide variety of roles. Great care is therefore needed to secure any commission on the right basis as it can no longer always be assumed that 'the normal services will apply', or that there will be a common understanding between architect and client as to what the 'normal services' might mean.

In any individual case the services will vary according to the expectations and requirements of the client. They will usually relate to a specific building project, however they could be in the form of general advice or consultancy work, in fields such as conservation, premises management, environmental or access auditing, or corporate image design or development.

If relating to a specific project the services will be affected by the nature and scale of the building project, the management structure set up for the project, and by the procurement method adopted. The architect could be engaged from inception through to completion, or perhaps for specific services at a single stage.

Given this wide diversity of potential roles, it is important that the services to be provided in each case are identified accurately and with care.

The job or commission can be secured through a variety of methods. For example, it could be as a result of a direct approach made to a potential client or an invitation to discuss and negotiate or to bid in competition. This might concern only the architect, or it might call for a joint submission with other professionals or partners from commerce and industry.

Where securing a commission is subject to competitive tendering, it is essential to know what criteria the client intends to apply when evaluating tenders, and what procedures will govern the submission. A careful assessment of resources required will be crucial to make realistic costings and establish viability before tendering.

Whatever the method of securing the commission, the importance of having an agreement in writing cannot be emphasised enough. It is a requirement of both the RIBA and the ARB Codes of Conduct, and it is normal practice to use one of the standard forms published by the RIBA. If these are not used then great care must be taken to allow for the effect of legislation which directly regulates many aspects of an architect's appointment, particularly payment provisions and dispute resolution.

If a quality system is maintained by the practice, ensure that the procedures for establishing the Forms of Appointment, and carrying out their subsequent review, are followed. (See Sections 2 and 3 of Tim Jefferies' (1999) *Model for a Quality Management System*, London, RIBA Publications.)

It may be that the client is interested in setting up a partnering agreement at an early stage. This may prove useful, particularly where a series of projects are envisaged. Partnering is a 'structured management approach to facilitate team working' (CIB (1997) *Partnering in the Team: A report by working group 12 of the CIB*) and would not replace the need for a clear written agreement with the client.

Sometimes, where the architect is contacted at a very early stage, the nature of the project and the scope of the services required may be so unclear that it is not practicable to use one of the standard forms. In these cases it may be better to agree the preliminary services by letter, but it is essential that the services are confirmed in writing.

A successful working relationship depends on the roles of all parties being established clearly from the outset, and without ambiguities that so frequently lead to misunderstandings and conflict. The actions listed below could be relevant before the appointment of an architect, whether for full or partial services, under any *Plan of Work* stage or part of a stage, and are generally applicable regardless of procurement method.

Actions

	Reference	To do
Prepare and activate strategy to target potential clients. This may include a practice statement.	PRE/CM1	☐

Initial discussions

Respond at once to approaches from potential clients.

If it is of interest, ask for further particulars, including details of the selection process to be adopted. Establish as much as possible by telephone or in writing.

PRE/CM2 ☐

Avoid spending unnecessary time on 'long shots' or unsuitable commissions. The client should be able to explain enough of what they have in mind, particularly with regard to how they feel an architect may be able to help them, to establish whether a meeting would be worthwhile. In particular, avoid being drawn into giving free advice.

Arrange a preliminary meeting, if appropriate, to discuss requirements.

☐

The initial meetings between client and architect will set the tone for the future working relationship. Clarify your respective roles and responsibilities.

Consider your reaction to the client and the project.

Are you in general sympathy with the client's needs and aspirations — if not, will this have an adverse effect on your work? Are the prospects good for building up a good understanding with the client? This is the stage at which key issues of a philosophical or political nature can be raised, such as the client's level of concern regarding environmental issues, or their interest and involvement in new procurement approaches such as partnering.

Be properly equipped with information about your practice and its work.

Remember that a professional appointment is a process of mutual selection: have ready a practice brochure with details of the practice's track record, personnel and a truthful statement about its expertise, experience and resources.

Take care when offering professional advice gratuitously to friends and acquaintances. The duty of care that you owe is not related to the size of fee. Even if there is no fee, you might still have a duty in tort.

Do not be casual in your dealings and inadvertently let yourself in for more than you intended. Under certain circumstances informal dealings can be construed as giving rise to contractual relationships. A contractual duty, if breached, could result in loss and an ensuing claim.

Warn the client at once if design requirements, timing and budget seem unrealistic. Remember that a failure to warn could leave you open to allegations of negligence. Explain fully what you advise should be done. Avoid jargon, and take care not to seem patronising or arrogant.

Identify the client, and the status and authority of any client representative. □

Note whether an individual is acting in a private capacity or representing a charitable organisation, consortium or a company, etc. If a representative, then is he or she acting under what authority and with what power?

In the case of a commercial or industrial client, make certain precisely where the ultimate authority resides. For example, the client's company might exist within a parent body. If the company fails and is unable to pay your fees, the benefits of your work could still be available to the parent body, which might have no legal obligation for the unpaid fees.

Where the client is a couple (married or unmarried), or a group of individuals who have formed some kind of association, be sure that you know who has authority to make decisions, give instructions and sign cheques.

Check whether the project is for direct occupation by the client or more in the nature of a speculative venture. Enquire about the possible involvement of a user client who may expect to be consulted. □

Bear in mind that working with a group of people on a community type project, or one which involves a user client, may entail a great deal of extra work, some of it outside normal working hours.

Check the experience of the client. □
Some clients know exactly what is needed and what they can realistically expect from consultants, while some may never have built before — this may be a once in a lifetime experience.

Be particularly careful in initial meetings with inexperienced clients. Remember that your legal duty of care can relate to the known experience or inexperience of your client.

Check the soundness of the client. ☐

Make discreet enquiries about the prospective client's business record, and apparent financial position. Is there any known tendency to questionable business dealings or hasty resort to threats of legal action? What nature of client are they? What previous projects have they commissioned? What were they like to work with?

Check whether any other architects were formerly involved with the project. If so, check that their appointment has been properly terminated and notify them in writing of your own appointment, when this has been formally concluded. Fig. PRE-AG 1 is a specimen letter. ☐

Fig. PRE-AG 1   Specimen letter to architect formerly engaged on project

We understand that you were engaged by (the clients) to work on this project but that the arrangement has been properly terminated.

Under Rule 3.5 of the RIBA Code of Professional Conduct we are obliged to notify you that (the clients) have now appointed us as architects for this project.

We would be pleased to have your written confirmation that there are no matters outstanding which should be drawn to our attention at this stage.

Bidding for the project

Check the client's requirements for the submission.   **PRE/CM2**   ☐

Make sure that if involved in competitive fee bidding, it is on fair and equitable terms, and that the given information is sufficient to permit preparation of a realistic bid. Confirm in writing any reservations or requests for further information.

Agree a common policy between fellow consultants if the fee bid is to be a team effort. Agree compatible working methods, procedures, and information format. ☐

Assess carefully what the project will require in terms of practice resources before you quote a fee. Do you have the necessary skills and staff? Can they be made available for the particular programme? If it looks as if you will be overstretched, can you buy in skills or sublet work? Fig. PRE-AG 2 is a project resource planning sheet. Whether prepared manually or as a spreadsheet this could provide essential information for a fee bid, and be a tool for monitoring small jobs.

☐

Decide whether it is realistic to undertake the commission with confidence that the timetable, quality of services and the budget can be met. What are the risks, and can they be traded off against likely benefits to the practice if the commission is won?

☐

Identify the likely role and nature of professional services needed. Will you be acting as lead consultant, as design leader, as a consultant team member, as consultant to the Employer Client in design and build, as provider of information to the Contractor Client in design and build, or even as coordinator or manager for separate trades contracts? Make an appraisal and consider carefully the implications.

PRE/CM3, CM4, CM5, CM6, CM7

☐

Examine carefully any terms or conditions proposed by the client.

☐

Be wary of conditions which might imply a level of services beyond what can be reasonably provided for the fee.

Check there is no conflict with professional Codes.

☐

Consider whether the terms and conditions follow normal practice or whether there is specially drafted wording which shows considerable client bias.

☐

Check what the client has asked for concerning indemnities, third party warranties, liability period, levels of professional indemnity cover, etc and consider whether these are reasonable or acceptable. If being considered for the commission depends on evidence of PII cover well in excess of that presently arranged, discuss with insurers the possibility of providing such cover as an interim measure, with the certainty of extending it if and when the commission is secured.

☐

Take expert advice from a construction lawyer and insurers if the client seeks to impose onerous conditions.

Design and build When acting for Contractor Clients in design and build, establish who carries the liability for design and to what extent. The contractor might not be insured against failures of design, and the liability might extend beyond the normal professional duty to exercise reasonable skill and care. ☐

Design and build When acting for Employer Clients in design and build, be wary if asked to check the Contractor's Proposals against the Employer's Requirements, and avoid 'approving' drawings submitted by contractor or sub-contractors. ☐

Take expert advice on whether terms proposed by the client comply with current legislation, unless it is clear that they follow those currently recommended by the RIBA. It is particularly important to check that terms regarding payment, notices and dispute resolution comply with the Housing Grants, Reconstruction and Development Act, and that a provision to deal with the Contracts (Rights of Third Parties) Act has been incorporated.

Remember that the law requires a professional to exercise reasonable skill and care. Resist any attempt to get you to guarantee what might not be attainable, e.g. that a building will be 'fit for the purpose intended'.

Do not enter into collateral agreements with third parties or give indemnities which impose greater liabilities than those which arise out of the agreement already entered into with your client.

If no terms are stipulated, draw up terms of appointment that could be proposed. ☐

Consider the minimum and maximum level of services which might be appropriate for the project, but in order to remain competitive keep strictly within the stated requirements when compiling the proposal.

Use a Standard Form of Appointment prepared by the RIBA, exactly as recommended in the guidance notes. If for some reason this is not possible, take expert advice on the terms to be proposed.

When setting out in writing the professional services you agree to carry out, make absolutely clear what is not included. Leave no room for misunderstandings, particularly when dealing with new or inexperienced clients.

Fig. PRE-AG 2   Specimen project resource planning sheet

Job no: _____   Job title: _____

Project resource planning sheet

Budget cost _____   Commencement _____   Completion _____

Estimated number of site visits _____

Stage		A–B	C	D	E	F–G	H	J	K–L	
Start										
Finish										
STAFF grade/name	£ per hr	Hours	Hours	Hours	Hours	Hours	Hours	Hours	Hours	Total £
Ivor Barch – partner	100	10	5							1,500
C. Smith – job architect	75	10	25	40	40	40			25	13,500
W. Bloggs – technician	25	2	10	10	120	200				8,550
Stage Total										
EXPENSES										

1. Estimate duration of Work Stages with start and finish entries.
2. List staff assigned to job, grade, unit rate and estimated hours under Work Stages. Rates should include for overheads, profit and reserves.
3. Enter estimated expenses likely to be incurred against headings such as car mileage, travel fares, subsistence, etc.

| **Total** | | | | | | | | | | |

With a consumer client, always arrange to meet and talk through the terms proposed in detail, and make sure your client fully understands them, otherwise under the Unfair Terms in Consumer Contracts Regulations 1994 certain terms may not be considered 'individually negotiated' and therefore become void.

Negotiating terms

Respond to the client with the fee proposal, be prepared to negotiate if appropriate.

Price the client's stated requirements at the outset, no more and no less. You will need to be competitive but if you quote a fee that is unrealistically low it might mean that you have to cut corners and the quality of service you are able to provide will suffer accordingly. There are obvious risks in putting yourself under this kind of pressure.

Take the time and trouble to explain fully to a client what you are proposing and why. For example, statutory obligations and necessary consents, production information, procedures for appointing contractor and sub-contractors may well seem daunting to the uninitiated. It is also sometimes wise to spell out the obvious — for example, that there is no such thing as a maintenance-free building and that regular and adequate maintenance is assumed when designing.

Be realistic when negotiating. A successful negotiator knows how far to go and when to stop. The aim should never be to secure a commission at any price.

Finalising the appointment

Decide whether to accept the commission if offered and confirm it in writing.

Submit appointment documents for signature before commencing work. Ensure that future review of the appointment is covered in case it is required. Where a standard form is used, follow the guidance notes exactly.

Should it prove premature to enter into a formal Memorandum at this point, when for example the extent of professional involvement cannot yet be determined, then enter into a preliminary agreement as an interim measure, clearly identified as such (see Fig. PRE-AG 3)

Keep adequate and appropriate records of all dealings connected with the project. Never sacrifice proper paperwork for the sake of assumed goodwill. File everything systematically so that items can be easily found and retrieved. Never rely completely on material held on computer: it is essential to have fail-safe back-up arrangements to protect both work in progress and records which may be needed for future reference.

Never assume that the commission is won until you have received written confirmation of acceptance.

Fig. PRE-AG 3   Specimen letter confirming preliminary agreement

An interim measure only to be used in particular circumstances.

We are writing about the terms of our appointment for this project.

You have asked us to undertake some preliminary services so that the project may proceed, and we confirm these as follows:

. . . .

. . . .

It is understood that if you subsequently instruct us to undertake other preliminary services, you will confirm this in writing. All these services will be charged on a time basis at the following rates:

Principals	£ .... per ....
Senior architectural staff	£ .... per ....
Other architectural staff	£ .... per ....
Administrative staff	£ .... per ....

In addition, the following expenses will be charged:

. . . .

. . . .

Invoices will be submitted monthly. VAT is chargeable, where applicable, at the current standard rate on all fees and expenses.

For the above services to be provided effectively, you will also need to appoint:

. . . .

. . . .

You should note that other financial commitments at this stage may include:

. . . .

. . . .

We will provide these services on the basis of the conditions included in the Form of Agreement, a copy of which is enclosed [if appropriate at this stage].

We envisage that this preliminary appointment will continue for approximately .... months while we conclude the principal Agreement. When the principal Agreement has been entered into, this appointment will be subsumed into it, and fees invoiced under this letter will rank as payments on account.

Please confirm your acceptance of the appointment set out in this letter by signing the enclosed copy and returning it to us.

References and further reading

Byrom, R. J. (2001) *Construction Companion to Terms of Engagement and Fees*, London, RIBA Publications.

CIB (1997) *Partnering in the Team: A report by working group 12 of the CIB*, London, Thomas Telford Publishing.

CIB (2000) *Selecting consultants for the Team: balancing quality and price*, London, Thomas Telford Publishing.

CIC/RIBA (1999) *Guidance for Clients to Quality Based Selection*, London, RIBA Publications.

Cox, S. (2002) *A Guide to Sound Practice*, London, RIBA Enterprises.

Cox, S. and Hamilton, A. (1998) *Architect's Handbook of Practice Management*, London, RIBA Publications.

Emmitt, S. (1999) *Architectural Management in practice: a competitive approach*, London, Pearson Education.

JCT (2001) Practice Note 4 (series 2): *Partnering*, London, RIBA Publications.

Jefferies, T. (1999) *A Model for a Quality Management System*, London, RIBA Publications.

Luder, O. (1999) *Keeping Out of Trouble*, London, RIBA Publications.

Lupton, S. and Stellakis, M (eds) (2002) *Guidance for Clients on Health and Safety: The Construction (Design and Management) Regulations 1994*, London, RIBA Enterprises.

Martin, I. (1999) *Marketing on a Shoestring*, London, RIBA Publications.

Philips, R. (1999) *The Architect's Contract: a guide to the RIBA standard forms of appointment*, London, RIBA Publications.

RIBA (1997) *Code of Professional Conduct and Standard of Professional Performance*, London, RIBA Publications.

RIBA (1999) *A Client's Guide to Engaging and Architect, including Guidance on fees*, London, RIBA Publications.

RIBA (1999) *A Client's Guide to Engaging and Architect: Small Works including Guidance on fees*, London, RIBA Publications.

PRE/CM1

Practice statement

Architects intending to approach, or being approached by new clients need to have information about their practice ready to hand. General information might be immediately accessible from a practice brochure, or from entries in the RIBA *Directory of Practices*. In some cases where the practice has a quality management system, the quality manual will contain much relevant information and could be issued to the client. Detailed information required in the context of a particular project might need to be specially assembled. Some client bodies may require all this information in a specific format, but nearly all will expect information to be included about the following:

- practice name, addresses, telephone, fax, e-mail;
- status of practice: whether sole principal, partnership, company, etc;
- directors or partners: names, CVs, photos;
- practice quality management systems, QA status;
- practice health and safety policy;
- practice environmental policy;
- specialist skills in-house;
- practice computer systems;
- professional indemnity insurance arrangements (subject to insurer's agreement);
- building type experience;
- recent commissions: details, illustrations, contact names;
- overseas experience and completed commissions, if relevant;
- languages in which the practice is fluent, if relevant;
- consultants with whom the practice normally collaborates;
- team being offered for the particular commission, with brief CVs.

PRE/CM2

Selection processes

The appointment of an architect may be handled directly by the client or indirectly through a project manager acting on the client's behalf. It could be for the full traditional services where the architect is lead consultant or for a limited appointment where the architect might be engaged as design leader, or simply to take on a design concept role. Regardless of the nature of the appointment or the procurement method adopted, the selection of an architect is likely to follow one of the following recognised procedures.

In *Constructing the Team* (1994), Sir Michael Latham recommended that 'consultants should be selected on a basis that properly recognises quality as well as price'. The Subsequent CIC/RIBA *Guidance for Clients to Quality Based Selection* describes a selection method primarily focused on quality, and the CIB report, *Selecting Consultants for the Team: balancing quality and price,* sets out a quality/price assessment mechanism for use in competitive tendering situations. Both of these documents are referred to below.

One to one negotiation

The architect is chosen on the basis of personal contact or recommendation, perhaps after a series of interviews. This procedure includes the following:
- suitable for any project;
- particularly suitable where services required are not yet formulated or the initial brief is still unclear;
- the client can have the opportunity of professional help in preparing an initial brief;
- negotiations over services, terms and fees can be carried out using a standard schedule of services as a focus for discussion.

Competitive interview

The architect is chosen primarily on the basis of a presentation to some stipulated form. The main features include:
- suitable for projects of any size;
- a limited number of architects are invited to make presentations;
- the architect can expect the client to supply a broad outline of the project and to state exactly what the presentation should cover;
- the presentation can be in written form only, or involve an interview, as stipulated by the client in the invitation. Any design content will not normally extend beyond broad concepts;
- after the presentation, the preferred firm can negotiate services and fees, etc.

Qualifications-based selection

The architect is chosen primarily on the basis of quality, by which are meant technical qualifications, design and performance potential and general suitability for the project in question. This approach to selection is widely and successfully used in the USA for public sector procurement following the introduction of The Brooks Act in 1972. A version of this system was developed by the CIC and is now published by the RIBA in the document *Guidance for Clients to Quality Based Selection*. The Guidance includes quality assessment forms and score sheets that can be used in the selection process.

After appropriate advertisement an initial list of firms is compiled from which a short list is invited for interview and discussion. The short-list firms are then ranked in order of perference. There is no mention of fees until the preferred firm is selected. If it proves impossible to agree a 'fair and reasonable' fee, negotiations with that firm are irrevocably terminated and fresh negotiations begin with the next preferred firm.

This approach has the undeniable merit of placing quality before any other consideration and, in the US at any rate, is perceived to be best value for taxpayers' money in the long term. Studies conducted by the American Institute of Architects has shown that the cost of architect selection and fees has a lower proportion of overall construction cost than when a 'quality plus price' method was used.

Quality/price selection

The system proposed by the CIB is similar to the above method but involves balancing quality/price at the outset. A ratio is agreed depending on the nature of the project, and indicative ratios are given as follows:

Type of process	quality/price ratio
Feasibility studies and investigation	85/15
Innovative projects	80/20
Complex projects	70/30
Straightforward projects	50/50
Repeat projects	20/80

Quality criteria are then set out and weighted (note if EC directives apply these will affect how this should be done). Submitted tenders are then assessed for quality by marking each of the quality criteria and summing the marks using the agreed weightings to give a total quality score. Candidates meeting an agreed threshold are then interviewed and their quality score adjusted. Their fees are then examined, the lowest is given a score of 100 and the others score 100 minus the percentage their fee is above the lowest fee. The final quality/price assessment is achieved by multiplying the quality and price scores by the quality/price ratio and adding them together to give a total score out of 100. The highest scoring candidate is awarded the contract.

Fee tender (without design)

The architect is chosen solely on the basis of the fee quoted, that is, the procedure is geared to the competitiveness of the fee.
- Unlikely to be suitable for more complex projects, and those under £500,000 capital value.
- A limited number of firms (say five or six) who accept invitations are sent tender documents. All must receive identical information.
- The information should state precisely which services are required and include an initial brief for the project.
- The tender may comprise a fee quotation and a resources schedule or other specified information.
- After receipt of satisfactory tenders, the client can be expected to enter into an agreement. There is little scope for negotiation, and undertaking 3.3 of the RIBA *Code of Professional Conduct* prohibits revising a fee quotation to take account of the fee quoted by another architect for the same service.

Fee tender (without design) using the Two Envelope System

The architect is chosen both on the basis of technical qualifications and on a fee quoted. Each is considered separately.
- Unlikely to be suitable for projects of less than £500,000 capital value.
- A limited number of firms (say five or six) who accept invitations are sent tender documents. All must receive identical information.

- The information should state precisely which services are required and include an initial brief for the project.
- The criteria to be used when evaluating the tenders should be stated.
- Two envelopes will normally be provided for tender submissions, clearly marked:
  (1) 'Qualifications' (the technical submission).
  (2) 'Fee' (the tender and quoted figure in a form stipulated by the client).

The Qualifications envelopes are opened first and the firms placed in order of preference. Then the Fee envelope from the preferred tenderer (only) is opened in the presence of that firm. Negotiation might subsequently be needed to arrive at a fair and reasonable figure. The second envelopes of the other firms should remain sealed and returned to those firms if negotiations are successful. Undertaking 3.3 of the RIBA *Code of Professional Conduct* must be observed. Only in the event of failure to reach a satisfactory outcome should the Fee envelope of the next preferred tenderer be opened.

Design submission with fee proposal

The architect is chosen both on the basis of a design submission and on a fee quoted. Each is considered separately under the Two Envelope System as described above.
- Suitable for larger projects (e.g. over £1 million).
- A limited number of firms (say three) who accept invitations are sent tender documents. All must receive full identical information.
- The information should state precisely which services are required and include an initial brief for the project.
- Clients should expect to pay a fee to all tenderers who submit detailed design ideas, and this will usually restrict the number of invitations. Architects taking part in such an arrangement would be wise to secure a formal agreement with the client to this effect.
- Two envelopes will normally be provided for tender submissions, clearly marked:
  (1) 'Design Proposals'.
  (2) 'Fee Tender'.

The Design Proposals envelopes from each of the tenderers is opened first and the firms placed in order of preference. Then the Fee envelope from the preferred tenderer (only) is opened. Negotiation might subsequently be needed to arrive at a fair and reasonable figure. The second envelopes of the other firms should remain sealed and returned to those firms if negotiations are successful. Undertaking 3.3 of the RIBA *Code of Professional Conduct* must be observed. Only in the event of failure to reach a satisfactory outcome should the Fee envelope of the next preferred tenderer be opened.

Design ideas competition

The architect is chosen solely on the basis of design ideas. The procedure does not involve fee tenders, for the fee is stated in the competition conditions.
- Suitable, in theory, for important projects regardless of size. In practice, application is likely to be restricted by the relative high cost to both client and architect.
- The architect can expect the client to provide a project brief, to define the professional services required, and to appoint a panel of assessors. This requires a professional input on the part of the client.
- Competition may be restricted to invited participants, and architects taking part in such an arrangement can expect to be paid a fee. A formal agreement with the client to that effect is advisable.
- Competition may be open but there is obviously a high cost risk for architects who participate.

Competitions are best run to procedures fully set out *in Architectural Competitions, an RIBA code of practice.* Undertaking 3.5 of the RIBA Code of Professional Conduct prohibits architects from entering competitions which the RIBA has declared to be unacceptable. Guidance on architects' fees may be found in *Engaging an Architect: Guidance for Clients on Fees*, published by the RIBA in 1999.

Note: Contracts for professional services may also be subject to The Public Services Contracts Regulations 1993 (SI 1993 No. 3228). Regulation 3 defines what is a 'contracting authority', and Regulation 21 sets out the criteria for awarding a contract. Regulation 24 is concerned with design contests. The Regulations only apply to services which are likely to be above a certain threshold, which at the time of writing is 200,000 ECUs.

PRE/CM3

Outline of possible roles for the architect

Some of the more common roles for the architect are described below, with a brief summary of the likely duties under such a role. The detailed duties will be as set out in the appointment documents, and the *Plan of Work* can be used as a model when discussing the services to be provided.

A standard appointing document should preferably be used (see PRE/CM5), but this should never be sent 'cold' to a client. It should first form a focus for discussion on the professional services which need to be commissioned, and only then be completed as a formal confirmation of what has been agreed.

If a preliminary appointment is needed pending formal agreement about the full services to be provided, a letter can be used incorporating the appropriate references. A letter activating appointment for specific stages can often be used in conjunction with a formal appointing document. A variation in services already formally agreed, or additional services to be provided, can often be imported by a letter supplementing the original document. It is important to be meticulous over such matters however, and to take legal advice where appropriate.

Appointment of architect as design leader, or lead consultant

The architect will normally act as design leader and as such is responsible for coordinating and integrating the work of other design consultants and specialists.

In the traditional or conventional appointment, and particularly on smaller projects, the architect will combine this role with that of lead consultant and contract administrator. On larger projects, the architect's commission is increasingly being confined to certain *Plan of Work* stages, or designated activities not necessarily to a *Plan of Work* format. Sometimes, particularly in construction management procurement arrangements, the role will be lead consultant working under a project manager who is the first point of contact for the client, and may take on the role of contract administrator. Sometimes the appointment will be for full services, but moving stage by stage. With arrangements where a more flexible approach to appointment is necessary, particular care is needed.

Typical duties

Typical duties of an architect acting as design leader might include:
- directing the design process;
- consulting the client about significant design issues;
- informing the client of duties under the CDM Regulations;
- investigating the feasibility of the requirements, and reporting;
- advising the client about any limitations on the use of land or buildings;
- preparing outline proposals, a scheme design, detail design drawings, etc;
- advising on the need for statutory and other consents, and preparing sufficient information for applications to be made;
- preparing sufficient production information for consultants and specialists to develop their proposals, coordinating these and integrating them into the overall scheme;
- bringing contract documentation to a final state for inviting tenders.

If the architect is also lead consultant and contract administrator, the following might be added:
- advising on the need for and appointment of other consultants;
- coordinating the work of other consultants;

- advising on methods of procurement, and on tendering and the appointment of the main contractor;
- administering the terms of the building contract and inspecting as relevant the performance of the contractor;
- issuing further reasonably necessary information, issuing empowered instructions, and acting as certifier as the contract requires, including issue of the final certificate;
- arranging for the preparation of record information and manuals.

Appointment of architect as consultant in design and build

A majority of design and build contracts, with the possible exception of package deals, involve an architect. This is a role quite different from that with the traditional commission, in that the architect acts solely as consultant to either an Employer Client or a Contractor Client at any one time. It is not uncommon for the architect to be engaged by both, but this would be sequential, never simultaneous, and would entail either the so-called consultant switch or novation. Even under this kind of arrangement it is often extremely difficult to separate clearly legal accountability and design responsibility. The degree of involvement with either Employer or Contractor will vary depending on the particular arrangements. An architect has no stated function in connection with the building contract.

Typical duties – Employer Client

Typical duties of an architect appointed as consultant to an Employer Client might include:
- advising on the initial brief;
- informing the Employer Client of duties under the CDM Regulations;
- carrying out a site appraisal;
- advising on the appointment of other consultants;
- advising on and taking part in discussions with statutory and other bodies;
- preparing outline proposals and making application for outline planning permission;
- advising on development of the brief for the Employer's Requirements;
- developing design concept drawings as appropriate for the Employer's Requirements;
- advising on tendering procedures;
- advising on contract matters;
- examining the Contractor's Proposals, including design and the contract sum analysis, and offering advice;
- acting as the Employer's Agent under the contract during the construction of the works;
- visiting the site during construction and reporting back to the Employer Client;
- advising the Employer Client on his or her obligations under the contract, and assisting in the drafting of statements;
- inspecting the works on behalf of the client prior to practical completion and advising the Employer Client;
- checking the contractor's as built drawings and operating/maintenance manuals;
- advising the Employer Client on the Employer's Final Account and Employer's Final Statement as appropriate.

Typical duties – Contractor Client

Typical duties of an architect appointed as consultant to a Contractor Client might include:
- examining the Employer's Requirements and all available information, and discussing a strategy for tendering;
- visiting the site, and noting all relevant constraints;
- checking arrangements for compliance with the CDM Regulations;
- advising on the appointment of other consultants;
- checking with authorities on statutory consents obtained and required;
- advising on the need for specialist sub-contractors;
- fulfilling the role of design leader;

- providing the Contractor Client with sketches, specification notes, etc for initial tendering purposes;
- advising about limitations or inconsistencies in the Employer's Requirements;
- providing the Contractor Client with drawings, specifications, samples, etc to support the Contractor's Proposals;
- after the contract has been awarded, developing and amending drawings and other documents in the Contractor's Proposals for contract documentation;
- developing design details;
- applying for statutory and other necessary approvals;
- preparing performance specifications and other detailed information for sub-contractor tendering;
- preparing production information drawings, details, schedules, specification notes for the Contractor Client;
- inspecting work during construction and reporting to the Contractor Client;
- preparing additional drawings, etc as necessary for submission to the Employer in the event of change orders;
- visiting manufacturers' workshops/factories as necessary and reporting to the Contractor Client;
- assisting in the preparation of as built drawings, operating/maintenance manuals, etc;
- inspecting the works prior to practical completion and advising the Contractor Client.

Appointment of architect as project manager

The project manager is the individual or firm primarily employed to look after the client's interests throughout the stages of a project in collaboration with the consultant team, including the cost consultant. The project manager's remit can be very wide, ranging initially from managing the brief through to managing the marketing or disposal of the completed project.

The project manager is usually responsible for the overall direction of the consultant team, specialists, contractor and sub-contractors. Administering the contract might be undertaken by the project manager or by a contract administrator working in close collaboration. The project manager's duties will vary considerably according to the nature of the project and the wording of the contract. The appointment of a project manager might be appropriate in traditional procurement, design and build, or for a management contract.

The role of project manager, for which some architects might well have the skills and aptitude, should be seen as separate and distinct from the architect's traditional role. It should not be confused with what many architects think of simply as managing the project.

Typical duties

Typical duties of an independent project manager might include:
- assisting in the preparation and development of the brief;
- informing the client of duties under the CDM Regulations;
- arranging for feasibility studies and reports;
- arranging for measures required by health and safety legislation;
- preparing the project management structure and plan;
- advising on the procurement method;
- arranging the appointment of consultants and specialists;
- checking professional indemnity insurances, warranties, etc;
- instructing consultants on feasibility studies, research, surveys;
- coordinating the design process;
- preparing and maintaining an overall cost plan;
- organising communication and information systems;
- arranging consultations/negotiations with statutory bodies;

- arranging monthly reports to the client on cost and completion forecasts;
- monitoring the performance, etc of the consultant team;
- arranging tender documentation;
- organising pre-qualification checks on contractors;
- evaluating tenders and preparing recommendations;
- participating in the selection and appointment of the contractor;
- arranging for the appointment of a construction supervisor/client's agent;
- assembling contract documentation;
- arranging for the appointment of an adjudicator and services as required;
- issuing instructions and variation orders;
- issuing extensions of time notices;
- preparing valuations and monitoring the budget;
- arranging commissioning and witness tests;
- developing a maintenance programme and staff training;
- organising handover/occupation procedures;
- issuing the practical completion certificate, preparing the final account;
- organising maintenance manuals and as built information;
- planning facilities management;
- advising on the marketing/disposal of the project;
- checking that defects are remedied, issuing the final certificate.

Appointment of architect as construction manager

The construction manager is the individual or organisation employed primarily to manage the construction stages of the project in collaboration with the consultant team, including the cost consultant. The appointee will be a specialist with contracting experience, paid by fee, and should preferably be appointed early (at the same time as the consultant team) so that he or she can participate in initial discussions. However, in practice the construction manager is often not brought in until the pre-construction stages are well advanced. Construction of the project is carried out by trades contractors, each having a direct contract with the employer but working under the direction of the construction manager. Alternatively, the construction manager may enter into a management contract with the employer, and each trade contractor will then enter into a separate 'Works' contract with the construction manager. If the architect is to undertake this role, he or she would usually set up a company specifically for this purpose.

Services, which can be provided by a construction manager, are held by some people to include helping to establish the client's requirements at pre-construction stages. A construction manager may certainly make a positive contribution at project design stage, but duties will vary considerably according to the nature of the project, the timing of the appointment and the wording of the contract.

Typical duties

Typical duties of a construction manager might include:
- arranging for meetings at design stages between client, consultant team and proposed trades contractors who will have a design responsibility;
- recommending the most economical materials and methods to meet the requirements of specification and sound construction practice;
- commenting on project drawings and project specification as appropriate, and advising on production information for issue by trades contractors;

- advising the consultant team on the division of the project into trades contracts;
- advising on the need for works at pre-construction stages, e.g. exploratory, mock-ups, tests of particular components, etc;
- arranging as appropriate for checks of the outline cost plan, the preparation of a project cost plan and cash flow forecasts;
- advising on measures necessary to satisfy statutory obligations, liaising with local and statutory authorities about construction and on site matters, and monitoring compliance by trades contractors;
- preparing a project programme showing lead times for trades contracts;
- preparing detailed week by week programmes, expanding and updating these during the progress of the works;
- advising the client on insurances to be taken out in respect of the project;
- preparing a schedule of tender events showing earliest start and anticipated finishing dates for all trades contracts;
- preparing, in consultation with the consultant team, a suitable tender list of trades contractors, checking references and resource capability;
- advising on tender procedures and participating in interviews, together with the client and consultant team as appropriate;
- evaluating tenders and preparing recommendations;
- advising the client on materials or plant to be ordered prior to placing trades contracts;
- arranging for adequate information for setting out, and coordinating this as necessary;
- issuing empowered instructions to trades contractors;
- receiving, reviewing and coordinating information, shop drawings, etc from trades contractors in consultation with the consultant team;
- providing management, administration and planning of trades contracts operations; monitoring methods, progress and quality;
- coordinating trades contracts operations in line with the project plan;
- arranging regular meetings with trades contractors to monitor progress and ascertain information requirements; chairing regular site meetings, issuing minutes and providing the client with monthly reports;
- preparing valuations and dealing with applications for payment from trades contractors;
- preparing interim and final accounts for each trade contractor;
- issuing certificates as required by the contract, including practical completion, in consultation with the consultant team;
- arranging for commissioning and testing;
- checking that defects are remedied;
- obtaining from each trade contractor relevant records, as built drawings and operating/maintenance manuals.

Acting in the role of the construction manager is unlikely to interest the majority of architects directly, who will only rarely have the necessary experience, skills and aptitude at least as far as projects of any size are concerned. Architects involved in this kind of procurement method are more likely to be acting as designer or lead consultant under the direction of the construction manager.

However, architects sometimes find themselves handling smaller projects where there is no main contractor and the work is carried out by direct labour, sometimes volunteers, or through a series of separate trades contracts. If asked to organise such operations they might be acting as the construction manager with all the attendant responsibilities for setting up the site, programming and coordination. This situation is not covered by standard appointing documents, and it would be well to check with insurers before undertaking to provide this kind of consultancy service. An appropriately drafted agreement would be needed.

Appointment of architect as planning supervisor

Under The Construction (Design and Management) Regulations 1994 the client in most jobs will be under a statutory duty to appoint a planning supervisor and a principal contractor.

Architects might wish to consider appointment as a planning supervisor either on a job where they are also acting as the architect or one where architectural services are provided by others. In all cases an appointment as planning supervisor should be seen as distinct from the provision of architectural services and the RIBA publishes a suitable Form of Appointment.

The planning supervisor will need a sound knowledge of design and construction processes and practice, and of health and safety matters relevant to the particular project. The appointment is to be made as soon as is practicable after the client has sufficient information about the project to be able to assess the appointee's competence and adequacy of resources for health and safety.

Typical duties

Typical duties of an independent planning supervisor might include:

- informing the client of duties under the CDM Regulations;
- advising the client on the competence and resources of designers as relevant to health and safety obligations;
- issuing statutory notices to the Health and Safety Executive;
- ensuring so far as reasonably possible that potential hazards are identified, eliminated or reduced at design stages;
- ensuring that all consultant team members and others contributing to the design (e.g. specialists/sub-contractors) cooperate over health and safety obligations;
- ensuring that a pre-tender Health and Safety Plan is ready for inclusion with tender information;
- attending pre-tender meetings with invited principal contractors to check adequacy of resources for health and safety obligations, and written health and safety policy statements;
- advising the client on the competence and resources of contractors relevant to health and safety obligations;
- checking that the principal contractor is provided with reasonably necessary health and safety information before construction commences;
- appraising the principal contractor's construction phase Health and Safety Plan and advising the client;
- monitoring the principal contractor's development of, or changes to, the Health and Safety Plan following variations or additional work, and advising the client as necessary;
- observing the principal contractor's compliance with the Health and Safety Plan during construction of the works, and advising the client if there are departures;
- obtaining necessary information for the Health and Safety File during the design and construction stages;
- preparing the Health and Safety File and advising the client on its safe keeping and future use.

The role of planning supervisor is one which on major projects might be undertaken by an independently appointed architect who has undergone the necessary training. On simpler projects the architect as lead consultant might be well placed to take on the additional but separate role of planning supervisor. However, this is a relatively new statutory appointment and the services to be provided need to be fully and precisely indicated. Any architect accepting such an appointment will need to understand fully the implications, be properly trained, and have appropriate indemnity cover. It is a function which could attract considerable liability in the event of injury to persons, or losses to clients should the works be delayed because of incidents or intervention by the Health and Safety Executive.

Architects should remember that even where a minor or domestic job is not notifiable to the Health and Safety Executive and there is no planning supervisor, the requirements on the designer under the CDM Regulations will still apply.

Appointment of architect as party wall surveyor

Under the RIBA Forms of Appointment the architect may undertake various duties in respect of party wall matters. These are described under *Architect's Guide to Job Administration: The Party Wall etc Act 1996*. The need for a party wall surveyor will only arise in the event of a dispute with an adjoining owner. If the architect is to act as the party wall surveyor, this should always be via a separate appointment. The party wall surveyor is a statutory appointment and the duties are as described or implied by the Act. In particular, the surveyor must uphold the rights and obligations of both parties, rather than serve the interests of the client alone.

The RIBA Standard Forms of Appointment are not suitable without significant modification. In addition to the quasi-arbitral nature of the role, some of the Act's specific requirements would conflict with the standard terms of appointment. For example, under the Act the appointment cannot be rescinded by the building owner, whereas the RIBA forms provide for termination. It is therefore preferable for the appointment to be by a specially drafted letter or document.

PRE/CM4

Current legislation relevant to appointments and fee recovery

Any or all of the legislation listed below may have an impact of the terms of appointment that can be agreed. The Standard Forms of Appointment published by the RIBA have already dealt with any implications of these Acts, but any bespoke terms should be checked carefully for possible conflicts with this legislation.

Supply of Goods and Services Act 1982

This statute covers contracts for work and materials, contracts for the hire of goods, and contracts for services. Most construction contracts come under the category of 'work and materials'. For services, the Act implies terms regarding care and skill, time of performance and consideration. For example s. 14 implies a term that where the supplier is acting in the course of business, the supplier will carry out the services within a reasonable time, provided of course, that the parties have not agreed terms regarding time themselves.

Defective Premises Act 1972

This Act applies where work is carried out in connection with a dwelling, including design work. It states that 'a person taking on work in connection with the provision of a dwelling owes a duty to see that the work which he takes on is done in a workmanlike or, as the case may be, professional manner, with proper materials and so that as regards that work the dwelling will be fit for habitation when completed' (s. 1(1)). This appears to be a strict liability, and is owed to anyone acquiring an interest in the dwelling.

The Housing Grants, Construction and Regeneration Act 1996

This requires that all construction contracts falling within the definition of the Act contain certain provisions including the right to stage payments, the right to notice of the amount to be paid, the right to suspend work for non-payment, and the right to take any dispute arising out of the contract to adjudication. If the parties fail to include these provisions in their contract, the Act will imply terms to provide these rights (s. 114) by means of The Scheme for Construction Contracts (England and Wales) Regulations 1998. The Act's definition of 'construction contract' includes the appointment of a professional. The Act is of broad application but with one important exception in the context of minor works — it does not apply to a 'construction contract' with a residential occupier. This means an appointment relating to operations on a dwelling which the client occupies or intends to occupy (s. 106). However, work on other residential properties, for example for landlords, Local Authorities or Housing Associations, will usually be covered by the Act.

Unfair Contract Terms Act 1977

This has the effect of rendering various exclusion clauses void including: any clauses excluding liability for death or personal injury resulting from negligence; any clauses attempting to exclude liability for Sale of Goods Act 1979 s. 12 obligations (and the equivalent under the Supply of Goods and Services Act); any clauses attempting to exclude liability for Sale of Goods Act 1979 ss. 13, 14 or 15 obligations (and the equivalent under the Supply of Goods and Services Act) where they are operating against any person dealing as consumer. It also renders certain other exclusion clauses void insofar as they fail to satisfy a test of reasonableness, e.g. liability for negligence other than liability for death or personal injury, and liability for breach of ss. 13, 14 and 15 obligations in contracts, which do not involve a consumer.

Unfair Terms In Consumer Contracts Regulations 1994

These only apply to terms in contracts between a seller of goods or supplier of goods and services and a consumer, and where the terms have not been individually negotiated (this would generally include all standard forms). A consumer is defined as a person who in making a contract, acting 'for purposes which are outside his business' (s. 2). An 'unfair term' is any term which causes a significant imbalance in the parties' rights to the detriment of the consumer, and the regulations state that any such term will not be binding on the consumer. An indicative list of terms is given in schedule 3 and includes, for example 'any term excluding or hindering the consumer's right to take legal action ... particularly by requiring the consumer to take the dispute to arbitration...' It is important, therefore, that if the arbitration option is selected, or if any other amendments are made which could be seen as limiting the employer's rights, that these have been explained and discussed, in order that they can be considered to have been individually negotiated.

Contracts (Rights of Third Parties) Act 1999

This Act provides that where a term of contract expressly confers, or purports to confer, a right on a person who is not a party to that contract, the party has the right to enforce that term. It is possible to exclude this right, and all Standard Forms of Appointment published by the RIBA contain an exclusion clause, to prevent third parties bringing claims against the architect. Architects should ensure that an exclusion clause is included in any non-standard terms which they agree to.

Late Payment of Commercial Debts (Interest) Act 1998

This Act implies a term into any contract to which the Act applies that any qualifying debt created by the contract carries simple interest in accordance with provisions of the Act. The contract may avoid the provisions of the Act being implied if it includes terms which give a 'substantial remedy' of interest on any late payment of an amount due. The contracts to which the Act applies would include most forms of construction contract or professional appointment. A debt could be created by the obligation to pay a certified amount or fee, and the interest will start to run the day after the debt became due. The Secretary of State has the power to set the rate of interest due.

PRE/CM5

RIBA Forms of Appointment

The RIBA publishes a comprehensive range of appointment documents as follows:

SFA/99 Standard Form of Agreement for the Appointment of an Architect
CE/99   Conditions of Engagement for the Appointment of an Architect
SW/99   Small Works
SC/99   Form of Appointment as a Sub-Consultant
DB1/99 Employer's Requirements
DB2/99 Contractor's Proposals
PS/99   Form of Appointment as Planning Supervisor
PM/99   Form of Appointment as Project Manager

SFA/99

This is the core document from which all the other Standard Forms of Appointment are derived. It is suitable for use where an architect is to provide services for a fully designed building project in a wide range of sizes and complexity and/or to provide other professional services. It includes notes on completion and an optional Services Supplement. There are Articles of Agreement and an attestation with provision for the agreement to be executed as a deed. The form can be adapted where the applicable law is the law of Scotland using text published by the RIAS for this purpose.

SFA/99 is clearly suitable for use on large projects following a traditional procurement route. In addition, unlike CE/99 and SW/99 this form differentiates between the role of architect as designer, design leader, lead consultant and contract administrator. This splitting of functions means that this form can be used in more complex or unusual procurement routes, for example construction management, where the architect is acting as design leader but the role of contract administrator may be performed by a separately appointed project manager.

If, after the appointment is agreed, it is decided to use a design build procurement, the parties can amend the agreement by executing DB1/99 (see opposite).

CE/99

Suitable for use where an architect is to provide services for a fully designed building project and/or to provide other professional services where a letter of appointment is preferred to the Articles of Agreement in SFA/99. It includes notes on completion, a draft Model Letter and an optional (modified) Services Supplement. The form can be adapted where the applicable law is the law of Scotland using notes and model letter published by the RIAS for this purpose.

CE/99 would normally only be used for straightforward projects using traditional procurement, and where there is no requirement to have the appointment executed as a deed. If necessary it can be adapted for design and build (appointment by employer client only) by use of DB1/99.

The Agreement comprises a letter of appointment from the architect to the client, to which a copy of the form is attached after completion of the schedules. The Model Letter should be carefully adapted for the particular circumstances of the project. Amongst other things, it deals with professional indemnity insurance and dispute resolution matters, in other words it covers the items included in the Appendix to the Conditions in SFA/99.

In the absence of signed articles, obtaining a written reply from the client accepting the terms set out in the letter of appointment is an important safeguard.

SW/99

Suitable for use where an architect is to provide services for a fully designed building project and/or to provide other professional services and where a letter of appointment is preferred to articles of agreement. It is suitable where:

- the services are of a relatively straightforward nature;
- the cost of the construction works is not expected to exceed £150,000;
- use of the JCT Agreement for Minor Works is appropriate;
- there is no requirement to have the contract executed under seal;
- the applicable law is the law of England and Wales (the Notes clearly state that it is not suitable for use where the applicable law is the law of Scotland).

The Agreement comprises a letter of appointment from the architect to the client, to which is annexed the Conditions of Appointment for Small Works and the printed Schedule of Services for Small Works, with Other Activities (not Services) listed on the reverse. SW/99 includes notes on completion, and a draft Model Letter which must be carefully adapted to suit the project. As with CE/99, obtaining a written reply from the client accepting the terms set out in the letter of appointment is an important safeguard.

SC/99

Suitable for use where a consultant wishes another consultant (sub-consultant) to perform part of his or her responsibility, but not for use where the intention is for the client to appoint consultants directly. It is used with Articles of Agreement and includes notes on completion and a draft form of Warranty to the Client. SC/99 is very similar to SFA/99, with the terms client and architect being replaced with consultant and sub-consultant. The form can be adapted where the applicable law is the law of Scotland using text published by the RIAS for this purpose.

The form is compatible with SFA/99, and with modification could be used with CE/99. The notes point out the importance of ensuring that the services are compatible with the services being provided under the head agreement, and that the warranty terms are harmonised with the head agreement and with any other warranties being provided.

DB1/99

An amendment for SFA/99 and CE/99 where an architect is employed by the employer client to prepare Employer's Requirements for a design and build contract such as the *JCT Standard Form of Building Contract with Contractor's Design* (JCT WCD98), and to act as the employer's agent during construction if required. It includes some modified definitions and work stages to suit the procurement method and a replacement Services Supplement. The notes give guidance on the procedure at initial appointment, on the need to vary the Agreement where a change to design and build has occurred after initial appointment, and on use with SFA/99 where 'consultant switch' or 'novation' is contemplated.

A 'consultant switch' arises where the employer requires the contractor to make a separate follow-on agreement with the contractor for professional services. After the consultant switch takes effect:

- the architect's services will be performed for the benefit of the contractor;
- the architect will remain liable to the employer client for services previously undertaken for the benefit of the employer client;
- the architect will not be liable to the employer client for services undertaken for the contractor (unless a warranty is executed).

A 'novation' arises where the employer requires the contractor to take over the employer's agreement with the architect. In a true novation the terms of the Agreement would remain unchanged but in practice the novation is often conditional. After the novation:

- the architect becomes liable to the contractor client for services already performed and to be performed in the future by the architect;
- the architect will not be liable to the employer client for services already undertaken or to be undertaken for the contractor (unless a warranty is executed).

In either arrangement a supplementary or tri-partite agreement will be needed, and the employer client may require a warranty. Model clauses for both of these are included in *The Architect's Contract: a guide to the RIBA standard forms of appointment*. However these are only intended as a basis for discussion and neither of these arrangements should be entered into without taking legal advice.

DB2/99

An amendment for SFA/99 where an architect is employed by the contractor client to prepare Contractor's Proposals for a design and build contract such as JCT WCD98, or in connection with the *Contractor's Designed Portion Supplement*. (Use with CE/99 is not recommended.) It includes replacement Articles, Appendix and Services Supplement and notes on completion for initial appointment and for 'consultant switch' and 'novation'.

PS/99

Used for the appointment as planning supervisor under the CDM Regulations 1994 of suitably qualified construction professionals. An appointment as a planning supervisor is distinct from the provision of architectural services under other RIBA Forms of Appointment. It is used with Articles of Agreement and includes notes on completion. The form can be adapted where the applicable law is the law of Scotland using text published by the RIAS for this purpose.

PM/99

This is for use where the client wishes to appoint a project manager to provide a management and/or other professional services. It is intended that this will not duplicate or conflict with the services as defined in other RIBA forms, particularly with the architect as design leader, lead consultant or contract administrator as set out in SFA/99.

Other appointments

Where specially drafted terms are being proposed these should always be checked against those in the standard forms. For small jobs the terms in SW/99 would form a useful checklist, otherwise legal advice may need to be sought. In all cases where non-standard terms are being proposed the architect should inform his or her insurers.

For certain specific roles not covered above, the following forms may be useful:
- *Adjudicator:* The JCT publishes a form of appointment for an adjudicator (with a version for a named adjudicator) which must be used where an adjudicator is appointed in a dispute relating to a JCT form. The CIC model Adjudication Procedure includes an agreement on appointment of an adjudicator.
- *Arbitrator:* normally arbitrators set their own terms of appointment.
- *Conciliator:* the RIBA has a standard form for use with the RIBA Conciliation Procedure.
- *Party wall surveyor:* this should be dealt with using a specially drafted letter or document. Guidance is set out in *Architect's Guide to Job Administration, the Party Wall etc Act 1996*, which includes a letter of authorisation which must be obtained from the Appointing Owner before proceeding.

- *Clerks of Works:* the Institute of Clerks of Works publish an appointment document.
- *Historic Buildings:* SFA/99 and CE/99 can be adapted for work on historic buildings. *The Architect's Contract: a guide to the RIBA Standard Forms of Appointment* includes a schedule of Special Services for this purpose.
- *Community Architecture:* SFA/99 and CE/99 can be adapted to community architecture projects. *The Architect's Contract: a guide to the RIBA Standard Forms of Appointment* includes a schedule of Special Services for this purpose.

A: APPRAISAL
B: STRATEGIC BRIEFING

Identification of client's requirements and of possible constraints on development. Preparation of studies to enable the client to decide whether to proceed and to select the probable procurement method.

Preparation of Strategic Brief by or on behalf of the client confirming key requirements and constraints.

Identification of procedures, organisational structure and range of consultants and others to be engaged for the project (RIBA Outline Plan of Work).

Description

Terminology

Key obligations from SFA/99

Actions

Stage input
Preliminary issues   architect
                            client
                            management and team working
Developing the Strategic Brief
Inspections/tests
Consultations
Approvals/consents
Cost planning
General procedures
Stage output

Core material

A-B/CM1	The briefing process
A-B/CM2	Strategic Brief checklist
A-B/CM3	Consultant team appointments and working
A-B/CM4	Planning permission, other consents and approvals
A-B/CM5	Health and Safety checklists
A-B/CM6	Inspecting the site
A-B/CM7	A project quality plan
A-B/CM8	Financial Appraisal

APPRAISAL AND STRATEGIC BRIEFING

Description

Stages A and B are often grouped for purposes of charging fees but although there is much overlap some distinction is possible, and they are separated in the *Plan of Work.*

The *Plan of Work* describes A: Appraisal as 'Identification of client's requirements and of possible constraints on development. Preparation of studies to enable the client to decide whether to proceed and to select the probable procurement method'.

Stage A is therefore the stage when requirements are clarified and a strategy for action prepared. It is important at this stage to raise fundamental questions regarding the project, for example whether there is a need for a new building, or whether adaptation and re-organisation of the client's existing premises may not satisfy existing needs. Key issues such as funding, budget, project duration and building life span should be addressed. This stage may not involve outside consultants; with larger or more experienced clients the process of appraisal may be handled by the client body itself. The stage should culminate in a 'statement of need' which will form the basis of the Strategic Brief.

The *Plan of Work* describes Stage B: Strategic Briefing as 'Preparation of Strategic Brief by or on behalf of the client confirming key requirements and constraints. Identification of procedures, organisational structure and range of consultants and others to be engaged for the project'.

Stage B includes such studies as may be relevant to determine what services will be necessary and whether it is feasible to achieve the project aims within the defined constraints. Such studies may be undertaken initially by the client organisation with in-house expertise or by a project manager before the appointment of other consultants. Professional advisers may be commissioned solely for Stage B, more particularly in the case of major projects where demonstrable impartiality and objectivity is required by a client body. However, for the majority of commissions the architect as designer is well placed to undertake feasibility studies, advise on alternative design and constructional approaches, and identify what might be imposed by legislative and other constraints.

Stage B begins the process of team assembly. Although this will continue through C and the remaining stages, it is essential to have the composition of the complete team and their various roles agreed at an early stage. The *Plan of Work* can be used as a model to identify the services needed. The architect engaged as lead consultant would play a key role in this process. Alongside setting up the team, it is at this stage that partnering agreements may be finalised and project quality control systems put into place.

Stages A and B are present in all procurement routes. With design and build the client must prepare a clear brief which may form part of, or evolve into, the Employer's Requirements under the design build contract. The architect may be appointed by the client to assist in its preparation (e.g. DB/1) or (less common) if the contractor has been approached at an early stage, may be engaged by the contractor to assist in preparing feasibility proposals or studies for the client.

SFA/99 assumes under basic services that the preparation of the Strategic Brief is the responsibility of the client and is 'received' by the architect at the start of Stage C, although the architect may contribute to its development through the preparation of studies, etc. If the architect is to be responsible for the preparation of this document, this must be identified in the terms of appointment as an 'Other Service'.

Fig. A-B1   Change in terminology between 6th edition and 7th edition of the *Job Book*

Work Stage	Plan of Work — reference	Job Book 7th — SFA/99	CIB terminology — document	description	CIB 'key step'	Job Book 6th	BS7000 terminology — document	description	use
A	term not used, instead states 'receive initial statement of requirements'	term not used, instead states 'receive initial statement of requirements'	Statement of Need	a document which defines the objectives and needs of the client organisation	1. Getting started	A (stage output)	initial brief	preliminary statement of client requirements	basis for feasibility studies
B	prepared during Stage B 'by or on behalf of client', input to Stage C	prepared during Stage B 'by or on behalf of client', input to Stage C	Strategic Brief	the statement of the broad scope and purpose of the project and its key parameters including overall budget and programme, agreed at an early stage of the project	2. Defining the project	B (stage output)	Project Brief	revised overall project objectives and main constraints	summarises feasibility studies, acts as a basis for outline proposals
C	development from Strategic Brief begins	development from Strategic Brief begins	Project Brief		3. Asembling the team (could cover A-C)	(stage output)	Design Brief	all design requirements	incorporates outline proposal results and acts as a basis for scheme design
D	output from Stage D	output from Stage D	Project Brief	the full statement of the client's functional and operational requirements for the completed project	4. Designing and constructing (could cover C-L)	D (stage output)	Consolidated Brief	all detailed design requirements	incorporates scheme design results, acts as a basis for detailed design and specialist designers
				Brief finalised at this point					
							Secondary Brief	detailed requirements for fittings etc.	records requirements agreed during production drawings
							residue		records all subsequent changes

Terminology

The RIBA *Plan of Work* refers separately to Stage A as Appraisal and Stage B as Strategic Briefing.

SFA/99 and CE/99 refer separately to Stage A as Appraisal and Stage B as Strategic Brief.

SW/99 refers to a combined Stage A-B Appraisal and Briefing.

DB1/99 and DB2/99 for design and build refer separately to Stage A as Appraisal and Stage B as Strategic Brief.

The terms 'statement of need' and Strategic Brief are defined in CIB (1997) *Briefing the Team: a guide to better briefing for clients*, London, Thomas Telford Publications.

The 6th edition of The Architect's Job Book *used the terminology set out in BS7000 Part 4 'Guide to managing design in the construction industry', and refers to an 'initial brief' and a 'project brief' as the outputs of Stages A and B respectively. The more recent CIB publication uses a different terminology which has been adopted in the* Plan of Work *and the RIBA Standard Forms of Appointment, and has therefore also been used in this edition of the* Job Book. *An approximate 'translator' is set out in Fig. A-B1.*

Key obligations which may apply	Reference	To do
- from SFA/99: design services		
Carry out studies to determine the feasibility of the client's requirements.	SFA/99/A/1	☐
Review with client alternative design and construction approaches and the cost implications, or	SFA/99/A/2A	☐
Provide information for report on cost implications.	SFA/99/A/2B	☐
[Strategic Brief prepared by or for the client.]	SFA/99/B/1	☐

In addition to the above, the architect should note the obligations set out in the SFA/99 Conditions of Engagement 2.1-2.8.

- from SFA/99: management services

(i.e. architect acting as design leader and lead consultant)

Advise on the need for, and the scope of services by consultants, specialists, sub-contractors or suppliers. ☐

Advise on methods of procuring construction. ☐

Actions

Stage input

Check that all information necessary during Stage A-B is available, which might include the following: ☐

- 'Statement of need' to include the client's requirements, budget,   (A-B/CM1).
  project timetable and timetable for services

- Information about the site and/or existing buildings to be supplied by the client. Legal aspects to be verified by the client's solicitors.

- Further information from the client, e.g. on manufacturing process, equipment, plant layout, accommodation schedule, etc.

- Information relating to the user client, e.g. location, security, particular needs, disabled access audits.

- Studies previously undertaken relevant to this project or site, e.g. social surveys, traffic or transport studies.

- Health and Safety File with information on site hazards or references to work carried out previously.

- OS maps, site and/or building survey drawings.

- Documents referring to local history of site, political and social context etc (e.g. as found in library archives or press cuttings).

- Environmental data, such as weather records, maps of the area, environmental studies, contaminated land investigations.

- Notes, sketches and photographs made during initial visits.

- Contributions, information and recommendations from consultants and specialists if as yet to be appointed.

Design and build   Employer's Requirements as issued to tenderers. *(Contractor Client)*   ☐

Preliminary issues – architect

Establish scope, content and context for Stage A-B activities.   ☐
Put it into context particularly if material produced is likely to be acted upon by others taking over subsequent stages.

Check appointing documents with respect to services and fees: ☐

- If the extent of professional services for Stage A-B is not yet settled, agree with client and confirm in writing.

- If the methods and levels of charging for Stage A-B are not yet settled, agree with the client and confirm in writing.

Establish, if possible, whether this is to be a continuing involvement for full services or likely to be a partial service confined to this Stage. *refer to Pre-Agreement section*

Check with professional indemnity insurers if the project seems likely to call for services outside those covered by the policy.
For example, the architect might find it necessary to engage other consultants direct, or might be called upon to give advice on self-build operations, or might act as manager for a series of separate trades contracts. Cover could also be called into question because of the nature or scale of operations, or because of stipulations by the client as to the amount or duration of cover required.

If the architect is to engage sub-consultants direct, check competence and resources, particularly with regard to CDM Regulations. Consider the use of SC/99.

Assess office resources needed for Stage A-B and ensure that they are adequate and available.

Review how in-house quality management procedures will be applied to the project. These may include the preparation of a project quality plan in an appropriate form. **A-B/CM7**

A project quality plan provides a mechanism to link the specific requirements of the project to an office quality management system which might already exist. It will not necessarily mean the development of a new document or procedures over and above those that already exist.

Preliminary issues – client

Check the identity of the client's project team/personnel/authorised agents.

Check that the client has made organisational arrangements to deal with questions, supply information and take decisions. Appointed representatives of the client should have the authority to act.

Appraise the client's requirements.

Obtain from the client the project requirements, budget and time-table. Check these carefully, question incompatibilities and agree priorities. **A-B/CM1**

Alert the client straight away to key issues that may be missing from these requirements and will need to be addressed in the client's Strategic Brief, for example strategy for disabled access, security policy, and environmental policy. **A-B/CM2**

Advise the client on the need to appoint a quantity surveyor and other consultants or specialists. Confirm who will make the appointments, the basis of agreements and the scope of such services. **A-B/CM3** ☐

Be clear about the professional services needed. If other consultants and specialists are needed, be prepared to explain their roles and responsibilities. The Plan of Work *may be a useful tool at this stage for mapping out the tasks that must be performed and identify who will perform them, although it should be noted that it does not list all appointments that may be needed, such as party wall surveyor or access auditor.*

Try to secure agreement that all professional appointments are on mutually interlocking agreements.

Explain to the client the options for procurement and note any matters which could affect the particular choice. **Fig. A-B/1-3** ☐

Check with the client whether tendering for the particular project is likely to be subject to legislative control. This could have an effect on procurement methods and procedures (see Fig. A-B/1-3). ☐

Advise the client on statutory and other legal obligations, including: ☐

- the need for various approvals under national legislation concerned with planning and building, and the additional requirements of any local legislation or legislation for the particular building type which might apply; **A-B/CM4**

- the fees payable to the relevant authority at the time of these applications;

- the obligations of a client under the CDM Regulations, and other health and safety legislation, as appropriate; **A-B/CM5**

- the need to appoint a planning supervisor, where the law requires this;

- the duties of the client as building owner under the Party Wall Act including the possible need to appoint a party wall surveyor, and the rights of adjoining owners to appoint their own surveyors;

- possible duties of the client under Part IIA of the Environmental Protection Act 1990, if the site may contain contaminated land.

Obtain from the client relevant information, including: ☐

- information about the site or existing buildings. This will first need to be verified by the client's solicitors. Such information might concern details of ownership, leases, boundaries, covenants, easements, party wall agreements and other land charges;

- copies of earlier studies or proposals for the site or buildings which might prove useful;

- any deposited Health and Safety File relating to the site or work carried out on the building previously.

Enquire whether the client wishes to ensure confidentiality for the project. If not, and publicity is sought, is this likely to involve wider consultation, e.g. presentations to a user client or local amenity bodies? ☐

A-B2: Traditional Procurement

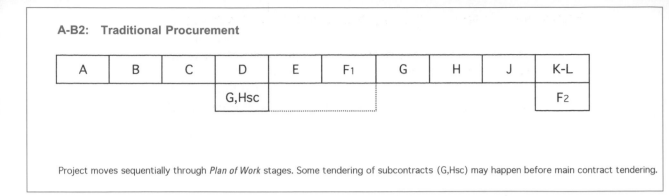

A	B	C	D	E	F1	G	H	J	K-L
			G,Hsc						F2

Project moves sequentially through *Plan of Work* stages. Some tendering of subcontracts (G,Hsc) may happen before main contract tendering.

A-B3: Design and Build

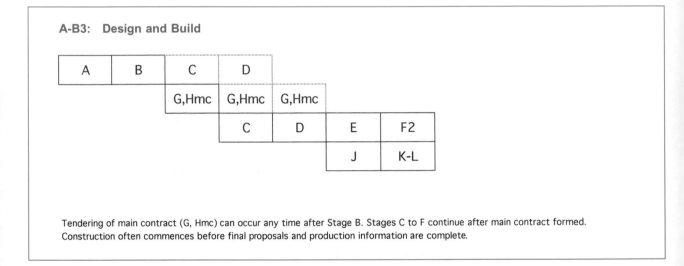

A	B	C	D				
		G,Hmc	G,Hmc	G,Hmc			
			C	D	E	F2	
					J	K-L	

Tendering of main contract (G, Hmc) can occur any time after Stage B. Stages C to F continue after main contract formed. Construction often commences before final proposals and production information are complete.

A-B4: Management Procurement

A	B	C	D	Ew1	Fw1	Gw1	Hw1	J	K-L
					Ew2	Fw2	Gw2	Hw2	
						Ew2	Fw3	Gw3	Hw3
							Ew4	Fw4	Gw4	Hw4
								etc	

Information/tendering of first Works contract (Ew1 - Hw1) is followed by mobilisation and commencement of work on site.
Information/tendering of subsequent Works contracts follows on a rolling programme, in parallel with work on site.

Preliminary issues – management and team working

Establish or review project quality management procedures in concert with relevant procedures of all consultant team members. ☐

Confirm the consultant team composition and identify a lead consultant. ☐

Identify functional relationship to planning supervisor and project manager (if appointed) and establish the authority of the lead consultant and design leader.

Identify need for a 'team' project quality plan and agree format with client and consultant team.

Check the scope of professional services agreed with other consultants as they are appointed. **A-B/CM3** ☐

Confirm agreed policy of consultants and specialists concerning accountability, warranties, professional indemnity insurance, etc. ☐

Appraise client requirements and agree input to the Stage by consultant team members. ☐

Confirm Stage timetable for services and note its relationship to the project timetable as agreed with the client. The timetable should show critical points by which information from the client and consultant team members will be required. ☐

Establish arrangements for communication between client, planning supervisor, project manager and consultant team leader. ☐

Agree working methods and procedures with the consultant team members, including: ☐

• means for integrating and coordinating effort and input.

• compatibility in systems, software, etc.

Establish programme and pattern for consultant team meetings. Fig. A-B6 is a specimen agenda for an initial consultant team meeting. ☐

Establish regular report procedures to the client. ☐

Procedures for consultant team members should be clearly set out and closely followed throughout the project.

Establish procedures for the client to 'sign off' the brief, design, etc at relevant stages. ☐

Be strict about keeping to deadlines for reports and other submissions to the client.

Set firm dates for approvals, instructions to proceed, and the supply of information.

Developing the Strategic Brief

Collate information from the QS, consultants and specialists. ☐

Prepare feasibility studies and reports and submit to the client. ☐

The feasibility reports to the client will establish the basis upon which the project should proceed. It may be that the job is not feasible at all, or that the client's requirements, programme and cost limits cannot be reconciled. Make sure your reports are comprehensive, soundly researched and objective.

Develop the client requirements into a Strategic Brief, or assist the **A-B/CM2** ☐
client in developing its Strategic Brief.

Inspections/tests

Obtain maps, studies and other contextual material. ☐

Make an initial visit to the site and/or existing building. **A-B/CM5,** ☐
A-B/CM6

Make a photographic record, notes and sketches as appropriate. File ☐
information and make an initial appraisal.

Advise the client about surveys needed and act as authorised. If ☐
independent surveyors are to do this, brief them fully.

Check for any reference in previous use or history of the site to con- ☐
tamination or presence of hazardous substances, geological problems, underground services, etc.

Advise client, if appropriate, to authorise special surveys to investigate potential health and safety problems on presence of contaminated land. ☐

It is important to identify at the earliest possible stage whether there are special conditions which will affect the viability of the project, e.g. contaminated land, asbestos in existing buildings, etc.

Inspect information provided by the client including the Health and Safety File, if applicable. ☐

Consultations

A-B/CM4

List authorities or bodies which may need to be contacted, identify particular officers, names, addresses, phone numbers, etc. ☐

Review relevant legislation to identify potential constraints to development. ☐

Obtain access to the text of Acts, SIs and Approved Documents or Approved Codes of Practice, and study them carefully. ☐

Make a preliminary assessment of the necessary consents, applications and relevant procedures. ☐

Check all information scrupulously; do not make assumptions. Consult the relevant authorities yourself and obtain or confirm their advice in writing.

Check the planning situation with the Planning Authority.
For example: ☐

- whether there is any existing relevant permission, approval or consent still current. Obtain the original notices if possible;

- whether the proposed work requires planning permission, and if so which applications would be relevant;

- whether there are special circumstances which need to be taken into account (e.g. Listed Building, Conservation Area, Enterprise Zone, Development Corporation, etc);

- whether an environmental impact assessment will be expected or helpful;

- whether there is a known existence of hazardous substances or conditions due to earlier uses, likelihood of archaeological remains, etc;

- whether there are plans for compulsory purchase, or land take proposals for, say, road improvements which could affect use of the site.

A-B/CM4

Hold preliminary discussions with the planning officer to discuss key issues arising from the above checks. Establish the approach of the planning officer towards the principle of development as proposed and enquire if serious difficulties might be expected. Establish the measure of consultation which the planning officer would welcome or expect.

☐

Note: consultation with statutory authorities is not included in SFA/99 until Stage D, although it appears in Stage C in the Plan of Work. *In practice, to establish feasibility of proposals, consultations are likely to be necessary at Stage A-C.*

Check whether, particularly in the case of alterations to an existing building, the local authority Building Control Department might be sympathetic to dispensations under building regulations.

☐

Check any concerns that the fire authority, police or military might have, particularly in an area of high sensitivity, and which might influence development or design.

☐

Check whether there are restrictions on site development potential due to mains or cables either below ground or overhead, and whether or not it is subject to easements or wayleaves.

☐

Check the position and capacity of mains drainage and supplies from statutory undertakers.

☐

Alert the client at a very early stage if it appears there may be issues concerning the development which may require approval/agreement of adjoining owners, e.g. whether rights of light, boundaries, rights of way such as for fires escape or access will be affected. These will normally be dealt with by the client's solicitors but may take a considerable time to negotiate.

Check whether notices under the Party Wall etc Act 1996 may be needed.

☐

Check whether third parties, e.g. landlord, estate surveyor, lessees, adjoining owners, etc, will need to be consulted. Initiate preliminary consultations if authorised by client. ☐

Consult with user groups as authorised. ☐

Note that consultations with users or third parties do not form part of the Services under SFA/99 unless identified under 'Other Services'.

Approvals/consents   A-B/CM4

Prepare an application to determine whether planning permission is required, or whether there is need for an Environmental Impact Assessment if appropriate. ☐

Prepare an application for outline planning permission, if appropriate. ☐

Note that applying for outline planning permission does not form part of the Services under SFA/99 unless identified under 'Other Activities', so unless it is included in the appointment it will be necessary to obtain client authorisation.

Prepare an application for certificates (e.g. Established Use) if appropriate. ☐

Submit applications (if instructed by client) with relevant documents, including a cheque from the client for the appropriate fee. ☐

Cost planning

Together with other consultants review the client budget figures and identify the sums included for actual construction work. ☐

Review the client requirements, programme and budget to assess compatibility. If not in balance report to client and seek clarification on priorities. ☐

Alert the client to the possible effects on the cost of the project due to inflation, and the application of VAT. ☐

Review with other consultants possible sources of funding or grant aid and, if instructed, help to prepare a case or application. ☐

This might take the form of assistance from government departments, statutory bodies, local authorities, English Heritage, etc, or charitable trusts, and many organisations with limited funds but still useful in aggregate. Financial assistance is often subject to conditions which could affect design and specification proposals.

Provide information for financial appraisal.   A-B/CM8   ☐

The report on cost implications should be structured under appropriate headings. It will normally be prepared by the quantity surveyor, if appointed. On jobs where there is no QS, cost estimates may need to be prepared by the architect — the appointment must make this clear.

General procedures

Set up an in-house project team. ☐

Establish who will lead the office design unit. Identify personnel, roles, accountability and lines of communication.

Establish office administrative procedures. ☐

Open project files and allocate code letter or number to the project in accordance with office practice. Check with the client the full project title to be used.

Begin to compile a record of all key persons involved in the project together with addresses, phone and fax numbers, etc. Check that names, titles or descriptions are correct and check spelling. Circulate to all concerned.

Set up procedures for checking progress against the timetable for services regularly, and for taking corrective action if needed. ☐

Monitor office expenditure against fee income: ☐

- Set up office procedures for recording time spent on the project, by whom and the rates chargeable, and for noting expenses and disbursements incurred.

- Set up procedures for checking expenditure against the office job cost allocation regularly.

Arrange for regular reports to the client on fees and expenses incurred, and for accounts to be submitted at agreed intervals.

☐

Update project quality plan as appropriate

☐

Stage output

Tangible results/material produced before the conclusion of Stage A–B might include the following as relevant:

☐

- A report to the client on studies to define the feasibility of the client's requirements. The report should analyse and appraise needs, give an environmental assessment and offer possible options, together with recommendations for the way forward. This might include conceptual drawings and diagrams.

- A cost appraisal sufficiently detailed to enable a cost strategy to be devised.

- Where appropriate, a report on the condition of the fabric of an existing (perhaps historic) building, and suggestions for future uses.

- Where appropriate, proposals developed sufficiently to allow an application for outline planning permission.

- Strategic Brief developed from the client requirements.

Design and build • Initial suggestions for the Employer's Requirements. *(Employer Client)*

Design and build • A report to the client on Employer's Requirements as received, and related matters pending preparation of Contractor's Proposals. *(Contractor Client)*

References and further reading

CIB (1997) *Briefing the Team: a guide to better briefing for clients*, London, Thomas Telford Publications.

Cox, S. and Hamilton, A. (eds.) (1997) *Architect's Guide to Job Administration under the Party Wall etc Act 1996*, London, RIBA Publications.

Cox, S. and Hamilton, A. (eds.) (1996) *Architect's Guide to Job Administration under the CDM Regulations 1994*, London, RIBA Publications.

Hyams, D. (2001) *Construction Companion to Briefing*, London, RIBA Publications.

Halliday, S. (2000) *Green Guide to the Architect's Job Book*, London, RIBA Publications.

Jefferies, T. (1999) *A Model for a Quality Management System*, London, RIBA Publications.

Penton, J. (1999) *The Disability Discrimination Act: Inclusion*, London, RIBA Publications.

RIBA (1996) *Model Safety Policy with safety codes, for architects, engineers and surveyors*, London, RIBA Publications.

A-B/CM1

The briefing process

Compiling the brief and developing the design are activities which interact as shown in Fig. A-B5. Briefing is really a continuous process through to Detailed Proposals but for convenience it can be regarded as evolving through three distinct phases. The client's 'statement of need' is the starting point, and it should never be forgotten that the client is at the core of the process. An inexperienced client, perhaps on a smaller size project, might welcome the assistance of the architect in preparing the statement of need.

The briefing process must be appropriate to the nature of the project. Some projects might depend upon planning and space standards which have already been widely researched and are generally available. Other projects might require considerable original investigation and extensive design studies. Such factors are likely to influence both the cost and duration of the design process and the development of the brief.

The statement of need

The statement of need should set out the objectives which the client wishes to achieve in the project and will probably refer to functional requirements, environmental standards, levels of quality, life span and maintenance.

The statement may be anything from a broad preliminary statement of interest to a comprehensive set of technical requirements. It will rarely be sufficiently clear or detailed for design work but it should be seen as the basis for feasibility studies. The CIB report *Briefing the Team* states that it should:
- state clearly the client's mission and objectives;
- set out the client's needs;
- indicate the impact of not meeting the needs;
- identify the triggers for change;
- place the client's needs in a historic context, e.g. a pattern of growth and change;
- state what is expected in response to this statement;
- state the sort of decisions needed and from whom.

Considerable further investigation and development work will be necessary to bring it to the level of a Strategic Brief by the end of Stage A–B. However, it should be seen as an important part of developing the brief, and as such should be a formalised document to be agreed with the client.

The Strategic Brief

The Strategic Brief should be a document which covers the technical, managerial and design intentions, and shows how these requirements are to be met. It is likely to be the result of research and development involving all the consultant team, with additional expertise and advice from commissioned specialists. It will be the outcome of activities such as:
- feasibility studies;
- site or building survey and studies;
- research into functional needs;
- accessibility audits;
- environmental impact considerations;
- statutory constraints;
- cost appraisal studies.

Fig. A-B5   The process of brief and design development

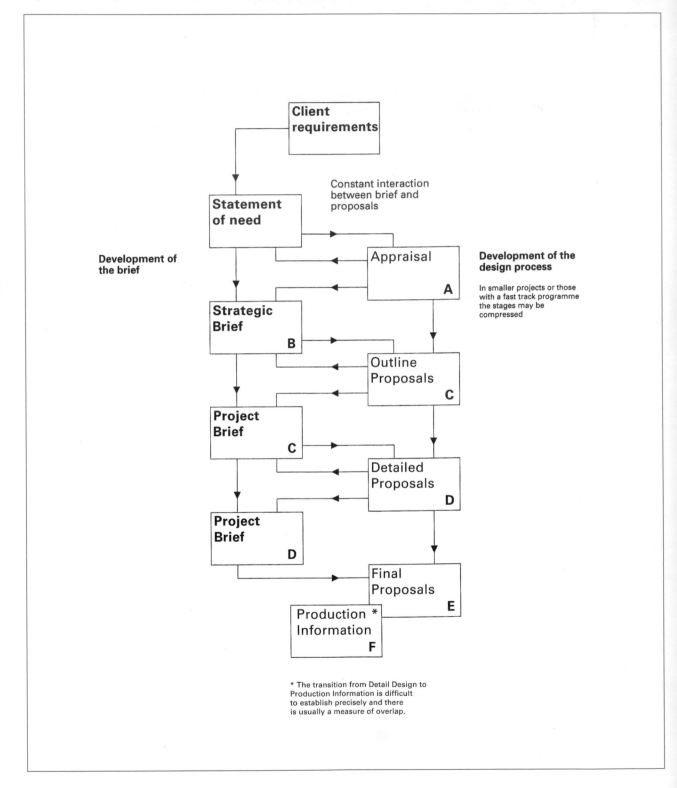

The CIB report *Briefing the Team* states that it should include:
* the mission statement;
* the context;
* organisational structure and function;
* overall scope and purpose of the project;
* programme, including phasing;
* statements on size and capacity requirements and functions to be accommodated;
* global capital expenditure budget and cash flow constraints;
* targets and constraints on operating expenditure and other whole-life costs;
* internal and external environmental requirements;
* technology to be incorporated or accommodated, including equipment, services, IT;
* quality requirements for design, materials, construction and long term maintenance;
* what is expected in response to the brief;
* how the success of the project will be measured;
* statutory requirements.

A detailed checklist for the Strategic Brief is given in A-B/CM2.

The Strategic Brief should be seen as a starting point for the development of the Project Brief and should be formalised by the end of Stage A–B.

The Project Brief

The Project Brief should define all design requirements. It should be prepared by the architect in collaboration with the client, and with coordinated contributions from all consultants and specialists, and the health and safety planning supervisor. Development of this Project Brief will probably require:
* assembly of all relevant information;
* design studies and investigations;
* preparation of detailed design proposals;
* preparation of a cost plan.

The Project Brief is the foundation on which the design will develop, and serves as a yardstick against which further design development can be measured. As such it is a factual record and a document of importance.

The Project Brief is the last stage in the briefing process and may be equated with the end of *Plan of Work* Stage D. It will evolve through Stages C and D, and an accurate record should be kept of the stage it reached at the end of Stage C. The Project Brief will be the basis for further detailed design work. The CIB report *Briefing the Team* states that it should cover:
* the aim of the design, including prioritised project objectives;
* the site, including details of accessibility and planning;
* the functions and activities of the client;
* the structure of the client organisation;
* the size and configuration of the facilities;
* options for environmental delivery and control;
* servicing options and specification implications, e.g. security, deliveries, access, workplace, etc;
* outline specifications of general and specific areas;
* a budget for all elements;
* the procurement process;

- environmental policy, including energy;
- the project execution plan;
- key targets for quality, time and cost, including milestones for decisions;
- a method for assessing and managing risks and validating design proposals.

A detailed checklist for the Project Brief is given in D/CM2

The Project Brief should be 'signed off' by the client after approval.

The steps outlined above are likely to be found in most projects of reasonable substance or complexity.

The briefing process is something that should always be developed systematically. It provides the framework within which the design can be developed and it is an indispensable part of quality management. However, on projects of a more domestic scale the design and briefing processes may be compressed. Nevertheless, sufficient time should be allowed for this work to be done thoroughly, and architects should resist jumping to quick design solutions which might not meet the client's requirements.

The process of brief development is cyclical, and it should be accepted that clients sometimes wish to modify their requirements even after approval of the Project Brief. Major changes could lead to the abandoning of design work already completed, or at least have a significant effect upon cost, time and statutory consents. It is therefore essential to have an identifiable approved Project Brief to start with, and to have a procedure for Brief Change Control as part of the quality management plan. This will enable the client to be aware of the implications of changes to the Project Brief before final instructions are given.

A-B/CM2

Strategic Brief checklist

A Strategic Brief checklist relevant at the end of Stage A–B might include the following:

General

- the client's objectives, requirements and established priorities and criteria;
- quality standards;
- the client's environmental policy;
- life expectancy of building and components;
- user client considerations;
- access requirements, including disabled access;
- security requirements;
- health and safety policy;
- budgets for security, energy, maintenance including cleaning (i.e. costs in use);
- detailed functional requirements of direct client/user client;
- site history, topography and geology;
- preferred spatial relationships and orientation;
- studies previously commissioned;
- plans for future expansion;
- exact location of boundaries;
- other parties known to have expressed an interest, e.g. English Heritage, Royal Fine Arts Commission, etc.

Planning and building considerations

- known constraints arising from previous consents or conditions;
- likelihood of planning gain or Section 106 Agreement;
- impact of Local Development Plan;
- leasehold/freehold interests and party walls, rights of light, access or other known easements.

Environmental

- services below ground and known restrictions on development;
- likely parking requirements;
- likelihood of archaeological or antiquarian discoveries;
- known road widening or development plans;
- known problems with the site, e.g. geological conditions, hazardous substances, presence of contaminated land;
- known problems with the buildings, e.g. presence of asbestos.

Financial

- funding or institutional requirements or restrictions;
- approximate cost per sq m if speculative development;
- grants, subsidies or information relating to tax advantages (e.g. VAT).

A-B/CM3

Consultant team appointments and working

Appointments

When acting as lead consultant, the architect should advise the client on the appointment of other consultants and specialists as necessary. The appointment and payment of consultants and specialists are matters best dealt with directly by the client; the services required should be identified in detail and recorded. The conditions of appointment for all consultants should be compatible and preferably to a common basis.

It is very important for the architect to know precisely what is included in the appointment terms of all consultants, so as to be able to minimise any overlap or duplication and to coordinate effectively the work of all the members of the consultant team. It is also desirable to ensure that all members are appointed under compatible conditions with a common policy concerning responsibilities, insurance, collateral agreements, etc.

The Latham Report, *Constructing the Team*, published in 1994, contained significant recommendations for a family of compatible documents to include the appointment of consultants, contractors and sub-contractors. These are under discussion by the various bodies who at present publish documents related to their own immediate interests, but to date no coordinated suite covering all appointments has yet been published. The *Plan of Work* serves as a useful table of the services that may need to be carried out, and could be referred to as the team is being appointed. It should be noted that, as explained in the Plan, not all of the services listed in the tables would be considered 'basic' or 'normal' by the relevant professional institution.

Depending on the nature and size of the project, a wide range of specialists and/or consultants may be needed at some stage. For example:

Surveyors
- Quantity surveyor
- Land surveyor
- Building surveyor
- Party wall surveyor

Engineering consultants
- Civil engineer (including geotechnics)
- Structural engineer

Building services consultants
- Heating and ventilating engineer
- Electrical engineer
- Lighting consultant

Other consultants and specialists
- Planning supervisor
- Landscape consultant
- Acoustic consultant
- Conservator
- Health and safety consultant
- Disabled access consultant
- Fire engineering consultant
- Public health consultant

- Drainage consultant
- Interior design consultant
- Facilities management consultant
- Security adviser.

Of these, the appointments most likely to be relevant at Stage A–B are:

Quantity surveyors
Standard conditions of engagement are published by the Royal Institution of Chartered Surveyors (RICS) relating to a wide range of services. These need to be examined carefully to establish which services are to be provided for the particular appointment.

Structural engineers
Standard conditions of engagement and a number of different forms of agreement are published by the Association of Consulting Engineers (ACE). Normal services for structural work are arranged broadly in accordance with the *Plan of Work* stages. These need to be examined carefully to establish which services are to be provided for the particular appointment.

Building services engineers
Standard conditions of engagement are published by the Association of Consulting Engineers. The basic range of services can include for Full Duties, Abridged Duties, or Performance Duties. The conditions need to be examined carefully to establish which services are to be provided for the particular appointment.

With engineering services, architects are reminded that:

(a) 'working drawings' as understood in architectural terminology are not produced by M & E consultants;

(b) 'builders work' drawings are for the architect to arrange, making sure that requirements for holes, shafts, access, insulation, etc are properly coordinated and integrated into the design;

(c) 'coordination drawings', where commissioned, should show detailed layouts and their relationship to plant rooms, spaces, structure, etc;

(d) 'installation drawings' (or 'shop drawings') are produced by the sub-contractors or suppliers, and may be expected to show only general lines of pipework, fabrication, and equipment installation details for comment by the engineering services consultant prior to fabrication or installation.

It is normally the architect's responsibility to coordinate and integrate the work of consultants and specialists into the overall design. To this end, architects will need to inspect drawings submitted by specialists. However, contract documents should clearly place the responsibility for coordination of work being carried out on site with the main contractor.

Sub-consultants

If the architect is to appoint sub-consultants direct, great care must be taken to check their competence and resources with respect to Health and Safety regulations and their PI insurance provisions. Reference can be made to Section 2 of Tim Jefferies' *A Model for a Quality Management System*. The RIBA Standard Form of Appointment for a sub-consultant SC/99 should be used wherever possible.

Consultant team roles and responsibilities

Quantity surveyor
The QS can assist the architect in assessing special site and other problems such as access, topography, economic site use and working. He or she can analyse cost information on other similar projects, local levels of building costs

and cost trends, etc, and can judge whether the client's budget is realistic and compatible with other stated requirements.

The QS should cooperate with the planning supervisor, liaise with other consultants and specialists, attend consultant team meetings, and prepare the financial appraisal for the feasibility report.

Structural engineer

The structural engineer can advise the architect about local conditions relevant to the site, such as soil and geotechnical factors, roads, sewers, water supply, etc. He or she can:

- obtain existing information and interpret it;
- identify hazards and hazardous substances;
- arrange for site, structural and drainage surveys;
- advise on alternative structural solutions;
- prepare cost planning information for the QS;
- prepare design criteria and calculations;
- advise on structural aspects of party walls, temporary structures and demolition work.

The structural engineer should cooperate with the planning supervisor, liaise with other consultants and specialists, attend consultant team meetings, and contribute to the feasibility report.

Building services engineers

The mechanical and electrical engineers should cooperate with the planning supervisor, and liaise with the architect and structural engineer to study climatic conditions, energy use and conservation, emission problems, etc, and should consult relevant authorities as necessary.

The M & E engineers can:

- provide details of load and space requirements for services;
- prepare feasibility studies, estimates, forecasts and maintenance cost options;
- assist in dealings with statutory bodies;
- prepare outline schemes;
- prepare energy management studies and report;
- prepare design criteria, and calculations;
- advise on installation options and cost implications;
- advise on energy, cost/benefit, and running costs.

They should attend consultant team meetings and contribute to the feasibility report.

Consultant team meetings

The consultant team will probably need to be enlarged during the development of the project. However, it is essential that it is formally constituted with proper definition of responsibility and clearly accepted roles. Regular consultant team meetings are important to review progress and to record decisions. A specimen agenda for the initial consultant team meeting is shown as Fig. A-B6, and although the list of items will need modifying as the project progresses, the main headings should remain consistent throughout. In this way the history of each aspect of job administration will be automatically recorded and can be easily traced.

A system of regular reporting can be established. For example, the client's representative will report under the heading 'Brief', the architect under 'Site' and 'Approvals', the quantity surveyor under 'Cost control', and so on. It is assumed that an architect acting as lead consultant will chair such meetings.

Fig. A-B6   Specimen agenda for initial consultant team meeting

1   Consultant team and reports
Appointments, personnel
Roles and responsibilities
Lines of communication for policy/day to day matters
Pattern and reporting procedures for future meetings
Project programme
Team members' programmes and progress

2   Brief
Client's requirements
Development of brief
Changes to brief, implications and control procedures
Pattern and procedures for reporting to client
Preparation of Stage reports to client

3   Site
Information from client about site, foreseeable hazards
Assessment of risks
Development constraints, physical and statutory
Surveys and consents

4   Approvals
Private individuals/bodies
Funders, insurers
Town and country planning
Building Regulations
Fire Officer
Legal (e.g. adjoining owners)

5   Health and Safety
Risk assessment
Health and Safety File
Health and Safety Plan

6   Design and cost control
Concepts
- feasibility assessment
- development of the brief
Coordination of design team effort
- general design
- structures
- services
Drawings
- agreed methods, scales, software, referencing
- cost control
- development of cost plan
- variations

7   Contract
Priorities and phasing
Programming
Procurement
Tendering procedures and documents, Health and Safety Plan
- main contract
- sub-contracts

8   Any other business

9   Date of next meeting

A-B/CM4

Planning permission, other consents and approvals

Consents may have to be obtained during Stages A–B, C, D and F from authorities, organisations or persons having jurisdiction over or rights affecting the project, or who are affected by the project. Consents which could affect feasibility should be applied for during Stage A–B.

Depending on the nature of the project, the site, and the amount of information available, each application for consent should be made at the earliest possible time in order to avoid abortive work.

Before initiating applications for consents:
- explain fully to the client what consents are necessary and what is likely to be involved;
- discover whether the client has contacts or lines of communication with authorities or individuals concerned;
- inform the client about fees payable direct by him;
- inform the client about the likely timescale for processing applications and the degree of consultation;
- make it clear to the client that architects do not obtain consents, this being beyond their power, but that they prepare submissions or make applications on behalf of their clients in accordance with the agreement for professional services.

Check the planning situation

Discover or confirm:
- the existing use of the site;
- whether the proposal is deemed to be 'development' under the Town and Country Planning Acts and so requiring planning permission;
- the planning history of the site, noting important issues such as the dates and decisions of any earlier planning permissions for the site;
- the effect on the site and the proposals of any policy statements or guidelines contained within the statutory Development Plan of the area;
- whether the proposals are within a Designated Urban Development Corporation, Enterprise or Simplified Planning Zone;
- whether the local authority has identified the site as containing contaminated land;
- any likely limitations to the proposals or impositions on the developer through the use of Section 106 agreements or planning conditions.

Check relevant procedures

Check which of the following applications are relevant:
- to determine whether planning application is necessary;
- for certificate of established use;
- for mining or working of minerals;
- for hazardous substances consent;
- for outline planning permission;
- for full planning permission to develop land;
- for listed building consent;
- for conservation area consent;

- for approval of 'conditions' on a planning permission;
- for varying or discharging conditions attached to listed building consent or conservation area consent;
- for varying or revoking conditions attached to a planning permission;
- for approval of reserved matters following an outline planning permission;
- for a scheduled monument consent;
- for a certificate of immunity from listing;
- to fell or lop a tree;
- to establish the need for an Environmental Impact Assessment;
- for permission to display signs and advertisements under the Control of Advertisement Regulations;
- for notification under Circular 18/84 where the Crown is developing on Crown owned land.

The planning application

Make preparations:

- prepare all documentation on the assumption that it might serve as supporting evidence in an Appeal;
- confirm by letter all meetings, phone calls, etc with the planning authority;
- make sure that the client's representative also attends all critical meetings with the planning authority;
- at an early stage consider project presentations to attract the interest and support of neighbourhood and parish groups, appropriate lobbies and news media.

Check the following:

- dates of planning meetings;
- probable date by which decision is to be given;
- number and types of drawings required;
- procedures, e.g. notices in the press, site notices, etc.

When making a planning application, check that:

- forms are carefully completed. Identify or list submitted drawings on forms or in covering letter;
- an accurate site plan identifies the land concerned, clearly defined in red;
- a covering letter accompanies the application, explaining features of the scheme;
- an Ownership Certificate A (or B, C, D as appropriate) is served;
- a cheque from the client for the appropriate sum is submitted at the same time (having checked the correct amount with the planning authority, as it usually increases year on year);
- the application is date-stamped by the planning authority (this defines the start of the period for determination);
- a copy of the written report by the planning officer to the planning committee is obtained;
- if permitted and appropriate, oral representation is made to the planning committee.

The planning meeting:

If appropriate, attend critical meetings with the client's representative. Arrange for a shorthand note to be taken by another person. If planning permission is refused and an Appeal is contemplated, send your account of proceedings to the Chief Executive of the authority. If not dissented from, it may have the status of 'agreed notes'. Examine the agenda and record of the meeting; these may constitute the basis for an Appeal.

A-B/CM5

Health and Safety checklists

Legislation

The principal legislation is the Health and Safety at Work etc Act 1974, which sets out general duties on the part of both employers and employees. These were reinforced with the introduction of the Management of Health and Safety at Work Regulations 1992.

The Workplace (Health, Safety and Welfare) Regulations 1992 are relevant at Stage A–B. Although they place a duty on employers in respect of workplaces under their control, there are implications for the way in which new workplaces are designed and fitted out. This can be in respect of planning (e.g. traffic routes, escalators, room dimensions, sanitary provisions, etc); finishes (e.g. floors, wall surfaces); and installations (e.g. lighting, heating, ventilation). The Regulations are concerned not only with the initial provision of safe conditions for staff but also with safety for cleaning and maintenance.

The RIBA used to publish a safety code for personnel visiting building sites (see Fig. A-B7) and this should be issued to staff and strictly observed.

The Construction (Design and Management) Regulations 1994 ('the CDM Regulations') implement an EC Directive which requires that account be taken of the general principles of prevention concerning health and safety during the stages of project design organisation, construction and future maintenance. The Regulations impose duties on the client, designer, planning supervisor and principal contractor. They apply to nearly all projects where construction work will be of more than 30 days' duration or where more than 500 person days of construction work are involved, except in the case of domestic clients undertaking work on their own residences solely for their own occupation.

The architect's role

The architect, when acting as lead consultant or 'Designer' (as referred to in the CDM Regulations) should carefully study the text of the Regulations and the Approved Code of Practice. It would also be wise to check the following:

- that the client is aware of his or her legal duty to appoint a planning supervisor 'as soon as practicable', and a principal contractor. The client must be satisfied as to the competence and resources of both concerning health and safety matters.
- that the client is aware of his or her legal duty to make available a Health and Safety File in respect of work previously carried out, and other relevant information concerning the site or premises.
- that any sub-consultants employed direct by the architect have the necessary competence and resources.
- that inspections and surveys of site or buildings cover all matters which might indicate potential health and safety hazards. This is a 'Designer's' duty, and if a detailed survey is thought necessary, the client must be prepared to pay for it.
- that when undertaking risk assessments, proper consideration is given to eliminating or reducing potential health and safety hazards when planning site layouts or development. This will include the way that the contractor's operations on site are to be planned.
- that there is full cooperation between the lead consultant and all others having a design input (including consultants and specialist sub-contractors) with regard to health and safety matters.
- that there is full cooperation with the planning supervisor over the production of information which may be relevant for the pre-tender Health and Safety Plan.

Fig. A-B7 Visits to sites and unoccupied buildings: RIBA safety code

Health and Safety legislation lays clear obligations on clients, designers, and principal contractors. The following code is complementary advice to all architects engaged in visits to buildings and sites.

Visits to building sites, unoccupied buildings and construction operations can be potentially dangerous. Consider the likely hazards. Follow the safety code.

1 Occupied building sites

● The Contractor or occupier has a responsibility for the safety of persons lawfully on site. Do not enter sites or buildings without permission, and immediately report to the person in charge. Comply with all requests from the contractor, his representative or other supervisory staff. See the contractor when you arrive, and when you leave the site.

● Wear suitable clothing, in particular protective headgear (a hard hat) and stout shoes or boots. Do not wear thin-soled or slippery shoes. Avoid loose clothes which might catch on an obstruction.

● Check that ladders are securely fixed and that planks are secure. Beware of overhead projections, scaffolding and plant, and proceed with caution. Particular care is necessary in windy, cold, wet or muddy conditions. Keep clear of excavations and beware of openings in floors etc. Do not lean on guard rails, scaffoldings etc. Do not interfere with any temporary barriers, guard rails or lights. Beware of ladders on which the rungs may have rusted or rotted, and never climb a ladder which is not securely fixed at the top.

● Do not touch any plant or equipment. Keep clear of machinery and stacked materials. Watch out for temporary cables, pumps, hoses and electric fittings.

● Do not walk and look around at the same time. Keep one hand free at all times when moving. Make sure that you are in a safe and balanced position whenever making notes or taking photographs.

● Report to the contractor anything that comes to your notice on the site as being unsafe.

2 Unoccupied buildings and sites

● As a general rule do not visit an empty building or unoccupied site on your own. Make sure that someone knows where you are, and at what time you expect to return.

● Do not take chances. Do not visit an empty building if you think it unsafe. Do not visit an unoccupied site if you think it dangerous. Anticipate hazards. Common dangers include:
– the possibility of partial or total structural collapse
– rotten or insecure floors and stairs
– hidden pits, ducts, openings etc, fragile construction, eg asbestos or plastic sheets on roofs
– space which has not been used or ventilated for some time
– live services
– contamination by chemicals or asbestos
– intruders who may still be around
– contamination by vermin or birds, or poisonous substances put down to control them.

● Plan the visit and make sure that you take with you appropriate equipment and protective clothing. Apart from stout shoes and a hard hat, remember that unoccupied buildings can be dirty, damp, cold and dark; so go prepared.

● Familiarise yourself beforehand with the plan of the building, particularly the exit routes. Make sure that security devices on exits will allow you to reach safety quickly.

● Look for defects in the floors ahead, eg wet areas, holes, materials that might be covering up holes.

● Walk over the structural members (eg joists, beams, etc) whenever possible – do not rely on floorboards alone.

● Do not walk and look around at the same time. Keep one hand free at all times when moving. Do not walk and try to take notes at the same time. Make sure that you are in a safe and balanced position when taking photographs or stretching out to take measurements.

● Check on protection when approaching stairwells, lift shafts, roof perimeters, etc.

● Do not assume that services (eg cables, sockets, pipes, etc) are safe or have been isolated.

● If you suspect the presence of gas, inflammable liquids, dangerous chemicals or free asbestos fibre leave the building immediately.

● If you sustain cuts, penetration by nails or other serious injury, seek immediate medical advice.

● Always heed these three golden rules:
– do not rush
– if uncertain do not proceed – seek advice or assistance
– do not smoke or use naked flame.

- that the planning supervisor is invited to attend consultant team meetings, and to comment as appropriate.
- that in all design development the issues of safe specification, safe buildability, and maintenance are kept fully in mind.
- that the pre-tender Health and Safety Plan is part of the tender documentation supplied to the principal contractor and sub-contractors.
- that tenders are carefully examined to make sure that the selected principal contractor has the necessary competence and resources available to deal with health and safety matters, and that price and programme reflect this.
- that the building contract has provisions for compliance with Health and Safety Regulations, and for the contractor to cooperate with the planning supervisor and provide 'as built' information, etc.
- that the client is aware that no work must start on site before a construction phase Health and Safety Plan has been produced by the principal contractor as a management document for the works.
- that a copy of any architect's instruction or variation with health and safety implications is passed to the planning supervisor, and that the construction phase Health and Safety Plan can be updated accordingly.
- that relevant information is passed to the planning supervisor from time to time for possible inclusion in the Health and Safety File.

The planning supervisor

Where this function is discharged by the architect on smaller contracts, it should be seen as a separate appointment, made via a separate appointing document and with an identifiable separate fee.

Where an independent planning supervisor is to be appointed, an architect not otherwise involved in the job might be a suitable person. In all cases such appointments should only be considered by architects who have undergone proper training, fully understand the risks, and have appropriate insurance cover.

Lead consultants or consultant team leaders working on a project where an independent planning supervisor has been appointed would do well to check that this appointee:

- gives proper notice to the Health and Safety Executive initially;
- cooperates effectively in structuring information for a pre-tender Health and Safety Plan;
- is thorough over the evaluation of health and safety aspects of the principal contractors' tenders, and is prepared to advise the client impartially;
- is thorough but reasonable in evaluating the acceptability of the construction phase Health and Safety Plan from the principal contractor and as updated from time to time;
- will prepare the statutory Health and Safety File for deposit with the client at the conclusion of construction, and will explain to the client his or her obligations concerning its safekeeping and future use.

These may not be statutory duties but such checks are very much in the spirit of the legislation and certainly demonstrate the use of reasonable skill and care.

The Health and Safety Notice

This notice, which is a statutory requirement, is normally submitted by the planning supervisor to the Health and Safety Executive. It should include the particulars listed below, as they become known:

- date of forwarding;
- address of construction site;
- name and address of client;
- type of project;

- name and address of planning supervisor;
- declaration confirming appointment of planning supervisor;
- name and address of principal contractor (when appointed);
- declaration confirming appointment of principal contractor;
- date for commencement of construction (when known);
- contract period for construction (when known);
- estimated maximum number of workforce;
- total number of contractors (i.e. principal contractor and nominated/approved sub-contractors) expected on site;
- names and addresses of nominated/approved sub-contractors already selected.

The Health and Safety Plan

The Health and Safety Plan, a document for which the planning supervisor should assume responsibility pre-tender, and for which the principal contractor is responsible, at construction phase might include the information listed below:

- name of client;
- nature of construction work and expected timetable;
- existing environment (e.g. land uses, planning restrictions, services which might have health and safety implications, traffic systems and restrictions which might affect site working);
- ground conditions and possible hazards;
- existing buildings: possible hazards, instability problems, special health problems associated with materials, etc;
- Health and Safety File particulars from previous works, supplied by client/owner;
- design principles (e.g. structural design precautions), risk hazards which are unavoidable, etc;
- construction information and choice of materials likely to cause health hazards and which cannot be avoided;
- site access, egress, organisation of working;
- particular precautions where exclusive possession is not available;
- procedures for dealing with unforeseeable circumstances, and updates to Health and Safety Plan.

The Health and Safety File

The Health and Safety File, a document for which the Planning Supervisor should assume responsibility, is to be deposited with the client at the completion of the contract. It will probably be assembled from information acquired gradually and steadily as the works progress. The client might need briefing as to its purpose, safekeeping, and future use.

The File will be part record and part maintenance manual. It should include the following:

- design criteria;
- general details of constructional systems and methods, materials used, and any potentially hazardous aspects;
- record drawings (as built);
- details of equipment, finishes, and maintenance facilities (e.g. window cleaning);
- maintenance procedures for the structure and finishes, including details and schedules by manufacturers and installers;
- operating instructions and maintenance manuals produced by consultants, sub-contractors and suppliers for services installations, with recommendations for renewal and replacement cycle of plant and equipment;
- information on location, setting and servicing of all services installations including alarms.

A-B/CM6

Inspecting the site

Proper inspections and surveys of sites and existing buildings are essential at Stage A–B. Rough preliminary surveys are not good enough and are an inadequate basis on which to judge feasibility. Ill-founded recommendations at this stage can lead to serious problems later.

When considering survey action, try to establish:
- the kind of survey needed and precisely what is to be surveyed;
- who will carry out the survey – the practice's own staff, external land or building surveyors, other specialists;
- who will pay for the survey and where liability will rest in the event of errors.

Identify the boundaries of the site to be surveyed or the limits of the building. Confirm with the client that access will be available and obtain keys if necessary. Notify persons on site as appropriate.

Do not overlook statutory obligations arising, particularly those concerning occupiers liability, and health and safety. Always heed the RIBA Safety Code for occupied building sites and unoccupied buildings and sites (see Fig. A-B7)

Information about immediate area

Check:
- general context and character, outstanding visual features;
- local development plan, action area plans, construction work currently under way;
- local authority Contaminated Land Register;
- evidence of social and economic patterns;
- traffic movement patterns, noise, pollution;
- derelict areas, nearby black spots, visually detracting features.

Visual inspection of site

Check:
- aspect, orientation, shelter, overshadowing from adjacent buildings or trees;
- hedges, ditches, ponds, wet/soft patches, underground streams;
- benchmarks, contours, and slope of site;
- paths, gates, stiles which might indicate rights of way;
- overhead cables, pylons and poles;
- possible health and safety hazards, e.g. flooding, exposure, unsafe trees, etc;
- properties adjoining the site, their condition, usage, evidence of subsidence, fire risks, party walls, etc;
- possible health and safety hazards such as radon or other gases, pollutants and contamination from previous use, filled basements, etc;
- adjacent waterways, railways, busy roads;
- possible restrictions on site access, delivery or site working;
- possible restrictions due to sensitive building uses adjacent, e.g. hospital, nursery school, law court.

Site survey information

If the site survey is to be undertaken by a surveying firm, make sure that this is agreed with the client as not a part of the architect's services, and is to be paid for direct.

Confirm:

- by whom the surveyors are to be engaged;
- how the surveying fees are to be paid;
- who is doing which part of the work;
- how the results are to be presented;
- arrangements for access, security, protection and insurance.

If appropriate, arrange for a survey of tree species and condition and an analysis of top soil.

The information presented in the survey plans and reports might be expected to include the following:

Plans, showing:

- existing and proposed boundaries;
- outline of existing buildings and roads;
- boundary fences, access ways, garden and adjacent walls, their height, profile, material, ownership and condition;
- ditches, ponds, waterways above or below ground;
- wet or bad patches (discover seasonal variations from local sources);
- rock outcrops and other geological features, their type and size;
- position of trial holes;
- rights of way/access (check with client's solicitors, local authority).

Sections, drawn on separate sheets taken along the full length of section lines on the key drawings, to the same scale as the plan.

Levels, showing:

- position and level of benchmarks or basis of datum;
- calculated levels in true relationship to an ordnance datum level;
- spot levels on a 10m grid related to ordnance survey grid, or closer where local variations occur, e.g. at changes of level, hillocks, etc.

Spot levels, indicating:

- the base of all trees;
- all services covers, etc;
- pavement kerbs and road crowns where they enter site.

Indicate contours, intervals (in metres) and position of section lines (on grid lines where possible).

Indicate all services above and below ground adjacent to, connecting into or crossing the site with relevant levels, falls, heights, access points, manholes (show cover levels and inverts). Also:

- pylons, posts (show headroom);
- soil and surface water drains;
- water mains;
- electricity cables;
- telecommunication cables;
- gas mains;
- any other services.

Indicate trees, hedges and large shrubs, their height and position, spread of branches and diameter of trunk 1m above ground level.

Soil investigations

On a domestic project or one which involves a relatively small and light structure, it might well be sufficient for the architect to instruct the digging of trial pits. These should be set out with regard to the siting of the proposed building. On anything larger, investigation by boreholes may be necessary to obtain information and data for the design and construction of foundations, underground structures, road works, earthworks, etc. On sites containing contaminated land or unstable landfill, specialist advice will be needed as to the surveying techniques to be used.

The structural engineer may be able to give preliminary advice by examining available information about the geology and history of the site, e.g. maps and memos produced by the Institute of Geological Sciences, Ordnance Survey maps, engineering data from earlier works in the area, aerial photographs.

The engineer should recommend the type and extent of investigations to be carried out, including the number of trial holes necessary to obtain an accurate assessment of the subsoil and water table conditions.

The investigating firm must allow for carrying out the work in accordance with any special requirements of the existing owners or occupiers of the site. They and/or their sub-contractor specialists should be made responsible for all security, protection and related insurance during execution of the work.

The field work should be supervised by the engineer, and daily liaison should be maintained so that any variations indicated by the borehole findings can be made. Daily site records of boreholes should be sent to the engineer stating:

- borehole numbers and location;
- date and times of boring;
- type of plant and method of boring;
- diameter of boring casing and core;
- description of strata and depth of base of each stratum;
- level at bottom of casing when sample taken, or in situ test carried out on each core drilled;
- depths at which each sample was taken and in situ tests made;
- water levels.

On completing the site work, the contractor should submit to the engineer preliminary borehole logs together with a list of samples so that instructions can be given for laboratory testing.

The final site investigation should be submitted as a draft (for approval of its form, not content). Unless otherwise specified it should contain:

- description of work carried out (i.e. site and laboratory work);
- borehole logs;
- laboratory test results, including geological classification, index properties, acidity, sulphate content, etc;
- records of water levels in standpipes and/or piezometers installed in boreholes, with notes of any variations;
- results of strength tests;
- diagrammatic cross-section through site showing trial holes related to a datum and assumed connecting geological structure, water table, etc;
- plan showing position of trial holes, incorporated with main survey plan if appropriate.

Surveys of existing buildings

It is essential that the architect personally walks through every room in the building to be surveyed, regardless of whether the survey is being done by in-house personnel or by a surveying firm. It is important to perceive the architectural character of a building and the way it has been constructed.

The measured survey drawings might show:

- plans, sections, elevations;
- elevational features, e.g. plinths, string courses, openings;
- precise levels at floors, datum, thickness and construction;
- levels of external ground;
- details of decoration, profiles, false columns, etc;
- finishes and colours;
- loose equipment, landlord's fittings, etc.

A written report might include information that cannot be shown graphically, such as:

- structural and other defects and their causes;
- dry rot, damp penetration, condensation;
- infestation by rodents, beetles and other insects;
- presence of asbestos (this may require a separate specialist survey);
- recent repairs and decoration;
- settlement cracks, mis-shapen openings, gaps at skirtings and windows;
- walls that are misaligned or have bulges;
- sagging roofs, defective roof coverings;
- deflection of beams or lintels, cracks at beam bearings.

The architects/surveyors should state whether or not they were able to see inside the structure of the building and how much they were able to see. It is important not to infer the state of the whole building from sight of one part of it. A statement on the following lines should appear at the end of the relevant part of the report (as stipulated in most professional indemnity insurance policies):

'It has not been possible to make a detailed examination of the floor or roof construction except at the positions described because material damage would have been caused in gaining access. It is therefore impossible to make any statement about the condition of the unexamined structure.'

Where appropriate, the client should be advised to call in specialists, e.g. mechanical, electrical, timber treatment, and should be asked for instructions regarding any fees, expenses and inconvenience arising from their investigations.

A-B/CM7

A project quality plan

References in this *Architect's Job Book* to setting up and developing a project quality plan are made against the background of the Standard for Quality Systems BS EN ISO 9001:1994. Quality management is concerned with consistent performance to stated requirements, and the system is essentially one of control. Likewise the project quality plan document should be seen as the principal instrument for control and communication on the project.

At the time of writing, a number of architects' practices have achieved certification status, and these will already be operating a system which includes for project quality plans. Such a system is set out in Jefferies (1999) *A Model for a Quality Management System*.

In addition to those who have formed third party certification, many other practices also have systematic procedures, whether or not they describe these as 'quality management', which constitute an effective framework for running the office and the individual jobs. There will probably be an office handbook or manual where the procedural framework is clearly set out. In addition to the office organisation, policy and review mechanism, the manual will probably describe general administrative procedures, the way appointments are to be formalised, job costing and fees, employing consultants, dealing with correspondence, management of design, producing and issuing drawings, administering contracts and keeping records. These and other matters are all part of the way a methodical practice carries on its business.

Accordingly, where a formalised quality system does not exist, a project quality plan can still be created either as a stand alone document or as part of a coordinated package making reference to other controlling documents or procedures. This may be provided in hard copy as well as software, written or diagrammatic. Many of the procedures might be described in detail elsewhere (e.g. in the office manual, handbook or other documents, such as this *Architect's Job Book*) and could be included by reference. Two alternative detailed and helpful project quality plans are set out in *A Model for a Quality Management System*. What follows is an outline of what a project quality plan might contain.

A typical project quality plan might include:

Project description
- the client's design requirements;
- a synopsis of brief and priorities;
- an intended life span of building overall and of components;
- constraints which arise from legislation or other sources.

Project organisation
- the identity of the client and representatives;
- an identified practice/project quality manager;
- agreed procedures for consultations/approvals;
- principal practice staff assigned to the project and their defined responsibilities;
- project timetable/programmes.

Consultant team
- consultants/specialists with design or other input;
- defined responsibilities, including review procedures;
- management, procedures for administration, including coordination.

Control procedures

- brief development control, and reviews;
- design input control, design management and development, and patterns of design review;
- design and information output control;
- project specification basis and development;
- project administration and document control procedures;
- procurement, and procedures for appointment of the project construction team;
- contract administration procedures;
- monitoring of contractors' quality management.

Change control

- agreed procedures for modifications or changes to approved brief;
- agreed procedures for modifications or changes to approved designs;
- records of modifications or changes;
- identification of documents subjected to revision and withdrawal to prevent unintended use.

Tests

- programme for inspections and tests, and personnel involved;
- procedures and check sheets or reports to be used;
- corrective action in the event of non-conforming work;
- programme for audits, personnel involved, and audit reports.

Particular instructions

- those items in the practice's quality system to be expressly excluded in the case of this particular project;
- items not covered by the practice's quality system to be specifically included in the case of this particular project.

Records

- end of project reviews;
- experience feedback studies and reports;
- maintenance manuals and operating instructions;
- as built information;
- job records and files.

To summarise, a project quality plan will be in the form most appropriate for the particular project. It should be a document which:

- defines activities and how they are to be carried out;
- should be adequate for submission to a client for acceptance and review;
- is reviewed regularly through the progress of the project, with amendments and revisions as necessary submitted for acceptance before implementation.

A-B/CM8

Financial appraisal

The financial appraisal is usually prepared by the quantity surveyor. The QS is the expert on costs and can call on an RICS or other information service, as well as his or her own knowledge and expertise. Such an appraisal could be a document to be developed as the design progresses, and form a basis for effective cost planning.

However, on a small project where no QS is appointed the architect may have to write an appraisal for inclusion in the feasibility report. This is likely to be little more than an estimate to test the viability of the client's budget figure. A proper cost plan will need to be developed later.

Where the architect undertakes to prepare this appraisal, the approach should be as follows.

Define status

Define the status of the appraisal, and set out the assumptions on which estimates are made. List any items of important information which were not available, and which items have not been included for.

State basis for estimates

State the basis for estimates (e.g. cost indices, £ per m^2 etc) on current or predicted rates (if projected, to what date).

Estimate capital cost

When estimating the capital cost of the building project, consider:
- location (e.g. whether remote) and access (e.g. a difficult, tight site);
- site investigation and abnormal site works;
- demolition or preliminary contracts for enabling works;
- programme and phasing;
- building substructure and superstructure (e.g. systems, cladding, etc);
- finishes (e.g. expensive or standard);
- engineering services installations;
- designers' and contractors' contingencies;
- fitting out and furnishings;
- landscape treatment — both hard and soft, including planting.

Other costs

Other costs to be taken into account might include:
- fees for statutory approvals;
- fees and expenses for the consultant team;
- fees and expenses for the planning supervisor.

An estimate should also clarify the VAT position, the possible effects of inflation, and warn that fluctuations are possible after the start of the building contract, even a lump sum contract. It might also be helpful to suggest the phasing of payments so that the client can begin to consider how best to manage his or her cash flow.

In addition to the estimate of the capital cost of the building project, the client will need to take into account the cost of the site, legal and other fees, finance costs, the risk and profit element, and an assessment of costs in use for the building.

C: OUTLINE PROPOSALS

Commence development of Strategic Brief into full Project Brief. Preparation of Outline Proposals and estimate of cost. Review of procurement route (RIBA Outline Plan of Work).

Description

Key obligations from SFA/99

Actions

Stage input

Preliminary issues   architect

client

management and team working

Developing the Project Brief and Outline Proposals

Inspections/tests

Consultations

Approvals/consents

Cost planning

General procedures

Stage output

Core material

C/CM1   Design and build documentation

C/CM2   Consultant team roles: Work Stage C

OUTLINE PROPOSALS

Description

This Stage starts with the receipt from the client of the Strategic Brief. The Strategic Brief may include details of any preferred option or feasibility study developed in Stage A-B which may form the basis for the outline proposals at Stage C.

The Strategic Brief is now the basis for the architect's services, which if different from the services, cost or time targets in the Agreement with the client, may require a formal variation by letter or deed.

With a traditional procurement method, during Stage C a design concept based on the Strategic Brief will usually be prepared. This will show the design analysis and options considered, and will be sufficiently detailed to establish in broad terms the outline proposal preferred. Presentation will normally entail drawings and a report, although more sophisticated techniques such as video or CD-ROM may be employed where appropriate.

Where no outline design concept is required, for example when conserving a historic building, then Stage C will involve the presentation of Outline Proposals appropriate to the commission.

In parallel with the development of the design, the Strategic Brief will be evaluated and developed to form the Project Brief, a document which is finalised by the end of Work Stage D.

Note that where the architect is appointed under the Small Works form, SW/99 Stages C and D are combined and that preparation of the Project Brief is not defined, although a record of any changes made to the original brief may be appropriate.

With design and build, where the architect is engaged by the employer for Stage C, an outline design may be developed to form part of the Employer's Requirements. The design will be taken to an extent related to the intended design contribution by the contractor.

With a Contractor Client, the employer's Strategic Brief may form a component part of the Requirements, and the architect will be involved in developing the Contractor's Proposals as a response to these Requirements. Tendering is often a two-stage process, and this might initially require outline design only, with design development left until a later stage.

Key obligations which may apply:

	Reference	To do
- from SFA/99: design services		
Receive Strategic Brief and commence development into Project Brief.	SFA/99/C/1	☐
Prepare Outline Proposals.	SFA/99/C/2	☐
Prepare an approximation of construction cost, or	SFA/99/C/3A	☐
Provide information for cost planning.	SFA/99/C/3B	☐
Submit to client Outline Proposals and approximate construction cost.	SFA/99/C/4	☐
Co-operate with planning supervisor where appropriate.	SFA/99/1.4	☐

In addition to the above, the architect should note the obligations set out in the SFA/99 Conditions of Engagement 2.1-2.8.

- from SFA/99: management services

(i.e. architect acting as design leader and lead consultant) ☐

Coordinating and monitoring design work. ☐

Establishing the form and content of design outputs, their interfaces and a verification procedure. ☐

Advising on methods of procuring construction. ☐

Reporting to the client. ☐

Actions

Stage input

Check that all information necessary during Stage C is available, which might include the following: ☐

- Brief developed to Strategic Brief stage including cost and time targets and any proposals accepted by the client, noting any agreed amendments.

- Further information as requested, supplied by client.

- Notes, sketches, details made on further visits to site and/or existing buildings.

- Published material, technical press articles as appropriate.

- Technical information (e.g. Planning or Design Guides, British Standards, Codes of Practice, etc). Manufacturers' trade literature.

- Results of surveys and tests conducted during Stage A–B.

- Relevant legislation, Circulars or Guides to assist in statutory compliance.

- Contributions, information and recommendations from consultants and specialists.

Design and build • Information as above for development into Employer's Requirements. *(Employer Client)*

Design and build • Employer's Requirements as issued to tenderers. *(Contractor Client)* **see C/CM1**

Preliminary issues – architect

Establish scope, content and context for Stage D activities. ☐
Put it into context particularly if previous Stages undertaken by others, or material produced is likely to be acted upon by others taking over subsequent Stages.

If coming new to the project at this Stage in the *Plan of Work:* ☐

- ascertain that relevant Pre-Agreement and earlier Stage checks have been carried out;

- allow for familiarisation and reviewing of all usable material when agreeing fees and timetable with the client;

- confirm the role of the architect in relation to the rest of the consultant team if appointed, i.e. whether appointed as lead consultant, design leader or member, or whether a project manager has been appointed. Direct access to the client, particularly at design stages, is highly desirable.

Check the client's instruction to proceed has been given and con- ☐
firmed in writing.

Check client has settled all accounts to date. ☐

Check appointing documents with respect to services and fees. ☐

- If the Services, cost or time targets are different from the Agreement with the client agree a formal variation by letter or deed as appropriate.

- If the extent of professional services for Stage C is not settled, agree with client and confirm in writing.

- If the methods and levels of charging for Stage C are not settled, agree with client and confirm in writing.

Enquire whether additional services will be wanted which are not included under the Agreement. These might extend to special studies, community surveys and participation exercises with a user client, attendance at meetings, presentation materials, etc.

Assess office resources needed for Stage C and ensure that they ☐
are adequate and available.

Carry out checks for compliance with in-house quality management procedures; including updated project quality plan. ☐

Review application of practice procedures to project. ☐

Preliminary issues – client

Alert the client to any matters raised during preliminary discussions with statutory or other bodies which seem likely to affect the brief or design proposals. ☐

Advise the client on the need to appoint further consultants and **C/CM2** specialists. Decisions may be needed for Outline Proposals which require specialist advice on structure, services environmental and other matters. ☐

Advise the client on Health and Safety matters.
Remind the client about the need to appoint a planning supervisor early to coordinate matters connected with the pre-tender Health and Safety Plan at this design stage. ☐

Make specific requests to the client for further necessary information if that provided is not adequate. ☐

Review with the client the options for procurement and note any matters which could affect the particular choice.
In particular it is important to identify at an early stage who will be carrying out all specialist areas of design, for example whether they will be handled by the consultant team or by specialist sub-contractors. This has implications for the consultant's terms of appointment, liability and warranty arrangements as well as affecting the procurement route to be adopted. ☐

Design and build Confirm with the client the extent of information to be included in the **C/CM1** Employer's Requirements. *(Employer Client)* ☐

Design and build Check the Employer's Requirements issued for tendering purposes, **C/CM1** and advise the client on any apparent omissions or inconsistencies. Confirm with the client the extent of information to be provided for inclusion in the Contractor's Proposals. *(Contractor Client)* ☐

Preliminary issues – management and team working

Establish or review project quality management procedures in concert with relevant procedures of all consultant team members. ☐

Check scope of professional services agreed with other consultants **C/CM2** as they are appointed. ☐

Agree input to the Stage by consultant team members. ☐

Remind consultant team members contributing at Stage C to identify current legislation (e.g. building regulations, health and safety) with which the project must conform to.

Discuss with consultant team members the performance standards, environmental provisions and budget allocation required to comply with the brief, and the presentation of material in a way which can be readily integrated into the overall design concept.

Confirm Stage timetable for services and note its relationship to the project timetable as agreed with the client. The timetable should show critical points by which information from the client and consultant team members will be required. ☐

Confirm arrangements for communication between client, planning supervisor, project manager and design leader. ☐

Cooperate with the planning supervisor and all other designers over carrying out risk assessments and in drafting the pre-tender Health and Safety Plan. ☐

Confirm programme and pattern for consultant team meetings. ☐

Developing the Project Brief and Outline Proposals

On receipt of the Strategic Brief, evaluate its content to establish that: ☐

- the client's stated objectives are reflected;

- an adequate basis for design is provided;

- the time and cost parameters are reasonable;

- all the information the client should provide before design commences is provided.

If changes to the brief are necessary, make sure that these are subject to the change control procedures established, for example in the project quality plan.

Advise the client of the results of the evaluation and seek instructions regarding any further information needed.   ☐

If the Strategic Brief varies from any submissions to the client during Stages A or B consider what action may be required.   ☐

Obtain relevant technical and trade literature.   ☐

Obtain project specific information from potential sub-contractors and suppliers.   ☐

Coordinate and integrate information from QS, other consultants and specialists.   ☐

Commence development of Strategic Brief into Project Brief.   ☐

Undertake design review as appropriate.   ☐

Prepare Outline Proposals.   ☐

Innovation in design, specification or selection of materials and methods can involve risk. Take care that risks are assessed before proposals are finalised. Check and test against known criteria — do not trust to luck.

Prepare report and submit to the client.   ☐

Inspections/tests

Make further visits to the site and/or existing buildings as authorised.   ☐

Carry out a visual inspection of the extent of existing buildings, site boundaries, etc before completing outline design or proposals. If necessary ask the client to ascertain the exact details of site boundaries, covenants, easements, etc. In the case of design and build particularly, the employer may carry total responsibility for accuracy.   ☐

Carry out or supervise further survey work if appropriate and instructed by the client.   ☐

If appropriate, construct contour or block models to demonstrate options in Outline Proposals.   ☐

Consider need for tests using physical or computer models (e.g. in research laboratory using a wind tunnel, heliodon, artificial sky, etc) to obtain and analyse information about environmental performance, air circulation, temperature distribution, etc.

Prepare models for testing, record and analyse results if instructed by client.

☐

Note that surveys, inspections or specialist investigations and preparation of special models do not form part of the Services under SFA/99 unless identified under 'Other Services'.

Consultations

Hold informal discussions with authorities as appropriate before making formal submission for permission, approval or consent.

☐

Note: consultation with statutory authorities is not included in SFA/99 until Stage D, although it appears in Stage C in the Plan of Work. *In practice, to establish feasibility of proposals, consultations are likely to be necessary at Stages A-C.*

Hold discussions as appropriate with the planning officer.

☐

Discuss with the client the potential benefits in obtaining Outline Planning Approval.

☐

Establish with the local authority Building Control department:

☐

- Whether the project is one which will require approval under Building Regulations and if so, whether this should be Building Notice or Full Plans submission.

- Whether it would be more beneficial to submit Building Regulations applications to the local authority or an Approved Inspector, and report to the client.

- Whether a dispensation would be likely where the legal requirements of Building Regulations could be particularly onerous and damaging to the architectural integrity of a historic building.

Check whether there is any local legislation or legislation particular to the proposed development or building type which should be complied with.

☐

Discuss with the relevant authorities the most satisfactory way of making provision for persons with a disability who could be expected to use the building. □

It is important to advise the client about the current and future implications of the Disability Discrimination Act 1995. Even though not all sections are yet in force, it is important to avoid the client being placed in a position where work may need to be altered in the near future.

Check whether bodies such as the National Rivers Authority, British Waterways Board, etc could have their interests affected by the proposed development. If this seems possible, they should be consulted. □

Check with relevant authorities concerning highways, drainage, water, gas and electricity, etc and note requirements for plant and meter housings, substations, etc. Consult with waste collection authorities regarding disposal and recycling of waste. □

Agree with the client the need and/or arrangements for discussions with authorised users in developing the Project Brief and the Outline Proposals. Consult with user clients authorised. □

Consult with third parties, adjoining owners, e.g. landlord, estate surveyor, lessees, adjoining owners, etc if authorised. □

Failure to agree party wall awards can lead to delays in start of work on site. Establish at an early stage whether notices under the Party Wall etc Act 1996 will be needed.

Note that consultations with users or third parties, and party wall matters, do not form part of the Services under SFA/99 unless identified under 'Other Services'.

Approvals/consents

Prepare an application for outline planning permission if appropriate and not yet obtained, and submit application if instructed by client. □

Submit applications for necessary approvals or consents required from third parties if instructed by the client. □

Note: applications for outline planning permission and approval of landlords, funders, etc do not form part of the Services under SFA/99 unless identified under 'Other Services'.

Cost planning

Provide information to QS for initial cost plan and cash flow projection (or prepare an approximation of construction cost if appointed to do so). **Fig. C1** ☐

Compare initial cost plan and cash flow forecast with the latest approved cost. ☐

Discuss with the consultant team and the client the effect of major design decisions on the allocations within the cost plan before they are taken. ☐

An increase in cost of one element, e.g. for a sophisticated external wall cladding system may require complementary savings in the mechanical services installation.

Report to the client on cost matters at agreed intervals. ☐

Design and build Provide information to the contractor's estimators for costing out design proposals. *(Contractor Client)* ☐

Fig. C1   Specimen cost plan/budget estimate

Job no: Job title:

Cost plan / budget estimate

		Cost of element	Cost per m² gross floor area	Element shown as % of whole
Substructure		_____	_____	_____
Superstructure	Frame	_____	_____	_____
	Upper floors	_____	_____	_____
	Roof	_____	_____	_____
	Stairs	_____	_____	_____
	External cladding	_____	_____	_____
	Windows and external doors	_____	_____	_____
	Internal partitions	_____	_____	_____
	Internal doors and windows	_____	_____	_____
Internal finishes	Ceiling finishes	_____	_____	_____
	Wall finishes	_____	_____	_____
	Floor finishes	_____	_____	_____
Fittings	Furniture and fittings	_____	_____	_____
Services	Sanitary installation	_____	_____	_____
	Mechanical installation	_____	_____	_____
	Electrical installation	_____	_____	_____
	Special installations	_____	_____	_____
	Elevators and hoists	_____	_____	_____
	Builder's work	_____	_____	_____
	Builder's profit and attendance	_____	_____	_____
Building work	**Sub-total**	_____	_____	_____
Additional	Site works	_____	_____	_____
	Drainage	_____	_____	_____
	External services	_____	_____	_____
	Extra temporary works (phasing)	_____	_____	_____
	Inflation at 3%	_____	_____	_____
	Preliminaries at 5%	_____	_____	_____
Total	**Excluding VAT and contingencies**	_____	_____	_____

Fig. C2   Specimen schedule of activities/spaces/rooms

Job no: Job title:

Schedule of activities/spaces/rooms

Activities/spaces/ rooms identified	Preferred aspect and location	Functional connections	Notes of specific requirements

Compiled by: Date

General procedures

Regularly check progress against the timetable for services. ☐

Continue resource control procedures for job: ☐

- Check expenditure against the office job cost allocation for Stage C;

- Monitor fee income against projected fee income.

Report regularly to the client on fees and expenses incurred, and submit accounts at agreed intervals. ☐

Check that the client settles all accounts promptly. ☐

Keep careful records of all conversations, consultations and design team meetings. File notes and sketches prepared during the outline design process. Keep all manufacturers' or trade literature to which reference was made. It might be needed later as proof of the 'state of the art' at the time. ☐

Always check with PI insurers if any aspects of Outline Proposals are innovative. ☐

Stage output

Check that all the agreed outputs have been produced before the conclusion of Stage C, which might include the following: ☐

- Partially developed Project Brief.

- Outline Proposals. These should show the design sufficiently developed for the client to comprehend, comment on and approve the proposals. A diagrammatic analysis of requirements, use of site, solutions to functional and circulation problems, relationship of spaces, massing, construction and environmental methods may be included.

- An estimate of the Construction Cost sufficient to allow a cost plan to be prepared (see Fig. C1).

- Where agreed, special presentation material.

Design and build Outline proposals for Employer's Requirements. *(Employer Client)* **C/CM1**

Design and build   Outline drawings for Contractor's Proposals. *(Contractor Client)*   **C/CM1**

Design and build   Notes, sketches, details to facilitate written material and estimates in connection with Contractor's Proposals. *(Contractor Client)*

References and further reading

CIB (1997) *Briefing the Team: a guide to better briefing for clients*, London, Thomas Telford Publications.

Cox, S. and Hamilton, A. (eds.) (1997) *Architect's Guide to Job Administration under the Party Wall etc Act 1996*, London, RIBA Publications.

Cox, S. and Hamilton, A. (eds.) (1996) *Architect's Guide to Job Administration under the CDM Regulations 1994*, London, RIBA Publications.

Halliday, S. (2000) *Green Guide to the Architect's Job Book*, London, RIBA Publications.

Jefferies, T. (1999) *A Model for a Quality Management System*, London, RIBA Publications.

Penton, J. (1999) *The Disability Discrimination Act: Inclusion*, London, RIBA Publications.

RIBA (1996) *Model Safety Policy with safety codes, for architects, engineers and surveyors*, London, RIBA Publications.

C/CM1

Design and build documentation

Employer's Requirements

The amount of information to be included in the Employer's Requirements can vary enormously. A straightforward project requiring a relatively simple design solution which can be left largely to the contractor may need little more than basic details of site and accommodation. With a more complex problem, or a design which needs sensitivity of detail, the Employer's Requirements might extend to a full scheme design.

The number and detail of documents which make up the Employer's Requirements will be influenced by considerations such as:

- how much design control the employer wishes to retain, for example in the interests of maintenance programmes or because of functional requirements;
- whether the employer regards the process as more of a develop and construct operation, where only constructional details are left in the hands of the contractor;
- whether contractor's standard unit types will form the basis of the scheme;
- whether the employer will require design continuity via novation or a 'consultant switch';
- whether the employer has appointed a planning supervisor and whether a pre-tender Health and Safety Plan exists.

Generally the Requirements will always need to include basic information, such as the following:

- site information and requirements (e.g. boundaries, topography, known subsoil conditions, existing services);
- site constraints (e.g. limitations of access, storage) and relevant easements or restrictive covenants;
- topographical surveys;
- geotechnical reports;
- planning permission obtained or conditions known (contractors will not usually tender until outline planning permission has been obtained);
- reports on other statutory consultations;
- existing Health and Safety Files, client's health and safety policy documents;
- functional nature of the building(s) (e.g. kind and number of units) and accommodation requirements;
- schematic layout of the building (or more developed design as appropriate);
- specific requirements as to forms of construction, materials, services, finishes, equipment, etc;
- specification information, probably including performance specifications;
- room data sheets;
- equipment and fitting schedules;
- details of special programming requirements (e.g. phased completion);
- contract data or special requirements (e.g. named sub-contractors, as built information);
- requirements concerning contractor's design liability, insurance cover, design team, requirement to use employer's designers, etc;
- clear statement of the extent of information and detail to be included in the Contractor's Proposals;
- content and form of the Contract Sum Analysis;
- if JCT WCD98 is to be used, information related to Supplementary Provisions S2-S7.

It is generally accepted that too specific an approach over design and constructional matters, or the specifying of proprietary systems and materials may reduce the contractor's design liability in the event of a failure.

Contractor's Proposals

These will be in direct response to the Employer's Requirements. Architects acting as consultants to a Contractor Client will first need to check the information provided to establish whether it is adequate. A query list is often necessary to obtain clarification on matters of conflict or omission.

Submissions sometimes take the form of an A3 brochure, and typically include the following:
* design drawings (e.g. site layout, floor plans, elevations, principal sections, some detailed drawings, landscaping);
* structural details (e.g. foundation and structure general arrangement drawings);
* mechanical services (e.g. layouts of ducts, pipe runs, schematic indications for all systems);
* electrical services (e.g. floor layouts showing lighting, power, alarms);
* specifications (e.g. particular for trades prescription and performance, general specification for workmanship, materials, finishes);
* programme (e.g. bar chart);
* method statements (e.g. general organisational matters and in particular Health and Safety Plan proposals).

The tender figure will usually be required to be made separately. With it will be the Contract Sum Analysis.

The structure of the Contract Sum Analysis will be in accordance with the Employer's Requirements. A typical breakdown could be:
* Design work
* Preliminaries
* Health and safety provisions
* Demolition
* Excavation
* Concrete
* Brickwork and blockwork
* Roofing and cladding
* Woodwork
* Structural steelwork
* Metalwork
* Mechanical and plumbing services
* Electrical services
* Glazing
* Painting and decorating
* Drainage and external works.

Architects involved with design and build should take note of information contained in:
* JCT Practice Notes CD/1A and CD/1B;
* NJCC Code of Procedure for Selective Tendering for Design and Build.

C/CM2

Consultant team roles: Stage C

Quantity surveyor

The QS can assist the consultant team in reviewing financial aspects of the Outline Proposals and monitoring costs against the budget. He or she should be involved continuously and should report regularly at consultant team meetings.

The QS will evaluate the Strategic Brief and advise on the cost implications of design and energy options. He or she will prepare an initial cost plan and cash flow forecast, relying on input from other consultant team members.

Structural engineer

The engineer can work with the architect to develop structural concepts which are integral with the overall design in the Outline Proposals. He or she will visit the site and advise on the structural constraints it imposes, and advise on surveys needed, for example where there are special conditions such as contaminated land. The structural engineer can advise on environmental issues such as excavation and landfill. He or she should also liaise with services engineers to ensure integrated design. Priorities should be established and conflicts resolved at design team meetings.

Building services engineers

At Outline Proposals stage, the architect will take into account orientation, climatic and other environmental factors. There will also be a need to establish performance, installation costs and costs in use. The services consultants can play an important role in contributing to an integrated design approach, including consideration of sustainability issues, for example where there are special conditions such as contaminated land. The structural engineer can advise on environmental issues such as excavation and landfill. They will identify surveys required and initiate preliminary consultations with statutory authorities. They should contribute regularly to design team meetings.

Health and safety

All consultant team members should cooperate with the planning supervisor in carrying out risk assessments, and starting to prepare material for inclusion in the Health and Safety File and the pre-tender Health and Safety Plan.

D: DETAILED PROPOSALS

Complete development of the Project Brief. Preparation of Detailed Proposals.
Application for full Development Control Approval (RIBA Outline Plan of Work).

Description

Key obligations from SFA/99

Actions

Stage input
Preliminary issues   architect
                 client
                 management and team working
Developing the Project Brief and Detailed Proposals
Inspections/tests
Consultations
Approvals/consents
Contract
Cost planning
General procedures
Stage output

Core material

D/CM1	Consultant team roles: Work Stage D
D/CM2	Project Brief: Final checklist
D/CM3	Detailed Proposals presentation

DETAILED PROPOSALS

Description

At Stage D, under traditional procurement, the Outline Proposals approved by the client are developed into Detailed Proposals and the development of the Project Brief is completed. As lead consultant the architect will need to be satisfied that there are no insurmountable problems ahead concerning the integration of the consultants' proposals into the overall design concept. As 'designer', within the meaning of that term in the CDM Regulations, the architect will also have to be sure that all health and safety implications have been properly considered at this stage.

With design and build, where the architect is acting for an Employer Client, Stage D might cover design formulation to the extent necessary for inclusion as part of the Employer's Requirements. If the project has been tendered at an early stage in the development of the design, Stage D may involve the architect in assessing the contractor's design proposals and reporting to the Employer Client.

With a Contractor Client, the architect may be involved in the development of the design information already included as part of the Contractor's Proposals. The development of Detailed Proposals will probably not take place until there is confirmation that the contractor's bid has been approved, or a second stage tender is invited.

Where management procurement is followed, there will still need to be an overall design scheme even though it is anticipated the detailed development will be phased. Thought should be given to how the works packages will be broken down, as this in turn might influence some design decisions.

Key obligations which may apply:

	Reference	To do
- from SFA/99: design services		
Complete development of Project Brief.	SFA/99/D/1	☐
Develop the Detailed Proposals from approved Outline Proposals.	SFA/99/D/2	☐
Prepare a cost estimate, or	SFA/99/D/3A	☐
Provide information for preparation of cost estimate.	SFA/99/D/3B	☐
Consult statutory authorities.	SFA/99/D/4	☐
Submit to client the Detailed Proposals and cost estimate.	SFA/99/C/5	☐
Prepare and submit application for full planning permission.	SFA/99/C/6	☐
Co-operate with planning supervisor where appropriate.	SFA/99/1.4	☐

In addition to the above, the architect should note the obligations set out in the SFA/99 Conditions of Engagement 2.1-2.8.

- from SFA/99: management services		
(i.e. architect acting as design leader and lead consultant)		☐
Coordinating and monitoring design work.		☐
Establishing the form and content of design outputs, their interfaces and a verification procedure.		☐
Advising on methods of procuring construction.		☐
Reporting to the client.		☐

Actions

Stage input

Check that all information necessary during Stage D is available, which might include the following:

- Partially developed Project Brief, derived from Strategic Brief.

- Stage C Outline Proposals as accepted by the client in written confirmation, incorporating any agreed design changes.

- Further information as requested by the architect and supplied by the client.

- Notes, sketches, details made on visits to other projects.

- Relevant published material, technical information, etc.

- Results of tests conducted during Stage C.

- Relevant legislation, Circulars or Guides.

- Further contributions, information and recommendations from consultants and specialists.

- Initial cost plan prepared by quantity surveyor.

Preliminary issues – architect

Establish scope, content and context for Stage D activities.
Put it into context, particularly if previous Stages were undertaken by others. If possible establish whether material produced now is likely to be acted upon by others taking over subsequent Stages.

If coming new to the project at this Stage in the *Plan of Work:*

- Ascertain that relevant Pre-Agreement and earlier Stage checks have been carried out.

- Allow for familiarisation and reviewing of all usable material when agreeing fees and timetable with the client.

- Confirm the role of the architect in relation to the rest of the consultant team.

Check the client's instruction to proceed has been given and confirmed in writing. ☐

Check the client has settled all accounts submitted to date. ☐

Check appointing documents with respect to services and fees: ☐

- If the Services, cost or time targets are different from the Agreement with the client agree a formal variation by letter or deed as appropriate.

- If the extent of professional services for Stage D is not settled, agree with the client and confirm in writing.

- If the methods and levels of charging for Stage D are not settled, agree with the client and confirm in writing.

Assess office resources needed for Stage D and ensure that they are adequate and available. ☐

Carry out checks for compliance with in-house quality management procedures, including updated project quality plan. ☐

Review application of practice procedures to project. ☐

Preliminary issues – client

Check whether the client has confirmed in writing acceptance of the Outline Proposals submitted at Stage C. Establish points to be discussed and developed during Stage D. ☐

Advise the client on the need to appoint further consultants and specialists. ☐

Alert the client about any matters raised during discussions with statutory or other bodies which might affect the proposals. Explain the implications and discuss what action should be taken. ☐

Alert the client to the design implications arising out of Health and Safety legislation (e.g. circulation, design of work stations, environmental comfort, etc) and implications for future maintenance, repair and replacement. ☐

Check that all information requested from the client concerning the site or existing buildings has been supplied.

Ask the client for information and requirements concerning pro- **Fig. D1** cesses, plant and other installations, room layouts and equipment, etc and record this information appropriately, if not already included in the Project Brief. Check on particular requirements concerning the life expectancy of components, fittings and installations, and performance requirements for environmental and services aspects, etc.

Check whether the client wishes the project to be planned to allow for phasing of completion or completion to a particular sequence. This might have design implications.

Check whether the client has decided the method of procurement, and confirm any decision in writing. If no decision is reached, explain the importance of reaching a decision before the detailed design is developed. This procurement method could affect the amount and type of design information needed at this Stage.

Preliminary issues — management and team working

Establish or review project quality management procedures in concert with relevant procedures of all consultant team members.

Check scope of professional services agreed with other consultants **D/CM1** as they are appointed.

Agree input to the Stage by consultant team members.

Confirm Stage timetable for services and note its relationship to the project timetable as agreed with the client. The timetable should show critical points by which information from the client and consultant team members will be required.

Confirm programme and pattern for consultant team meetings.

Appraise input from specialist firms, including potential sub-contractors and suppliers.

Confirm arrangements for communication between client, planning supervisor, project manager and design leader.

Monitor, coordinate and integrate input from consultant team members and specialists.

Fig. D1   Specimen room data notes sheet

Job no: Job title:

Room data notes

Room reference

Function/
functional requirements

User requirements

Relationships and
connections

Critical dimensions

Layout and flexibility

Floor loadings

Technical performance
standards

Lighting

Power

Heating/ventilation

Engineering installations

Finishes

Fittings

Other particular
requirements

Compiled by: Date

Maintain close collaboration with consultants and specialists. The architect might not be responsible for their individual performances, but will be responsible for the coordination and integration of their work into the overall design.

Check the designers' cooperation with the planning supervisor with respect to the Health and Safety Plan and File. □

As lead consultant or design leader, the architect has an obligation to check that every designer pays regard to the CDM Regulations and avoids foreseeable risks, or takes steps to combat them at source when designing.

Developing the Project Brief and Detailed Proposals

Review with the consultant team the client's response to Stage C Outline Proposals and decide what action is necessary. □

Review with team the developing Project Brief. Check that the Stage C changes have been recorded, authorised by the client and dealt with by the change control procedures established (e.g. those set out in the project quality plan). □

Check that the brief as presently developed still meets the client's stated objectives. Further amendments should be agreed with the client and confirmed in writing. □

The client must be advised that the Project Brief will be finalised during Stage D and warned that any modifications thereafter could mean abortive work and additional expense.

Obtain Codes, Standards, Digests, etc relevant to the project. □

Note: when designing to meet legislative standards or codes of practice, these must be the current versions.

Obtain project-specific information from potential sub-contractors and suppliers. □

When adopting proprietary systems or components for a design, take care that proposals will satisfy British Standards or other technical standards prescribed. Manufacturer's test results, as published, might relate to tests carried out under circumstances quite unlike those which might apply to a particular project. Check that products specified are suitable for the purpose and location, and obtain verification, certificates, warranties as appropriate before making a design commitment.

Coordinate and integrate information from QS, other consultants and specialists. ☐

Finalise Project Brief. **D/CM2** ☐

During this stage it is wise to draft preliminary specification notes, and to collate information as it comes to hand. Specification writing is part of the design process, and should be undertaken by the designer.

Develop the Detailed Proposals. ☐
When developing the Detailed Proposals it will be necessary to make regular checks against the brief as last updated. It is all too easy to overlook small but crucial requirements in the excitement of designing.

Advise the client about any proposals to introduce innovative design ☐
or construction ideas or the specifying of relatively new materials, and ask the client to confirm awareness of these in writing.

Always check with PI insurers if any aspects of the Detailed Proposals are innovative.

Undertake design review as appropriate. ☐

Finalise Detailed Proposals. **D/CM3** ☐
The presentation to the client of Stage D proposals is particularly important. Establish early how this is to be effected, and prepare the material accordingly. It will usually entail a written report and visual material. It may require an oral presentation.

At the conclusion of Stage D, get the satisfied client to 'sign off' the Detailed Proposals and the Project Brief. Clearly, beyond this point any changes which are client-originated might mean abortive work and additional expense.

Prepare report and submit to client. ☐

Inspections/tests

Make further site/building visits as authorised. ☐

Arrange to inspect similar projects elsewhere if appropriate, perhaps accompanied by the client. Appraise and analyse the schemes. It would be wise to check first that expenditure is authorised by the client. ☐

Arrange for testing, record and analyse results if instructed by the client. These tests might include production prototypes, mock-ups, sample components and panels to be tested under specified conditions and to stipulated methods as appropriate, for example testing for structural performance, durability, consistency, etc of components, fittings and finishes. ☐

Note that surveys, inspections or specialist investigations and preparation of special models do not form part of the Services under SFA/99 unless identified under 'Other Services'.

Consultations

Hold further meetings with statutory bodies as necessary. ☐

Discuss with the planning officer any difficulties or conditions arising from an outline planning permission, and any problems likely to occur with a full planning application. Check whether the authority operates particular planning policies, issues its own supplementary guidance notes, etc. ☐

Enquire whether the planning authority requires information additional to that of the usual form of application for full planning permission, and whether additional copies could speed up the consultation process. ☐

Enquire whether representation at planning committee when the application considered is possible, should this be thought desirable. ☐

Continue discussions with Building Control and the fire authorities over matters where overall design could be fundamentally affected, e.g. compartmentation, atrium design, fire resistance of elements, escape routes, smoke lobbies, active systems such as sprinklers, etc. ☐

Consult insurers as appropriate regarding the application of Codes of Practice or Design Guides relating fire safety which might have design implications, e.g. compartmentation, atrium design, fire resistance of elements, active systems such as sprinklers, etc. ☐

Check Health and Safety legislation requirements likely to affect detailed planning. Continue to cooperate with the planning supervisor and other designers over design implications of the pre-tender Health and Safety Plan required under the CDM Regulations. ☐

Continue checks with relevant authorities for highways, drainage, water, gas, electricity supplies, etc. ☐

Consult further with user clients/third parties, adjoining owners, if authorised. ☐

If instructed, issue party wall notices as soon as the proposals are sufficiently finalised, on behalf of client.

Note that consultations with users or third parties, and party wall matters, do not form part of the Services under SFA/99 unless identified under 'Other Services'.

Approvals/consents

Monitor that necessary third party consents are being obtained. ☐

Prepare and submit application for Approval of Reserved Matters following an outline planning permission if appropriate. ☐

Prepare and submit application for full planning permission, listed **A-B/CM4** building consent, conservation area consent as relevant and if instructed by client. Ensure all applications are accompanied by relevant documents including a cheque from the client for the appropriate fee. ☐

Prepare and submit application for Express Consent to Display an advertisement, application or notification to fell or lop trees covered by a Tree Preservation Order or in a Conservation Area, as relevant. ☐

Contract

Confirm in writing with the client the procurement method and type of contract to be adopted. ☐

Discuss with the client and consultant team whether any preliminary tender action for specialist sub-contractors and suppliers will be required. ☐

Discuss with the client and consultant team whether any action will be needed on advance orders. ☐

Identify works packages where applicable. ☐

Identify any performance specified work or contractor's designed portion items. ☐

Discuss with the client any particular requirements for phased or sectional completion. ☐

Cost planning

Discuss with the consultant team and the client the effect of major design decisions on the allocations within the cost plan before they are taken. ☐

There must be regular two-way exchange of information if designers are to keep within cost targets or limits.

Provide the QS with information on the cost plan and cash flow projection (or prepare a cost estimate if appointed to do so). ☐

Report to the client on cost matters at agreed intervals. ☐

Design and build Provide information to other consultants and contractor's estimators to cost detailed proposals. *(Contractor Client)* ☐

General procedures

Check progress against the timetable for services regularly. ☐

Continue resource control procedures for job: ☐

- Check expenditure against the office job cost allocation for Stage D;

- Monitor fee income against projected fee income.

Report regularly to the client on fees and expenses incurred, and submit accounts at agreed intervals. ☐

Check that the client settles all accounts promptly. ☐

Stage output

Check that all agreed outputs have been produced before the conclusion of Stage D, which might include the following: ☐

- Project Brief developed from the Strategic Brief.

- Detailed Proposals showing coordinated design intentions, site **D/CM1** layout, planning and spatial arrangements, elevational treatment, construction and environmental systems and buildability.

- Developed proposals for existing, perhaps historic, buildings with information from conservators and other consultants.

- A firm cost plan including a cash flow forecast.

- Prototypes, mock-ups, models, sample panels, etc.

- Proposals developed sufficiently to allow an application for full planning permission/listed building consent/conservation area consent, etc as applicable.

Design and build • Detailed Proposals for incorporation into Employer's Requirements (part of Stages D–G). *(Employer Client)*

Design and build • Further notes, sketches, details and drawings as necessary to develop the scheme included in the Contractor's Proposals (part of Stages D–E). *(Contractor Client)*

References and further reading

Anstey, J. (1998) *Party Walls and what to do with them*, London, RICS.

CIB (1999) *Briefing the Team*, London, HMSO Publications.

Cox, S. and Clamp, H. (2000) *Which Contract? 2nd edn.,* London, RIBA Publications.

Duxbury, R. M. C. (1999) *Planning Law and Procedure*, 11th edn., London, Butterworths.

JCT (2001) Practice Note 5 (series 2): *Deciding on the appropriate JCT Form of Main Contract*, London, RIBA Publications.

D/CM1

Consultant team roles: Work Stage D

Quantity surveyor

The QS should collaborate with the architect and other consultants to develop and refine the full cost plan as the design is developed and outline specification notes are prepared.

The QS will prepare an elemental cost plan followed by a firm cost plan and cash flow forecast, relying on input from other consultant team members. He or she will advise on cost effects of compliance with statutory requirements. The QS should contribute information and advice for inclusion in the Stage D report to the client.

Structural engineer

The structural engineer should collaborate in developing the design and advise on structural options and preferred solutions. The architect is responsible for coordination and integration into the overall design concept. This will include checking that structural proposals are compatible with the space and access requirements of the services installations.

The structural engineer should produce the initial structural design, prescribe profiles, basic specifications, building tolerances, define basic rules for voids and holes which might need to be provided and which might affect the structure and take steps as necessary to establish compliance with statutory requirements. He or she will provide information for the elemental and firm cost plan. The structural engineer should contribute information and advice for inclusion in the Stage D report to the client.

Building services engineer

The services engineers should have developed proposals sufficiently to establish performance specifications and to ensure satisfactory integration of services into the overall design scheme. This will mean working within the constraints set by the architect as lead consultant and the structural engineer. Decisions will need to be made on the services layouts and their coordination in relation to the building structure generally; ceiling, floor and wall layouts; and providing satisfactory access for commissioning.

The engineers should liaise closely with the architect on all services aspects, including the location and installation of equipment and plant, services voids, building tolerances, and access for maintenance and repairs. They will provide information for the elemental cost plan and an outline specification, and will negotiate with statutory authorities the provision of incoming services.

The building services engineers should contribute information and advice for inclusion in the Stage D report to the client.

D/CM2

Project Brief: Final checklist

By the end of Stage D the Brief should be finalised and signed off by the client. The Project Brief should normally address the following:

(a) the aim of the design, including:
- prioritised project objectives
- accommodation requirements, including disabled access policy
- space standards
- environmental policy, including energy
- environmental performance requirements
- image and quality
- flexibility to accommodate future reorganisation
- allowance for future expansion or extension
- life span for structure, elements, installations
- operational and maintenance requirements
- special considerations (e.g. security)

(b) the site, including details of accessibility and planning
- site constraints (physical and legal)
- legislative constraints

(c) the functions and activities of the client
- schedule of functions or processes
- activities
- spatial relationships
- schedule of installations

(d) the structure of the client organisation

(e) the size and configuration of the facilities

(f) options for environmental delivery and control

(g) servicing options and specification implications, e.g. security, deliveries, access, workplace, etc

(h) outline specifications of general and specific areas

(i) a budget for all elements

(j) the procurement process

(k) the project execution plan

(l) key targets for quality, time and cost, including milestones for decisions

(m) method for assessing and managing risks and validating design proposals.

D/CM3

Detailed Proposals presentation

Presentation to the client at Stage D will be in the most appropriate form, or may have to be in a form directed by the client. A decision should be made as early as possible, and might be influenced by context.

The medium of presentation

Decide how presentation of the scheme design is to be made, e.g. by:
*   the architect in person;
*   written report and drawings;
*   electronic means.

The intended recipients

Establish who is to be the immediate recipient of the scheme design presentation (e.g. client in person or client body committee) and whether the same material will also have a secondary presentation (e.g. to the Planning Committee, public meetings, user client groups).

The end users

Establish the use to which presentation material is likely to be put initially and in the longer term (e.g. for public display, fund raising, media coverage). This might require production of specially commissioned particular material, or simply multiple copies of the original material being available.

The content

The content of information to be presented, and the media to be used might include, for example:

Written report
*   presenting facts for information;
*   suggesting and comparing solutions;
*   making recommendations;
*   including or accompanied by illustrations, drawings and a financial report.

Drawings
*   orthographic plans at all levels;
*   elevations and cross-sections;
*   perspectives, etc to give a realistic view of the building exterior;
*   computer-generated visual images or analytical diagrams.

Models
*   block model (working tool);
*   presentation model to show architectural quality, form and colour, landscape setting, etc;
*   detail model of building part or particular feature, etc;
*   interior arrangement model to show spaces, arrangements, furniture layouts, etc;
*   computer-generated models.

Multi-media

• Computer animation, video, CD-ROM.

The scheme design presentation will also be influenced by factors such as:

• whether material is to be produced in-house or by outside professionals;

• whether the presentation is covered by a budget allocation, or is to be paid for direct by the client;

• the anticipated life of the material and its subsequent storage;

• costs associated with circulation, transport (particularly if overseas), insurance, etc.

E: FINAL PROPOSALS

Preparation of Final Proposals for the Project sufficient for co-ordination of all components and elements of the Project (RIBA Outline Plan of Work).

Description

Key obligations from SFA/99

Actions

Stage input
Preliminary issues   architect
                                  client
                                  management and team working
Developing the Final Proposals
Inspections/tests
Consultations
Approvals/consents
Contract
Cost planning
General procedures
Stage output

Core material

E/CM1	Design information: Implications of procurement method
E/CM2	Procedures for the issue of drawings
E/CM3	Consultant team roles: Work Stage E

FINAL PROPOSALS

Description

At Stage E under traditional procurement, the approved Detailed Proposals are developed into Final Proposals, the last stage in the design development before the production information is prepared. The Final Proposals will include the required construction details, choice of materials and standards of workmanship. Consultation with the client will be needed throughout the process. The client may be expected to contribute information or comments on finishes, furnishings and equipment. Design work by consultants and specialists must be coordinated, and relevant information passed to the planning supervisor for inclusion in the Health and Safety Plan or File. Cost checks are essential at this stage to ensure that the design development does not exceed budgetary limits or depart from the approved cost estimate.

In design and build procurement with an Employer Client, the design will be developed to the level of detail previously agreed. It is relatively rare for the Employer Client to require Final Proposals as part of the Employer's Requirements. However, some exploratory detail design is often necessary before the Employer's Requirements can be finished.

With a Contractor Client, Final Proposals will usually closely overlap production information. They may overlap for inclusion in the Contractor's Proposals, or if the contract has already been let, the information may be solely for the Contractor's design development. The detail design development will be associated with the work of other consultants to the contractor, specialist sub-contractors and the estimators within the contractor organisation.

With the management procurement approach, the Final Proposals are more difficult to resolve. A significant proportion will depend on the input of the specialists involved with the works packages, and not all their contributions will be available at this stage. Stage E cannot be equated with traditional procurement, as much will remain to be resolved after the contract and works packages have been let. Great reliance has to be placed on the management contractor or construction manager, and an early appointment will help the Final Proposals Development. Close attention should be given to the appropriate number of packages and control maintained to minimise the risk of overlap or duplication. Monitoring of detail design will continue well into the construction phase, and the Health and Safety Plan might require regular adjustment.

Key obligations which may apply:

	Reference	To do
- from SFA/99: design services		
Develop Final Proposals from approved Detail Proposals.	SFA/99/E/1	☐
Revise cost estimate, or	SFA/99/E/2A	☐
Provide information for revised cost estimate.	SFA/99/E/2B	☐
Consult statutory authorities.	SFA/99/E/3	☐
Obtain Client approval to Final Proposals and revised cost estimate.	SFA/99/E/4	☐
Advise on consequences of subsequent changes.	SFA/99/E/5	☐
Co-operate with Planning Supervisor where appropriate.	SFA/99/1.4	☐

In addition to the above, the architect should note the obligations set out in the SFA/99 Conditions of Engagement 2.1-2.8.

- from SFA/99: management services

(i.e. architect acting as design leader and lead consultant)

Directing, coordinating and monitoring design work. ☐

Establishing the form and content of design outputs, their interfaces and a verification procedure. ☐

Considering with the client a list of tenderers for the Works. ☐

Developing and managing change control procedures. ☐

Reporting to the client. ☐

Actions

Stage input

Check that all information necessary during Stage E is available, which might include the following: ☐

- Project Brief as accepted by the client in written confirmation, incorporating any agreed amendments.

- Detailed Proposals as accepted by the client in written confirmation, incorporating any agreed amendments.

- Cost plan prepared by quantity surveyor.

- Published material. Technical information including samples relevant to the project.

- Results of tests conducted during Stage D.

- Relevant legislation.

- Further contributions, information and recommendations from consultants and specialists including possible sub-contractors and suppliers.

Preliminary issues – architect

Establish scope, content and context for Stage E activities. ☐
Put it into context, particularly previous Stages undertaken by others.
If possible establish whether material produced now is likely to be acted upon by others taking over subsequent Stages.

If coming new to the project at this Stage in the *Plan of Work:* ☐

- Ascertain that relevant Pre-Agreement and earlier Stage checks have been carried out.

- Allow for familiarisation and reviewing of all usable material when agreeing fees and timetable with the client.

- Confirm the role of the architect in relation to the rest of the consultant team.

Check the client's instruction to proceed has been given and confirmed in writing. ☐

Check the client has settled all accounts submitted to date. ☐

Check appointing documents with respect to services and fees: ☐

- If the Services, cost or time targets are different from the Agreement with the client agree a formal variation by letter or deed as appropriate.

- If the extent of professional services for Stage E is not settled, agree with client and confirm in writing.

- If the methods and levels of charging for Stage E are not yet settled, agree with client and confirm in writing.

Assess office resources needed for Stage E and ensure that they are adequate and available. ☐

Carry out checks for compliance with in-house quality management procedures, including updated project quality plan. ☐

Review application of practice procedures to project. ☐

Preliminary issues – client

Check whether the client has confirmed in writing acceptance of the Project Brief and Detailed Proposals submitted at Stage D. Establish points to be discussed and developed during Stage E. ☐

It is important to remind the client that any changes to the approved Project Brief which are client-originated might mean abortive work, additional expense and delays

Continue discussion with the client on more detailed aspects of procurement, and confirm decisions in writing. The decisions will affect the finalisation of the design during this Stage, the amount and type of design information needed at this Stage, and the role of the consultants. ☐

Note: the client should be given reasonable notice to supply detailed final requirements concerning access, facilities, furnishings, fittings, etc. Likewise take into account users' requirements as relevant.

Check whether client has given authority for any preliminary tender action for specialist sub-contractors and suppliers that will be required, and confirm in writing. ☐

Advise the client on the need to appoint further consultants and specialists.

Ensure the client is alerted to the possible need to appoint party wall surveyors. ☐

Preliminary issues – management and team working

Establish or review project quality management procedures in concert with relevant procedures of all consultant team members. ☐

Check scope of professional services agreed with other consultants as they are appointed. ☐

Agree input to the Stage by consultant team members. **E/CM3** ☐

Remember that the procurement method chosen will greatly affect the amount of detail design information necessary at this stage.

Confirm Stage timetable for services and note its relationship to the project timetable as agreed with the client. ☐

Confirm arrangements for communication between client, planning supervisor, project manager and design leader. ☐

Confirm arrangements for communication between consultant team members. ☐

Have an agreed policy for issuing and exchanging drawings and **E/CM2** other information.

Have an agreed policy for coordinating information on drawings and between documents. Use of Coordinated Project Information was recommended by Sir Michael Latham and should be introduced at the earliest possible stage in information preparation. ☐

Be careful when using networked CAD systems that there is a clear procedure for updating and circulating base drawings to be used by the whole team.

There must be an organised flow of information between the architect and other consultants, particularly with the QS.

Confirm programme and pattern for consultant team meetings. ☐

Confirm with consultant team members arrangements for inviting specialist tenders. ☐

Monitor, coordinate and integrate input from consultant team members. The architect needs to bring both design and management skills to Stage E. Collaboration with other consultant team members and coordination of their contributions is often difficult to achieve in practice. ☐

Check the designers' cooperation with the planning supervisor with respect to the Health and Safety Plan and File. ☐

Check that any design changes now instructed are recorded and subject to established control procedures. ☐

No consultant team members should attempt to make decisions unilaterally!

Developing the Final Proposals

Review with the consultant team the client's response to Stage D Detailed Proposals and decide what action is necessary. ☐

Appraise input from specialist firms, including potential sub-contractors and suppliers. ☐

Coordinate and integrate information from consultant team members. ☐

Obtain the client's approval of materials and finishes. ☐

Obtain samples, etc and submit to client for comment.

Prepare special presentation panels, etc for client.

Draft preliminary notes for Bills/Spec/Schedules of Work.   **E/CM3**   ☐

This should be done systematically as further materials are chosen and standards of workmanship set.

Undertake design review as appropriate.   ☐

Complete Final Proposals.   **E/CM2, E/CM3**   ☐

Prepare report and submit to client.   ☐

Design and build   Check whether the client has confirmed in writing acceptance of proposals and information supplied so far to form part of the Employer's Requirements. *(Employer Client)*   ☐

Design and build   Check whether the client has confirmed in writing acceptance of design proposals to form part of the Contractor's Proposals. *(Contractor Client)*   ☐

Inspections/tests

Make such visits as necessary to supply sources (e.g. quarries, brickyards, stoneyards) and manufacturing sources (e.g. foundries, factories, workshops) before making final design choices.   ☐

Arrange for further tests to be conducted on components, panels and finishes, if appropriate and authorised by the client.   ☐

Consultations

Review with the design team implications of any conditions attached to full planning permission.   ☐

Discuss with the planning officer the implications arising from any planning permission conditions. If permission was refused, discuss the reasons for the refusal and prepare for the client recommendations as to the best course of action.   ☐

Note: revision of documents to comply with planning or other statutory authority requirements do not form part of the Services under SFA/99 unless identified under 'Other Services'.

Continue discussions with the Building Control and fire authorities before making a formal application for approval under the Building Regulations.   ☐

Review adequacy of information on building services from statutory undertakers for detail design. ☐

Continue discussions with relevant authorities for highways, drainage, water, gas, electricity supplies, etc on matters concerning detail design. Check adequacy of information on building services from statutory undertakers for detail design. ☐

Consult insurers as appropriate regarding the application of Codes of Practice or Design Guides relating to construction, materials, standards and finishes in detail design, and their requirements for fire prevention during site operations which might have design implications. ☐

Consult user clients/third parties, if authorised. ☐

If instructed issue party wall notices on behalf of client. ☐

Note that consultations with users or third parties, and Party Wall matters, do not form part of the Services under SFA/99 unless identified under 'Other Services'.

Approvals/consents

In the event of a refusal of planning permission, amend the scheme and re-submit the application as appropriate. ☐

Note that exceptional negotiations with planning or other statutory authorities do not form part of the Services under SFA/99 unless identified under 'Other Services'.

Check whether minor amendments to the Detailed Proposals at this Stage go beyond the scope of the planning permission granted. If so, it may be necessary to deposit amended drawings. ☐

Prepare a Building Notice for submission under the Building **F-G/CM4** Regulations, or prepare an application for approval by deposit of Full Plans. Prepare a submission to an Approved Inspector for issue of an Initial Notice for acceptance by the local authority, if this is the chosen option. ☐

Application for Building Regulation approval is not included in SFA/99 until Stage F, although 'statutory approvals' appears in Stage E and Stage F of the Plan of Work. *In practice, it is advisable to submit for all necessary approvals at the earliest possible date. However the Stage at which the submissions can be made will depend on how much detail the authority requires – there is an increasing tendency to ask for a high level of detail so that submission may not be possible until Stage F.*

Prepare material for submission to the client's insurers if necessary and instructed by the client.   ☐

Contract

Note: SFA/99 refers to tender action at Stage H only. In projects where there are to be many specialist sub-contractors, particularly where these are undertaking some design obligations, it may be necessary to initiate some tender action of sub-contractors at an earlier stage. This will enable design proposals to be integrated into the overall design and quotations to be checked against the cost plan. This information may be needed before the main contract tender documentation can be finalised at Stage G.

Review/update standing lists or register of specialist tenderers and check written confirmation from client. Check willingness and availability of firms included as listed sub-contractors, and if necessary decide on additional names.   ☐

Initiate tender action for quotations from specialist sub-contractors **H/CM2** and suppliers if appropriate.   ☐

Check tender invitation documents for sending to specialists.

Invite further tenders as appropriate.

When inviting tenders for specialist subcontract work which includes a design element, make certain that the client consents in writing, and that his interests are properly protected by warranty.

Inspect tenders and information submitted by specialist sub-contractors and suppliers.   ☐

Refer specialist tenders to the planning supervisor and relevant consultants for comment. Refer all tenders to the QS for cost checking.

Approve specialist tenders and notify all tenderers of this decision.

Follow meticulously the procedures stated in the main contract to be used for the appointment of specialist sub-contractors.

Only place advance orders with specialist sub-contractors or suppliers as provided for in the sub-contract documentation, and only if authorised in writing by the client, as advised by the planning supervisor.

Discuss list of potential main contractors (or construction managers if appropriate) with client and consultant team. Check whether the client holds a General List of Approved Contractors from which tenderers must be selected. Make preliminary enquiries with contractors if appropriate.

Tender lists should only include firms well known to the architect, or firms which have been satisfactorily investigated.

Discuss with the client tender procedures, including: **H/CM1**   ☐

- whether firms who wish to be considered as tenderers should complete a tendering questionnaire;

- whether the client will require tenderers to complete a non-collusion or other similar certificate.

Discuss with the client and the planning supervisor the tendering period, procedures to be followed in opening tenders and notifying results.   ☐

Continue discussion with the client on the inclusion of any special clauses or amendments to the contract. Remind the client of the need to take legal advice before amending standard forms of contract. Discuss with the client the implications of any advice obtained.   ☐

Cost Planning

Discuss with the consultant team and the client the effect of detailed design decisions on the allocations within the cost plan before implementation.   ☐

Provide information to QS for revision of cost estimate and cash flow projection (or revise cost estimate if appointed to do so).   ☐

Report to the client on cost matters at agreed intervals. ☐

Design and build Provide any further necessary information to the contractor's estimators. *(Contractor Client)* ☐

Design and build Review estimates received from specialist firms either direct or through consultants for inclusion in tender documents or as basis for provisional sums. *(Contractor Client)* ☐

General procedures

Check progress against the timetable for services regularly. ☐

Continue resource control procedures for job: ☐

- Check expenditure against the office job cost allocation for Stage E;

- Monitor fee income against projected fee income.

Report regularly to the client on fees and expenses incurred, and submit accounts at agreed intervals. ☐

Check that the client settles all accounts promptly. ☐

Stage output

Check that all the agreed outputs have been produced before the conclusion of Stage E, which might include the following: ☐

- Detail design drawings. **E/CM3**

- Specification notes (prescriptive and performance) on materials and workmanship, and notes for draft preambles or preliminaries for Bills of Quantities/Specification/Schedules of Work.

- Further detailed information on proposals for existing, perhaps historic, buildings.

- Information for preparation of Full Plans submission for approval under Building Regulations.

- Non-production information for use in dealings with third parties, landlords, tenants, funders, etc (eg in connection with leases, boundaries, party walls, etc).

Design and build • Detail design information for incorporation into Employer's Requirements (part of Stage D–G). *(Employer Client)*

Design and build Further design development drawings and design team members' work on scheme submitted in the Contractor's Proposals (part of Stage D–E). *(Contractor Client)* ☐

References and further reading

Powell Smith, V. and Billington M.J. (1999) *The building regulations explained and illustrated*, Oxford, Blackwells.

E/CM1

Design information: Implications of procurement method

The production of information, its amount, type and timing, is likely to be directly affected by the procurement method chosen, and ultimately by the type of contract selected.

For example, the extent to which there is to be contractual reliance on drawings might determine their form and detail. Whether Bills of Quantities or schedules of work will be needed will depend on the form of contract and the nature of the work.

It is important to identify at detail design stage who will have responsibility for producing what information — architect, consultants, or contractor, specialist firms, etc.

The more complex the pattern of information required, the greater the risk of omissions, errors and inconsistencies between documents. Greater, too, is the need for collaboration in order to bring about integration and coordination of design information.

Ideally all information necessary for the construction of the project should be completed before construction work begins. In practice this ideal is rarely, if ever, achieved but if a great deal is left to be prepared during the construction stage, then very high levels of management skills will be needed from all those involved.

Even in traditional procurement it is rarely possible to bring a lump sum project to a fully designed state pre-tender. Most building contracts accept the need for further information to be issued during progress of the works.

With design and build, or management contracts, it is recognised that a substantial amount of detail design work will take place after the main contract has been let.

In an attempt to control the amount and flow of information, and recognising that everything will not always be available at the start of a contract, a schedule of information still to be provided is sometimes agreed beforehand by the architect and the contractor. This has now been embodied in many JCT standard form contracts as an optional 'Information Release Schedule'.

Sometimes the successful tenderer is required to inspect the documentation and provide the client with verification that it will be sufficient to carry out and complete the project. Then, should it be necessary to produce further drawings or calculations, this will be the contractor's risk. However, the architect will then be involved in checking the contractor's submissions to ensure that detail design is not compromised.

Design information flow: Traditional procurement

1. Origination

Design information can originate from the:

- architect
- design team members
- specialist sub-contractors and suppliers
- main contractor (to the extent provided for in the contract).

2. Coordination and integration

Responsibility for coordinating and integrating such information into the overall design rests with the architect as lead consultant, or design team leader.

3. Detail design work

Some detail design work is necessary for all projects and should be started as soon as practicable. The transition from the final proposals of Stage E to the Stage F production information is not easily defined. There will inevitably be a measure of overlap which might vary from project to project. With small projects the two stages might be merged.

4. Design development

With traditional procurement where a project is to be fully designed before work on site commences, Stage E provides an opportunity to develop and refine the design intentions. The scheme can be systematically explored and parts expanded to a larger scale in plan, section or three dimensions. Potentially awkward junctions can be identified and resolved. Zones may be introduced and a grid discipline imposed.

5. Avoidance of conflict and overlap

Design information originating from various sources should be coordinated to eliminate any conflict between structure and services, to make sure that different services are not competing for the same duct spaces, or that holes are not expected at critical structural points. Design integrity and quality should not need to be sacrificed because of the requirements of other design team members, but achieving acceptable compromise and satisfactory integration can be a demanding process.

Smaller projects which might need only a dozen or so drawings, and very limited input from consultants, are unlikely to present real problems in terms of integration and coordination.

Larger and more complex projects will need a more formalised set of procedures. The design concept is likely to be founded on a totally integrated approach. There should be an agreed strategy for the coordination of information between the architect and other consultant team members.

Fig. E1   Design information flow: traditional procurement

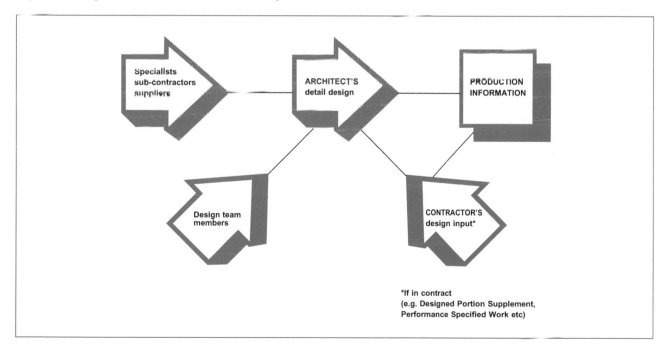

Design information flow: Design and build procurement

1. Origination

Design information can originate from:

- the Employer Client (through Employer's Requirements with input from his or her consultant team);
- the Contractor Client (through Contractor's Proposals and subsequent development of these, with input from his or her consultant team).

2. Coordination and integration

If acting as lead consultant or design leader appointed by either the Employer Client or the Contractor Client, responsibility for coordinating and integrating the relevant design information may rest with the architect, always depending on the terms of appointment.

3. Employer Client's design in Employer's Requirements

Where an Employer Client includes a scheme devised by his or her own consultant team as part of the Employer's Requirements, some Stage E detail work might be relevant. The extent of the commitment should be agreed with the client before work is undertaken. In the event that novation or a 'consultant switch' is envisaged, particular care might be needed to establish design viability. The point of changeover for design liability from one client to the other must be carefully defined.

4. Contractor Client's design in Contractor's Proposals

Where a Contractor Client is expected to offer a scheme design as part of the Contractor's Proposals, this may involve only a fairly limited design exercise, or require a more developed design approach, particularly in the case of two stage tendering. Either way, some exploratory detail design work is necessary to establish the viability of the proposal. The extent of the commitment should be agreed with the client before work is started.

Contractor's Proposals sometimes entail the preparation of a considerable number of architectural drawings — general arrangement, plans, sections and elevations, sectional and elevational details and landscape proposals. There may also be full structural details and a substantial number of services drawings. Obviously effective coordination and integration of the information is very important.

5. Detail design work

Stage E, insofar as it might be relevant for a Contractor Client, could continue intermittently throughout the early stages of construction. It might be difficult to distinguish at times from production information work. Detail design might be subject to fairly liberal interpretation, with last minute amendments, revisions or substitutions by the Contractor Client. The client might also have a particular preference for detail design solutions which are familiar, will wish to use materials or components which are available to suit the programme, and wish to keep in line with the estimator's calculations.

Stage E, insofar as it might be relevant for an Employer Client, will probably apply mainly to the development of the Employer's Requirements. Once the contract has been let, any changes in these are likely to be costly and weighted heavily in the contractor's favour.

6. Avoidance of conflict

Once the contract is under way, should any conflict between the Employer's Requirements and the Contractor's Proposals emerge, then depending on the wording of the contract, the latter is likely to take precedence. Careful scrutiny at Stage E is therefore advisable, whether the architect is acting for the Employer Client or the Contractor Client.

Fig. E2   Design information flow: design and build procurement

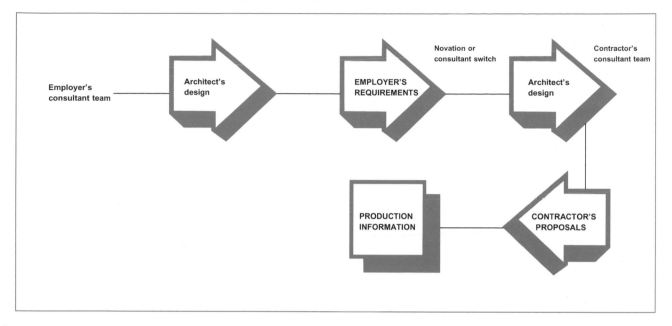

Design information flow: Management procurement

Management procurement is likely to be particularly suitable where the project is fairly large or complex, where there is need for early completion, and where the requirements of the client might change or perhaps only be formalised in detail during work on site. Design is still in the hands of the professional team. The management contractor is appointed early enough to advise the team on buildability but carries no responsibility for the design. As lead consultant or design leader, responsibility for coordinating and integrating information into the overall design rests with the architect, although considerable design input will normally come from the specialist works contractors.

1.   Origination

Design information can originate from:

• the architect
• professional team members
• specialist works contractors.

2.   Detail design work

Two general lines of the design will be shown in the project drawings and project specification produced by the professional team. Some Stage E detail design is an essential precursor to information issued when inviting tenders for works packages.

Further detail design work will arise when the works contractors are appointed. Each discrete work package must be placed in the context of the overall design. The information flow can produce management problems if not effectively controlled. Risk of frustrated design work and perhaps abortive fabrication can occur unless agreed procedures are adopted by the management contractor and the professional team.

3.   Coordination and integration

The management contractor can expect to be closely involved in the appointment of works contractors. This might be on the basis of developed detail drawings, specifications and perhaps Bills of Quantities. Drawings prepared by the works contractors will be mainly installation or shop drawings, and should be passed to the architect by the management contractor for inspection with regard to their integration and incorporation into the overall design.

Fig. E3   Design information flow: management procurement

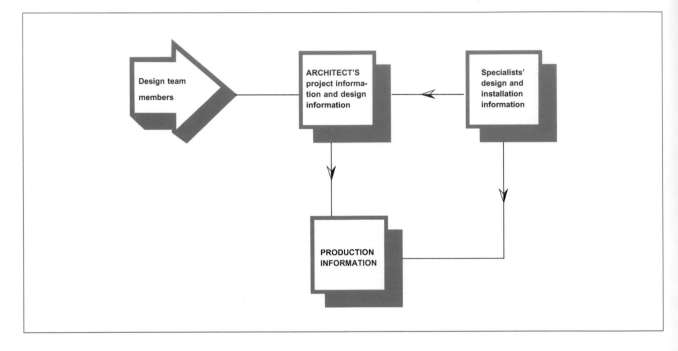

E/CM2

Procedures for the issue of drawings

Commencing at Stage E in particular, collaboration between the architect, other members of the consultant team and specialists is likely to lead to a regular exchange of drawings. The project quality plan should include procedures for the recording and issue of all drawings, receipt of incoming drawings, and a controlled way of dealing with changes to design decisions already agreed. Fig. E4 is a checklist of the parts of a building for which drawn information might be required.

Fig. E4 Checklist of necessary drawn information

Summary		Site layouts General arrangement drawings	
Substructure		Excavation Floor beds	Foundations Pile foundations
Structure	Primary	External walls Internal walls Floors and galleries	Stairs and ramps Roofs Frames
	Secondary	External wall openings Internal wall openings Floor openings	Balustrades Suspended ceilings Roof openings
	Finishes	External wall finishes Internal wall finishes Floor finishes	Stair finishes Ceiling finishes Roof finishes
Services	Piped and ducted	Refuse disposal Drainage Hot and cold water Gases	Refrigeration Space heating Ventilation and air conditioning
	Electrical	Power Lighting Communications	Transport Security
Fittings	Fixtures	Circulation General room Culinary	Sanitary Cleaning Storage
	Loose equipment	Circulation General room Culinary	Sanitary Cleaning Storage
External		Substructure Structure Finishes	Services Fittings

Register of drawings

Most practices will already have a standard Register of Drawings (see Fig. E5), which might record amongst other things:

- job number and title;
- drawing number, title, date, revisions (A, B, etc);
- scale of drawing, size of drawing (A3, A4, etc);
- number of copies sent, distribution, and date sent.

Where recipients are to be charged for copies, the Register might also allow entries indicating the charge made and by whom payable. Great care must be taken to keep the register updated, particularly where networked CAD systems are being used.

Fig. E5 Specimen registers of drawings and prints

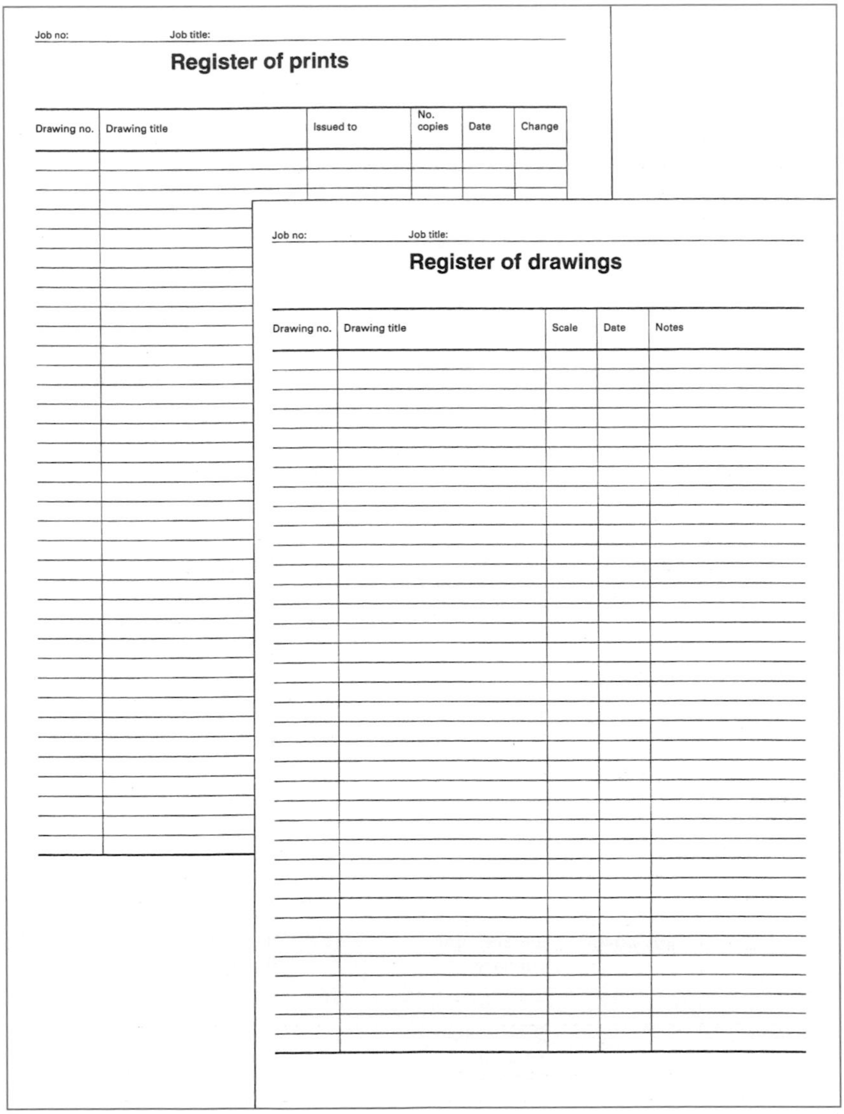

Job no: Job title:

Register of prints

Drawing no.	Drawing title	Issued to	No. copies	Date	Change

Job no: Job title:

Register of drawings

Drawing no.	Drawing title	Scale	Date	Notes

Schedules of drawings

Drawing schedules can be a convenient record for several purposes:

- for listing at the start of Stage E what drawings or drawn schedules need to be prepared;
- for listing at the start of Stage F–G what Production Information needs to be prepared (see Fig. E6);
- for listing drawings or drawn schedules issued for tender purposes;
- for listing necessary information still to be prepared by the architect and/or the contractor during progress of the works;
- for listing drawings or drawn schedules supplied to the client on completion – either for record purposes or for incorporation in the Health and Safety File.

Fig. E6   Specimen schedule of drawings required

Job no:	Job title:			
Schedule of drawings required (prepared before drafting starts)				
Drawing no.	Drawing title	Sheet size	Scale	Notes
L00	Site location plan	A3	1:1250	
01	Site plan	A1	1:200	
02	Site plan – contractor's fencing	A1	1:200	

Distribution _____ _____ (date)

Drawings received

A practice should also have its standard record of drawings received. All incoming drawn or scheduled information should be entered, and the sheets might record amongst other things:

- job number and title;
- drawing number, title, date, revision;
- name of originator;
- date received;
- whether response required and if so by when;
- response made and date achieved.

Drawings issued

Drawings should never normally be issued simply under cover of a compliments slip. It is better practice to use a drawing issue sheet (see Fig. E7) which indicates the purpose of the action and allows a proper record to be kept.

Fig. E7   Specimen architect's drawing issue sheet

Design Change Notice

Drawings or other documents indicating proposed design changes should be circulated under cover of a Change Notice (see Fig. E8) which invites comments from recipients. These photocopied (if not sent in duplicate) forms should then be filed and the action taken recorded. Following the adoption of design changes, amendments might be needed to the entries in the Register of Drawings.

Fig. E8   Specimen design change notice and record

Job no:

Job title:

Design change notice and record

TO:

Enclosures:

Please find enclosed the documents listed below.
Please enter comments, photocopy, and return original notice by

_____ (date)

Issued by _____   _____ (date)

COMMENTS:

Signed _____   _____ (date)

Implementation record

Change adopted   YES/NO   Included in contract   YES/NO

Covered by Architect's Instruction   No. ____ issued _____ (date)

E/CM3

Consultant team roles: Work Stage E

Quantity surveyor

The QS should be in close collaboration with the architect during this time of detail design. Choices of materials and specification notes concerning standards and workmanship need to be watched carefully and checked against the cost plan. The QS will be closely involved in discussions regarding the selected procurement route. The QS will provide an updated cost plan and cash flow forecast for inclusion in the Work Stage report.

Structural engineer

The structural engineer should cooperate closely with the architect to ensure a satisfactory integration of structural considerations into the overall design. The engineer should have regard to the location and requirements of all service installations, the building envelope, and the construction process.

The engineer will consult with statutory authorities as appropriate, and provide information as necessary for statutory or third party approvals. Where necessary, the engineer should develop drawings and specifications for tendering documentation for nominated sub-contract work or enabling contract works.

Building services engineer

The building services engineers should assist the architect in finalising design integration. Their proposals should develop information drawings and specification notes sufficient to allow tendering documentation for nominated sub-contract work or nominated supply items. They should consult with statutory authorities as appropriate.

They should also prepare builders' work requirements in detail for incorporation in the architect's and structural engineer's drawings. All information should be passed to the QS through the architect for checking against the cost plan.

F: PRODUCTION INFORMATION

F1 Preparation of Production Information in sufficient detail to enable a tender or tenders to be obtained.
F2 Preparation of Further Production information required under the building contract (RIBA Outline Plan of Work).

Description

Key obligations from SFA/99

Actions

Stage input
Preliminary issues   architect
                                        client
                                        management and team working
Developing the Production Information
Inspections/tests
Consultations
Approvals/consents
Contract
Cost planning
General procedures
Stage output

Core material

F/CM1	Production Information: Drawings
F/CM2	Production Information: Specification and Schedules of Work
F/CM3	Production Information: Bills of Quantities
F/CM4	Building control approval checklist
F/CM5	Consultant team roles: Work Stage F

PRODUCTION INFORMATION

Description

At Stage F under traditional procurement, the Final Proposals are translated into precise technical instructions sufficient to allow for pricing and for construction of the proposed works. This information will normally be conveyed by means of written descriptions, drawings and schedules. The RIBA *Outline Plan of Work* recognises that with many contractual arrangements some of this information may be prepared and provided after the main contract has been entered into, and the Stage is split into F1 and F2 accordingly.

Responsibility for production information in design and build procurement is more difficult to establish and will depend on the particular circumstances. It would be very unusual for an Employer Client to arrange for Production Information direct, although he or she might retain a consultant team to monitor Production Information prepared and submitted by the contractor. Alternatively, the employer might require the continued use of his or her team by the successful contractor through a consultant switch. The Contractor Client will require Production Information to be prepared. An architect engaged in this context might well find it advisable to establish exactly how much work, how many drawings, etc will be required before agreeing a programme or fee. The contractor might wish to impose restrictions in respect of the method of structuring and supply of Production Information, preferred technical solutions, materials, etc.

With management procurement, the amount of Production Information available at the commencement of the project will be limited to the extent that much detail information will be supplied by the works contractors by way of shop or installation drawings. Nevertheless, the general Production Information will originate from the consultant team, and the process of coordinating and integrating information will continue throughout the construction of the project.

Key obligations which may apply:

	Reference	To do
- from SFA/99: design services		
Prepare production information.	SFA/99/F/1	☐
Prepare schedules of rates, quantities, etc, or	SFA/99/F/2A	☐
Provide information for tender pricing documents.	SFA/99/F/2B	☐
Prepare and make Building Regulations submissions.	SFA/99/F/3	☐
Co operate with planning supervisor where appropriate.	SFA/99/1.4	☐

In addition to the above, the architect should note the obligations set out in the SFA/99 Conditions of Engagement 2.1-2.8.

- from SFA/99: management services		
(i.e. architect acting as design leader and lead consultant)		
Directing, coordinating and monitoring design work.		☐
Establishing the form and content of design outputs, their interfaces and a verification procedure.		☐
Considering with the client a list of tenderers for the Works.		☐
Developing and managing change control procedures.		☐
Reporting to the client.		☐

Actions

Stage input

Check that all information necessary during Stage F is available, which might include the following:

☐

- Final Proposals prepared during Stage E.

- Amendments recommended by local Building Control and fire authorities during consultations, particularly relating to construction details and fire prevention including finishes.

- Further contributions, information and recommendations from consultants and specialists. In particular, documents submitted by approved sub-contractors and suppliers.

- Technical information from manufacturers and recommendations or test results relevant to the particular use intended, context and location.

- Relevant legislation.

Preliminary issues – architect

Establish scope, content and context for Stage F activities.
Put it into context, particularly if previous Stages were undertaken by others. If possible, establish whether material produced now is likely to be acted upon by others taking over subsequent Stages.

☐

If coming new to the project at this Stage in the *Plan of Work:*

☐

- Ascertain that relevant Pre-Agreement and earlier Stage checks have been carried out.

- Allow for familiarisation and reviewing of all usable material when agreeing fees and timetable with the client.

- Confirm the role of the architect in relation to the rest of the consultant team.

Check the client's instruction to proceed has been given and confirmed in writing.

☐

Check the client has settled all accounts submitted to date. ☐

Check appointing documents with respect to services and fees. ☐

- If the extent of professional services for Stage F is not yet settled, agree with the client and confirm in writing.

- If the methods and levels of charging for Stage F are not yet settled, agree with the client and confirm in writing.

- Assess office resources needed for Stage F and ensure that they are adequate and available.

Carry out checks for compliance with in-house quality management procedures, including updated project quality plan. ☐

Review application of practice procedures to project. ☐

Preliminary issues – client

Check whether the client has confirmed in writing acceptance of the Final Proposals submitted at Stage E. Establish points to be discussed and developed during Stage F. ☐

Check whether any necessary detail information to be supplied by the client is still outstanding. ☐

Discuss with the client any outstanding matters of detail design which need to be resolved before preparing Production Information. ☐

Check whether the client has confirmed in writing the tender procedure to be followed, and whether this is subject to legislative control. ☐

Advise the client on the use of preliminary contracts for enabling works, demolition, etc if appropriate. ☐

Review with the client the appointment of sub-contractors and specialists at this stage and whether it might be advantageous to place advance orders for materials, design or fabrication. ☐

Nomination or naming of sub-contractors or suppliers should only be made with the written consent of the client.

Advise the client on the need for a clerk of works if appropriate, and explain the role of such a person and appointing procedures. ☐

Advise the client on the need for a party wall surveyor if appropriate. ☐

Note that if the architect is to be appointed as party wall surveyor, this appointment must form a separate agreement.

Discuss with the client whether interviews with potential contractors should take place at this stage. Under certain circumstances their views on operational methods and health and safety during construction could be valuable. ☐

Check with the client when the site will be available to the contractor, and that nothing is likely to prevent possession or commencement on that date. ☐

Discuss with the client any intention to impose restrictions on the contractor's working methods (e.g. sequence, access, limitation on hours, noise, etc). This could have an effect on production information and would be essential information for tenderers. ☐

Discuss with the client any proposal for work not forming part of the contract to be carried out by other persons (e.g. the client's own work force) whilst the contractor is in possession. Take account of any such confirmed instructions when preparing production information and programming. ☐

Discuss with the client essential information for completing contract documents (e.g. Appendix) and which will need reference in Preliminaries or Preambles of Bills of Quantities/Specification/ Schedules of Work. ☐

Check with the client any special or optional contract provisions. ☐

Check with the client and advisers on insurance for works, etc. ☐

Preliminary issues – management and team working

Agree input to the Stage by consultant team members. ☐

Confirm Stage timetable for services and note its relationship to the project timetable as agreed with the client. ☐

Establish a cut-off point for information to be passed to the QS. This will become information for tenderers. Any subsequent changes are then to be treated formally as contract variations at the appropriate time.

Confirm arrangements for communication between client, planning supervisor, project manager and design leader. ☐

Confirm programme and pattern for consultant team meetings. ☐

Monitor, integrate and coordinate input from consultant team members and specialists. Continue to appraise input from specialist firms, including potential sub-contractors and suppliers. ☐

The lead consultant is responsible for all information coordination and integration into the general scheme. A formal approach to 'question-and-answer' procedures should be adopted with the QS as soon as possible. Ask the QS to state priorities for receiving information for billing purposes.

The CPI system for Production Information should be used wherever **F/CM1-3** *practicable by all consultant team members. Remember to request this at an early stage.*

Continue to cooperate with the planning supervisor. Review designers' cooperation with the planning supervisor with respect to the Health and Safety Plan and File. ☐

Discuss with the planning supervisor any outstanding matters of designers' contributions to pre-tender Health and Safety Plan including, where appropriate, site traffic movements and layout for site operations. ☐

Remember that the pre-tender Health and Safety Plan, as prepared by the planning supervisor, will need to be issued at tender stage.

Developing the Production Information

Check whether the client has any further comments on the Final Proposals as developed at the end of Stage E. It is not always easy or practical to distinguish Final Proposals from Production Information, but there should be no significant design changes during Stages F–G without client approval. ☐

From now on any changes made to the brief, even apparently minor ones, might cause delay and abortive work. The client should be warned of this.

All alterations should be subject to the change control procedures established (e.g. in the project quality plan).

Obtain necessary information in good time from firms to be named or nominated, and place reliance on it only after having secured a design warranty in favour of the client. Check on availability and delivery before including particular materials or sources named in Production Information. ☐

Complete information with respect to prescriptive/performance items in Bills, etc. ☐

Take care when including provisional sums that the figure is adequate, and that wherever possible it is for defined work.

Draft preliminaries, preambles, specifications for materials and workmanship. ☐

Use standard specification clauses which are clear and precise. It should be normal practice to use the appropriate version of NBS.

Use a specification in addition to Bills of Quantities by incorporating it so that it forms part of the contract documentation.

Provide information as agreed to the QS for preparation of tender pricing documents (or prepare pricing documents if appointed to do so). ☐

Consider requirements for commissioning of engineering services by sub-contractors, main contractor, and provisions for testing for inclusion in tender documents. ☐

Consolidate detailed information for production drawings, sub-contract **F/CM1-3** specifications and preliminaries to Bills of Quantities/Specification/ Schedules of Work. ☐

Prepare report and submit to client. ☐

Design and build   Check whether the client has confirmed in writing acceptance of proposals and information supplied so far in Stages D–E which are to form part of the Employer's Requirements. *(Employer Client)* ☐

Design and build   Review any client's comments on the detail design or development, and note any adjustments which may be unavoidable due to modifications introduced lately by component manufacturers or specialist sub-contractors. Detail design amendments might also be necessary because, for example, of substitutes forced by long delivery times. Check what action is to be taken as a result. *(Contractor Client)* ☐

Inspections/tests

Decide on the provisions for testing to be included in the Bills of Quantities/Specification/Schedules of Work, including contractor's testing and commissioning of building services before completion (note in particular the new requirements and provisions for testing included under the Building Regulations Part L1 and L2). ☐

Determine provisions for the client to witness testing if required, and whether this is to be part of the contract period. Establish the contractor's obligations for attendance and rectification if necessary. ☐

Decide on the method statement required from the appointed contractor on quality management testing, verification, audit and records. ☐

Review quality management of potential suppliers and sub-contractors and their general compliance in health and safety matters. Pass relevant information to the planning supervisor. ☐

Consultations

Check all necessary information has been obtained with respect to Building Control approval. Hold further discussions with authorities as necessary to resolve outstanding points. ☐

If appropriate, continue discussions with highways authority on matters such as access to site, waiting or off-loading restrictions, siting and design of temporary fencing, hoardings, etc. ☐

Discuss, if appropriate, with relevant body (e.g. English Heritage) protective measures for existing works during site operations. ☐

Approvals/consents

Submit Building Notice or application for approval by deposit of Full **F/CM4** Plans, if not already submitted, together with relevant documents including a cheque from the client for the appropriate fee. ☐

Check that all Party Wall notices have been served. ☐

Contract

Agree with the client and the planning supervisor the tendering period and procedures to be followed in opening tenders and notifying results. ☐

Allow adequate time for tendering, and for the assessment of tenders. The most acceptable tender must be thoroughly checked for errors, and this takes time.

Allow time for checking by the planning supervisor.

If necessary, send out preliminary enquiries to firms selected as potential tenderers, as agreed with the client. **H/CM1** ☐

Arrange interviews to select principal contractor if relevant and necessary. ☐

Pre-tender meetings and interviews should only be held if considered essential, and always with a strictly limited agenda.

Arrange for interviews, if appropriate, for selection of contractors by negotiation. ☐

Take action on advance ordering as authorised. ☐

Check that the form of contract to be used has been confirmed with the client in writing. ☐

Discuss with the client the need to use Supplements to cover, for example, Sectional Completion, Contractor's Design, Fluctuations, etc. ☐

Discuss with the client the appropriate choice for optional provisions in the contract. Advise on the particulars which need to be entered in the appendix to the contract, and referred to in the tender documents, e.g. dates, insurances, liquidated damages, option clauses, etc. ☐

Check, in particular, that the client is aware of the requirements of insurance provisions in the contract and that he or she appreciates the advisability of seeking specialist advice from his insurers or brokers. ☐

It is very important that the client should be fully aware of the insurance requirements well in advance of the tender process.

Confirm with the client the inclusion of any special clauses or amendments to the contract, bearing in mind legal advice obtained. ☐

Review the position with respect to advance orders for design, materials, and fabrication by specialist sub-contractors and suppliers, including nominated sub-contractors. If authorised, take further necessary action.

Always obtain authorisation before taking action on advance orders.

Confirm with the client any arrangements to employ persons direct to carry out work not forming part of the contract during the contractor's occupation.

Confirm with the client the details of any preliminary contracts for enabling works and if authorised, take the necessary action.

Design and build Advise on completion and content of tender documents and the final form and content of the Employer's Requirements. *(Employer Client)*

Design and build Inspect drawings and information received from specialist sub-contractors and suppliers for checking against Contractor's Proposals, and advise the client. *(Contractor Client)*

Cost planning

Provide information for the QS to review cost plan and monitor cost implications of decisions during the preparation of Production Information (or revise cost estimate if appointed to do so).

QS (or architect if appointed to do so) to review quotations received from specialist firms and check against provisional sums or budget figures.

Design and build Provide revised information if relevant for corrected cost estimates. *(Employer Client)*

Design and build Provide revised information if relevant to contractor's estimators. *(Contractor Client)*

General procedures

Regularly check progress against the timetable for services.

Continue resource control procedures for job:

- Check expenditure against the office job cost allocation for Stage F;

• Monitor fee income against projected fee income.

Report regularly to the client on fees and expenses incurred, and submit accounts at agreed intervals. ☐

Check that the client settles all accounts promptly. ☐

Stage output

Check that all the agreed outputs before the conclusion of Stage F have been produced, which might include the following: ☐

• Production Information coordinated documents – probably **F/CM1-CM3** including location, component and assembly drawings, drawn schedules, Bills of Quantities/Specification/Schedules of Work.

• Information prepared specially for use in self-build or semi-skilled operations.

• Information for issue to specialist sub-contractors and suppliers in connection with tender invitations.

• Information for inclusion in pre-tender Health and Safety Plan – to be passed to the planning supervisor.

• Information for inclusion in Health and Safety File – to be passed to the planning supervisor.

• Non-production information for use in dealings with third parties, landlords, tenants, funders, etc (e.g. in connection with leases, boundaries, party walls, etc).

Design and build Detail design information for incorporation into Employer's Requirements (part of Stages D–G). *(Employer Client)* ☐

Design and build General arrangement drawings, interface details, performance speci-fication and other technical information (part of Stages F–G). *(Contractor Client)* ☐

References and further reading

Co-ordinating Committee for Project Information (1998) *Common arrangement of works sections for building works*, London, CCPI.

Co-ordinating Committee for Project Information (1987) *Code of pro-cedure for building works: a guide with examples*, London, CCPI.

Co-ordinating Committee for Project Information (1987) *Production Drawings: a code of procedure for building works*, London, CCPI.

Co-ordinating Committee for Project Information (1987) *Production Information: a code of procedure for building works*, London, CCPI.

JCT (2001) *JCT Guide to the use of Performance Specification*, London, RIBA Publications.

Lupton, S. and Stellakis, M. (2000) *Performance Specification: a guide to its preparation and use*, London, RIBA Publications.

F/CM1

Production Information: Drawings

Coordinated Project Information

Sir Michael Latham in *Constructing the Team* recommended the adoption of Coordinated Project Information (CPI) for all projects regardless of procurement method. The CPI publication *Production Drawings: A Code of Procedure for Building Works*, should be followed wherever possible. The code is for use by all members of the design team who have the task of preparing and issuing production drawings. It is complementary to BS 1192:1984, Construction Drawing Practice.

Architects' drawings are best structured as follows:

Location drawings (for example, block plan, site plan, general arrangement plans, sections, elevations).
Where the project is so large that at a suitable scale these will not fit easily on to single sheets, it might be necessary to split the project into suitable blocks or zones. They should enable users to gain an overall picture of the building, give setting-out dimensions, locate and identify the parts of the building, and refer out to more specific information.

Assembly drawings
These will be divided into groups representing parts of the building, e.g. walls, stairs, roofs, openings, ceilings, fittings, external works. They should show the construction of the building, particularly at selected junctions, and refer out to more specific information as necessary.

Component drawings (for example, purpose-made windows, doors).
These should be referred to from the location drawings. They should show the shape, dimensions and assembly of various parts, and identify components which are not described adequately elsewhere.

Drawings from the structural engineer and the building services engineers should be structured in a compatible manner despite the fact that information in their cases is likely to come from a number of sources, including specialist sub-contractors and suppliers.

Purpose of drawings

Drawings at this Stage are produced for three main reasons:
- because they must accompany Bills of Quantities for tendering purposes as stipulated by SMM7;
- because they will later become contract documents;
- because they may need to be developed or issued as other 'necessary information' to the main contractor when work on site commences.

The number of drawings required is likely to be influenced by the size of the project, the procurement method to be adopted (i.e. who actually produces the drawings), and the relative significance of drawn information in relation to other contract documents.

Whatever drawings are produced it is important to be clear about their intended purpose and the needs of the user of the drawing. Any drawing should provide such information as shape or profile, dimensions (notional or finished), position, composition and relation to other parts including tolerances, fixing methods, etc. On a small project where only a small number of drawings is necessary, these might embrace the needs of all trades and suppliers and be annotated to the extent that no other supporting document is required.

Conversely, larger projects will require a considerable number of drawings and schedules, each devised with a particular trade or element in mind, and cross-referencing to other drawings will need to be carried out with great care.

A checklist of the parts of a building which may need to be covered in a Production Information drawing and schedule programme is given in Fig. E4

Drawn schedules

In addition to the drawings, some information is more clearly and conveniently conveyed in drawn schedule form. Schedules commonly include:

- ironmongery (with location and fixings);
- doors;
- windows (to include glazing);
- finishes (floor, walls, ceilings);
- precast lintels and sills;
- inspection chambers and manhole covers;
- colours.

Any elements or components which are repetitive or can be grouped may be suitable for scheduling. The exercise is a good coverage check for compilers but information should not be repeated on the drawings as this might lead to confusion and inconsistencies.

Actions for architects

Architects producing drawings and drawn schedules should:

- draft a schedule of drawings and other information needed;
- work out a realistic timetable after assessing the amount of work involved and resources available;
- confirm a system for recording and distributing information and revisions;
- arrange for printed sheets, title panels, etc as appropriate;
- compile specification notes as relevant during the production of drawn information.

F/CM2

Production Information: Specification and Schedules of Work

CPI procedures

The introduction of Coordinated Project Information (CPI) procedures has created an efficient way of achieving integrated architectural and engineering drawings, specifications and Bills of Quantities. The Common Arrangement of Work Sections for building works (CAWS) has been adopted throughout the documents. The National Building Specification (NBS), National Engineering Specification (NES) and the Standard Method of Measurement (SMM7) all use this arrangement. The architect and the QS will find it easier to prepare and interpret a specification where it shares a common arrangement with the method of measurement used in preparing the bills.

Some architects' practices might use a system of specification clauses developed for use with particular types of work (e.g. housing refurbishment). Care must be taken to keep such clauses relevant and up to date, and it is generally safer and more convenient to adopt a well-developed system such as NBS. This allows for consistent description of materials and workmanship with full reference to British Standards and other codes and standards. NBS also enables performance specifications to be developed.

NBS is available in hard copy or software in Full, Abridged or Minor Works versions. The software versions include a word processing base package or more sophisticated packages such as the specification writer and the specification manager. The CPI publication, *Project Specification*, provides a code of procedure which should be followed wherever possible.

The specification

A specification is a written document which may describe the materials or products to be used, standards of workmanship required, performance requirements, and the conditions under which the work will be carried out.

Specification can be prescriptive, in that there is precise description of the materials, workmanship, etc which leaves no area of choice to the tendering contractor. Specification can also be by stated performance requirements either for the building components or engineering services, in which case there will remain an area of choice on the part of the contractor as to how the stated performance will be achieved. If performance specification is to be used, great care needs to be taken in ensuring that the contractual terms recognise this additional responsibility of the contractor.

Under CPI the specification is the core document to which the other production information refers. The description of materials and workmanship contained in the specification should therefore not be repeated on the drawing or in the Bill — these documents should refer to clause numbers in the specification. A specification will therefore be needed even when there is a separate Bill of Quantities. CPI advocates give it contract document status by making it part of the Bill. This can be done by calling the specification 'Bill Number 2'. Alternatively it can be done by including the specification at the start of the Bill, or by introducing the relevant parts of the specification as preambles to the various measured work sections of the Bill of Quantities.

Where there is no Bill of Quantities, it may be wise to append a schedule of work to the specification for pricing purposes, possibly supported by a schedule of rates, or to require the tendering contractor to provide a Priced Activity Schedule. If the specification has been prepared using the CAWS system then a breakdown according to works sections may not be very helpful when it comes to valuing variations or certificates.

The architect as designer is responsible for the method of specification selected, and the content. Specification notes will normally be compiled during the design process. The specification is a key document and will provide information to:

- the contractor's estimator when preparing a tender;
- the QS when preparing Bills of Quantities;
- the clerk of works or contractor during construction work.

Members of the design team might prepare the specification for those parts of the work which require specialist knowledge but the architect as design team leader should remain responsible for overall content and coordination.

Schedules of work

Schedules of work comprise lists of the various items of work to be carried out, usually on a room by room basis. It is customary to introduce a number or area alongside the items to encourage systematic pricing by tenderers. Items in respect of each room are usually listed under headings such as doors, ceilings, wall finishes, floor finishes, fittings, etc. Schedules of work should not contain quantities, for they are not exact documents by nature. A contractor, when pricing, should be expected to include everything necessary to complete the works.

Schedules of work might be a contract document where there is no Bill of Quantities. They are sometimes regarded as an alternative to a specification, particularly when used for housing refurbishment or alteration work. However, CPI would recommend that the specification is used, and that the Schedule of Work items refer to the detailed descriptions in the specification.

Actions for architects

Architects responsible for the preparation of specifications should:
- agree with the consultant team a strategy including a programme for the production of appropriate documents (e.g. specification/schedules/Bill of Quantities);
- assemble specification notes during detail design Stage E;
- prepare a checklist to show which headings or sub-headings might be relevant for the particular project;
- select from the library of standard specification clauses (preferably NBS);
- identify sections or items which are not covered adequately and which will require special draughting;
- allocate responsibilities for writing particular parts of the specification;
- establish which parts will be by prescription and which by performance requirements;
- if specifying by reference, obtain the documents and carefully read the relevant parts;
- review selection of materials, descriptions of workmanship, etc and check with cost plan;
- mark up a library of clauses and produce a draft copy of the specification;
- decide on the presentation of the specification;
- check final copy for errors, omissions and possible inconsistencies either within parts of the document or between the specification and other Production Information;
- establish the number of copies required and distribute as appropriate.

F/CM3

Production Information: Bills of Quantities

Pricing a Bill of Quantities is the traditional method of obtaining comparable tenders for projects where the design has been fully detailed beforehand. Where an accurate or full Bill of Quantities becomes part of the contract documentation, it usually means that quality and quantity included in the price will be as that stated in the Contract Bills. It is therefore important to ensure that the Bill accurately reflects the intentions of the architect and does not conflict with information shown on the drawings.

Notional bills or approximate quantities

Where it is not possible to present the QS with a completely detailed design and specification, it may be possible to invite tenders on the basis of notional bills or approximate quantities. These should be reasonably accurate as to description and items, with only the amounts left subject to measurement after completion.

Work which cannot be quantified with certainty, even in an accurate Bill of Quantities, may be covered by the introduction of provisional sums (for either defined or undefined work), prime cost sums (where an accurate figure can be placed on a sub-contract or supply item), or an approximate quantity (where the item is certain but the quantity is not). The once frequent inclusion of a contingency sum is nothing more than a provisional figure for undefined work of an unforeseeable nature. All such items require later instructions from the architect before the contractor can act on them.

Standard Method of Measurement

A uniform basis of measuring work for inclusion in a Bill of Quantities may be found in the *Standard Method of Measurement of Building Works*, currently in a seventh edition (SMM7). Although it is usually the prerogative of the QS to decide which method of measurement to adopt and how the Bill will be structured, for building work this is most likely to be using the Common Arrangement, and in accordance with SMM7. The contents of a Bill prepared in this way are likely to include:

Preliminaries/General conditions
• Items which are not specific to work sections but which have an identifiable cost (e.g. site facilities, insurances).
• Items for fixed and time related costs (e.g. plant, temporary works).

Work sections

(also incorporating cross-references to drawings and specification)

C	Demolition/alteration/renovation
D	Groundwork
E	In situ concrete/large precast concrete
F	Masonry – brick, block, stonework, etc
G	Structural/carcassing – metal and timber
H	Cladding/covering – patent glazing, plastics, etc
J	Waterproofing
K	Linings/dry partitions
L	Windows/doors/stairs
M	Surface finishes – screeds, tiling, decorating, etc

P   Building fabric sundries – trims, ironmongery, etc
Q   Paving/planting/fencing/outdoor furniture
R   Disposal systems – pipework gutters, drainage
Y   Mechanical and electrical services.

Actions for architects

To assist the QS during preparation of the Bill, the architect might be expected to supply the following:

- Specification or specification notes for incorporation as preambles to work sections.
- Information for inclusion in Preliminaries such as:
  - form of contract, supplements, option clauses, amended clauses, etc;
  - content and use of contract documentation;
  - method statements required;
  - pre-tender Health and Safety Plan;
  - work to be done by employer direct;
  - requirements concerning sequence, time limitations, etc;
  - provisional sums to be included;
  - provision for named/nominated sub-contractors/suppliers.
- Diagrams for inclusion in the Bill (e.g. extent of retaining structures, cornice profiles, multi-coloured paintwork, etc). SMM7 Rule 5.3 refers to the use of dimensioned diagrams in place of a dimensioned description.
- Drawn information to accompany the Bill:
  - location drawings (i.e. block plan, site plan, floor plans, sections and elevations);
  - component drawings (i.e. showing information necessary for manufacture and assembly);
  - drawn schedules.
- Dimensions, which will normally appear on the drawings listed above. In particular the QS will require overall dimensions, and internal dimensions of all rooms and spaces.

SMM7 Rules 5.1, 5.2 and 5.4 refer to drawn information. These might be expected to apply to most of the Work Sections listed above. In many cases it will simply show the scope and location of the work. In other cases (e.g. E, H, etc) it will require the supply of detail drawings.

The QS will almost certainly expect a rapid response to the Query Sheets directed at the architect during Bill preparations. It will also assist the QS if information is despatched to suit the taking-off process, that is to ensure that the right information is received in the right sequence.

The CPI publication, *SMM7*, contains a full set of the General Rules. There is also the *SMM7 Measurement Code* published by CPI which includes a commentary on particular rules and contains illustrative material likely to be of assistance to the architect.

F/CM4

Building control approval checklist

Preparing an application for Building Regulations approval is normally one of the services provided by the architect. In many cases, although informal consultations may well have taken place earlier, the drawings and calculations necessary to support a formal submission will not be sufficiently developed until well into Production Information.

For England and Wales, the principal legislation is The Building Act 1984, which empowered the making of Building Regulations (currently 1991). Health and Safety legislation is quite separate, as is Fire Precautions legislation. These latter areas of law, although administered by different authorities, closely affect building and should be regarded as complementary.

Approval procedures

Building Regulations approval may be sought by application to the local authority using either the Full Plans or the Building Notice procedure. Using the former means that you can seek a Determination if you consider that your work complies with the Regulations, or a Dispensation if you consider that the strict legal requirements are too onerous in a particular set of circumstances. Using the Building Notice procedure means that you do not have to submit full plans but you must be reasonably confident that the work complies, because there is no opportunity to seek a Determination.

If you elect to use an Approved Inspector and do not make an application to the local authority, then you must follow the Initial Notice procedure. This takes the place of both the local authorities procedures described above.

The Building Regulations 1991

The Regulations include the following:

Regulation 4 states the requirements relating to building work. It refers to Schedule 1 which sets out the Functional Requirements, and it is the 'practical guidance' on meeting these requirements which is found in the Approved Documents (S6 Building Act 1984). Regulation 4 refers to building work, and Regulation 6 extends the application to material change of use.

Regulation 9 states that the Building Regulations will not apply to all building work, and the exemptions (mostly uninhabitable, small, temporary or ancillary buildings) are set out in Schedule 2.

Regulation 8 makes it clear that there is a legal obligation to go beyond that which is necessary to secure reasonable standards of health and safety for persons in or about buildings. It may include the welfare and convenience of persons. It may also include the conservation of fuel and power, prevention of waste, etc.

Regulation 7 supplements the requirements of Schedule 1 and is concerned with materials and workmanship. Architects should carefully consider what to specify and contractors should ensure that specified standards are achieved by effective quality control. The Approved Document on materials and workmanship is very general. Guidance is given on fitness and adequacy by reference to past experience, Agrément Certificates, British Standards, EC Construction Products Directives and testing. The emphasis seems to be on selecting materials and methods that are known and proven. In the event of a failure, it would be for the architect to demonstrate that the requirements of Regulation 7 have been met.

Regulation 10 establishes that applications for relaxation or a dispensation may be made to the local authority. An appeal may be made to the Secretary of State.

Regulations 1–15 set out the procedural requirements where application for approval is made to the local authority. If the application is made to an Approved Inspector, then the Building (Approved Inspectors, etc) Regulations will apply.

Applications to the local authority may be by Full Plans (*Regulation 13*) or Building Notice (*Regulation 12*). The latter is not an option where the proposed work is in shops or offices, or is subject to rules for means of escape in the event of fire.

The technical requirements under the Building Regulations are set out in Schedule 1. They aim to ensure that buildings meet reasonable standards of health and safety, although additionally Part L is concerned with energy conservation and Part M is concerned with access for the disabled. The requirements are stated in broad terms of performance standards, and guidance as to what might satisfy these are given in the Approved Documents.

Submitting an application

When preparing or submitting an application to the local authority, note the following:

- Assuming that the work is not 'exempt' (check against Building Regulation 9 and Schedule 2), either deposit Full Plans (Regulations 11–14) or give a Building Notice in the case of small works.
- A prescribed fee is payable. This is revised fairly frequently. Check with the local authority.
- The Secretary of State has power (through the local authority) to dispense with or relax a Regulation (see Building Act 1984, s. 8), and to make Determinations (s. 16).
- The local authority must pass or reject a Full Plans application within five weeks (unless a longer period not exceeding eight weeks is agreed).
- The local authority must be given two days' notice before commencement of work, one day's notice must be given before certain work is covered up, and notice is required within five days of completion.
- Where work is not commenced within three years of approval, the local authority may hold that the notices or deposited plans are of no effect (Building Act 1984, s. 32).
- When work is carried out without Building Regulations approval, or in contravention of the Regulations, the local authority is empowered to require its removal or alteration to comply. The local authority may, if necessary, seek a court injunction.

F/CM5

Consultant team roles: Work Stage F

Quantity surveyor

The QS should be supplied with drawings and specifications for all the contract works. Any observed discrepancies or omissions should be raised with the architect, preferably by question-and-answer sheets. The QS will carry out cost checks and keep the architect informed of the results. Contract particulars and other information for the preliminaries should be supplied to the QS. Once the billing and tendering documentation is complete, the QS should provide the design team with an updated cost plan for the project.

Structural engineer

The engineer should prepare production drawings and specifications for the relevant construction and operations on site. Documents might also be needed for preliminary contracts or enabling works which usually have a structural content.

The engineer should provide the QS with drawings and specifications for billing, and with reinforcement lists or schedules as relevant. It might also be necessary to supply copies of surveys, soil reports and geotechnical information to accompany tender enquiries.

Building services engineer

The services engineers should prepare the necessary drawings and specification. Tendering procedures for named or nominated sub-contract work should be finalised. Where work is to be subject to performance specification and is intended to be the direct responsibility of the main contractor, albeit via some domestic arrangement, then the services engineer should alert the consultant team to this as the main contract will need to include appropriate terms.

All necessary information should be passed to the QS for inclusion in the specification and Bill of Quantities. Where the services engineers are responsible for obtaining tenders from sub-contractors and suppliers, evaluation of these should be in collaboration with the architect, QS and planning supervisor.

G: TENDER DOCUMENTATION

Preparation and collation of Tender Documentation in sufficient detail to enable a tender or tenders to be obtained for the construction of the project (RIBA Outline Plan of Work).

Description

Key obligations from SFA/99

Actions

Stage input
Preliminary issues   architect
                               client
                               management and team working
Cost planning
Approvals/consents
Contract
Preparing the Tender Documents
General procedures
Stage output

Core material

G/CM1   Tender Documentation checklist

TENDER DOCUMENTATION

Description

Stage G under traditional procurement involves the assembly and coordination of all the Production Information into the tender package. In addition, it is the Stage when the pre-cost estimate is prepared by the quantity surveyor. This is an essential final check before proceeding to tender that the design as currently developed still meets the client's budget. If the estimate reveals any unanticipated problems then some adjustment of the Production Information may be needed, requiring careful management and collaboration from all concerned.

In design and build procurement, Stage G (and H) may be out of sequence with the other Work Stages. Although in cases where the client wishes to tender on detailed information the Stages may follow something close to the normal sequence, in others, where the design and build contract is entered into on minimal information, Stage G may follow Stage C, with Stages D–F occurring after the contract is let and sometimes during construction.

With management procurement, the amount of production information available at the commencement of the project will be limited to the extent that much detail information will be supplied by the works contractors by way of shop or installation drawings. Nevertheless, the general Production Information will originate from the professional team, and the process of coordinating and integrating information will continue throughout the construction of the project.

Key obligations which may apply:

	Reference	To do
- from SFA/99: design services		
Prepare and collate tender documents.	SFA/99/G/1	☐
Pass information for pre-tender Health and Safety Plan.	SFA/99/G/2	☐
Prepare pre-tender cost estimate, or	SFA/99/G/3A	☐
Provide information for pre-tender cost estimate.	SFA/99/G/3B	☐
Co-operate with planning supervisor where appropriate.	SFA/99/1.4	☐

In addition to the above, the architect should note the obligations set out in the SFA/99 Conditions of Engagement 2.1-2.8.

		To do
- from SFA/99: management services		
(i.e. architect acting as design leader and lead consultant)		
Directing, coordinating and monitoring design work.		☐
Establishing the form and content of design outputs, their interfaces and a verification procedure.		☐
Considering with the client a list of tenderers for the Works.		☐
Developing and managing change control procedures.		☐
Reporting to the client.		☐

Actions

Stage input

Check that all information necessary during Stage G is available, which might include the following:

- Production Information prepared during Stage F.

- Any further conditions imposed by the local Building Control and fire authorities, particularly relating to construction details and fire prevention, including finishes.

- Further contributions, information and recommendations from consultants in relation to documents submitted by approved sub-contractors and suppliers.

Preliminary issues – architect

Establish scope, content and context for Stage G activities.
Put it into context, particularly if previous Stages were undertaken by others. If possible, establish whether material produced now is likely to be acted upon by others taking over subsequent Stages.

If coming new to the project at this Stage in the *Plan of Work:*

- Ascertain that relevant Pre-Agreement and earlier Stage checks have been carried out.

- Allow for familiarisation and reviewing of all usable material when agreeing fees and timetable with the client.

- Confirm the role of the architect in relation to the rest of the consultant team.

Check the client's instruction to proceed has been given and confirmed in writing.

Check the client has settled all accounts submitted to date.

Check appointing documents with respect to services and fees.

- If the Services, cost or time targets are different from the Agreement with the client, agree a formal variation by letter or deed as appropriate.

- If the extent of professional services for Stage G is not settled, agree with the client and confirm in writing.

- If the methods and levels of charging for Stage G are not yet settled, agree with the client and confirm in writing.

Assess office resources needed for Stage G and ensure that they are adequate and available. ☐

Carry out checks for compliance with in-house quality management procedures, including updated project quality plan. ☐

Review application of practice procedures to project. ☐

Preliminary issues – client

Check whether the client has confirmed in writing acceptance of any proposals and information submitted at Stage F. Establish any points to be discussed and developed during Stage G. ☐

Advise the client on the need for a party wall surveyor if appropriate. ☐

Note that if the architect is to be appointed as party wall surveyor, this appointment must form a separate agreement.

Check whether any necessary contractual information to be supplied by the client is still outstanding. ☐

Confirm with the client the details of any preliminary contracts for enabling works, demolition, etc. ☐

Confirm with the client the details of any advance appointments of sub-contractors and specialists. Ensure the client has copies of relevant warranties. ☐

Confirm with the client the details of any clerk of works' appointments if appropriate. ☐

Arrange with the client for further interviews of potential contractors if appropriate. ☐

Confirm with the client the details of any phasing, restrictions and implications. ☐

Confirm with the client the details of any proposal for work not forming part of the contract to be carried out by other persons. ☐

Confirm with the client the details of contract appendix entries. ☐

Confirm with the client the details of any special or optional contract provisions. ☐

Confirm with the client and advisers that arrangements for insurance for works, etc are being made. ☐

Preliminary issues – management and team working

Agree input to the Stage by consultant team members. ☐

Confirm Stage timetable for services and note its relationship to the project timetable as agreed with the client. ☐

Confirm timetable for receipt of any revisions to tender information required from consultant team members. Establish a cut-off-point for revised information to be passed to QS. ☐

Confirm patterns for communication between the client, planning supervisor, project manager and design leader. ☐

Confirm programme and pattern for consultant team meetings. ☐

Integrate and coordinate input from consultant team members and specialists. Continue to appraise input from specialist firms, including potential sub-contractors and suppliers. ☐

Coordinate and provide final information for pre-tender Health and Safety Plan and pass to the planning supervisor. ☐

Discuss with the planning supervisor any outstanding matters of designers' contributions to pre-tender Health and Safety Plan, including appropriate site traffic movements and layout for site operations. ☐

Coordinate production of Information Release Schedule if appropriate. ☐

Confirm with consultant team members any further arrangements for inviting specialist tenders. ☐

Continue to appraise input from specialist firms, including potential sub-contractors and suppliers. ☐

Cost planning

Provide information for the QS to prepare pre-tender cost estimate (or prepare pre-tender cost estimate if appointed to do so). ☐

The pre-tender estimate is an essential check prior to inviting tenders. At this point the estimate should be an accurate prediction of the tender figures. The design and tender documents may need to be amended if the estimate does not match the project brief.

Review with the client implications of the pre-tender estimate prepared by the QS. ☐

Discuss possible options with the client. Explain implications for time-table and consultants' fees if amendments are required to change (or comply with) brief.

Design and build Provide revised information if relevant for corrected cost estimates. *(Employer Client)* ☐

Design and build Provide revised information if relevant to contractor's estimators. *(Contractor Client)* ☐

Report to the client on cost matters at agreed intervals. ☐

Approvals/consents

Monitor progress on statutory and other consents. Submit additional information if necessary. ☐

Monitor progress on Party Wall Awards. ☐

Contract

Confirm any outstanding details of the contractual terms, including: ☐
- supplements;
- optional provisions;
- particulars which need to be entered in the appendix to the contract.

Discuss with the client the results of any pre-selection interviews or **H/CM1** other selection procedures, and take any necessary further action. ☐

Confirm with the client the final tender list, and inform all tenderers of their inclusion. ☐

Check that the client has finalised all insurance arrangements. ☐

Check that all advance orders for design, materials and fabrication by specialist sub-contractors and suppliers, as agreed, have been placed. ☐

Check that any preliminary contracts for enabling works are under-way and on schedule. Administer the preliminary contracts, if author-ised. ☐

If appropriate, confirm with the client that the appointment of a clerk of works is in hand. ☐

Confirm with the client that any arrangements to employ persons direct to carry out work not forming part of the contract are in hand. ☐

Review, with other consultant team members, any further tenders received from specialist sub-contractors and suppliers. Include in tender documents as appropriate. ☐

Certify to the planning supervisor or the client, as appropriate, readi-ness to proceed to tender. ☐

Design and build Advise on completion and content of tender documents and the final form and content of the Employer's Requirements. *(Employer Client)* ☐

Design and build Inspect drawings and information received from specialist sub-contractors and suppliers for checking against Contractor's Proposals, and advise the client. *(Contractor Client)* ☐

Preparing the tender documents

Obtain from sub-contractors and suppliers any outstanding project information. ☐

Provide final information to the QS for Bills and the pre-tender cost estimate. ☐

Consolidate the final detailed information for production drawings, sub-contract specifications and preliminaries to Bills of Quantities/ Specification/Schedules of Work. ☐

Prepare, coordinate, collate and check tender documents. ☐

Prepare report and submit to the client. ☐

Request authority of the client to invite tenders. ☐

Design and build Check whether the client has confirmed in writing acceptance of pro- posals and information supplied so far in Stages D–G which are to form part of the Employer's Requirements. *(Employer Client)* ☐

Design and build Review any client comments on the detail design or development, and note any adjustments which may be unavoidable due to modifi- cations introduced lately by component manufacturers or specialist sub-contractors. Detail design amendments might also be necessary because, for example, of substitutes forced by long delivery times. Check what action is to be taken as a result. *(Contractor Client)* ☐

General procedures

Regularly check progress against the timetable for services. ☐

Continue resource control procedures for the job: ☐

- Check expenditure against the office job cost allocation for Stage G;

- Monitor fee income against the projected fee income.

Report regularly to the client on fees and expenses incurred, and submit accounts at agreed intervals. ☐

Check that the client settles all accounts promptly. ☐

Stage output

Check that all the agreed outputs have been produced before the conclusion of Stage G, which might include the following: ☐

- Finalised tender documents – probably including drawings, drawn **F/CM1-CM3,** schedules, Bills of Quantities/Specification/Schedules of Work, **G/CM1** pre-tender Health and Safety Plan, terms of bonds and warranties, sub-contractor information and tenders.

- Information prepared specially for use in self-build or semi-skilled operations.

- Information for issue to specialist sub-contractors and suppliers in connection with tender invitations.

- Information for inclusion in Health and Safety File – to be passed to the planning supervisor.

- Non-production information for use in dealings with third parties, landlords, tenants, funders, etc (e.g. in connection with leases, boundaries, party walls, etc).

Design and build   Detail design information for incorporation into Employer's Requirements (part of Stages D–G). *(Employer Client)*

Design and build   General arrangement drawings, interface details, performance speci-fication and other technical information (part of Stages F–G). *(Contractor Client)*

References and further reading

Cox, S. and Clamp, H. (1999) *Which Contract? 2nd edn.,* London, RIBA Publications.

G/CM1

Tender Documentation checklist

(Note: there is a separate list for Employer's Requirements at C/CM1)

When sending out for tender, any of the following documents and information may be relevant:

- a list of all tender documents so that the tenderers can check they have received the complete package;
- tender forms and details of procedure to be followed, e.g. type of tender required, submittals required, how the tender should be packaged and identified, to whom it should be sent;
- site information and surveys;
- drawings;
- drawn schedules, e.g. for doors;
- specification;
- Bill of Quantities;
- list of items to be paid for prior to delivery on site;
- schedule of works;
- schedule of rates;
- activity schedule;
- information release schedule;
- the Health and Safety Plan;
- programmed dates for proposed work;
- details of any phased commencement or completion;
- details of the contract terms and conditions, including insurance provisions;
- details of advance payment arrangements;
- details of any bonds or guarantees required from the contractor or to be provided by the employer;
- details of any warranties to be provided.

H: TENDER ACTION

Identification and evaluation of potential contractors and/or specialists for the construction of the project.
Obtaining and appraising tenders and submission of recommendations to the client (RIBA Outline Plan of Work).

Description

Key obligations from SFA/99

Actions

Stage input
Preliminary issues   architect
                          client
                          management and team working
Sending out for tenders
Inspections/tests
Approvals/consents
Contract — tender review
General procedures
Stage output

Core material

H/CM1	Selective tendering principals
H/CM2	Selective tendering lists
H/CM3	Selective tendering: Specialist sub-contractors and suppliers
H/CM4	Selective tendering: Main contract – Traditional procurement
H/CM5	Selective tendering: Main contract – Design and build procurement
H/CM6	Selective tendering: Main contract – Management procurement

TENDER ACTION

Description

Tendering is an activity not wholly confined to Stage H. For example, there will often be the need to obtain tenders from specialist sub-contractors or suppliers at an earlier stage. Sometimes it may be advantageous if the main contractor is appointed earlier to advise pre-construction, followed by a second stage tender for the full contract works. Obviously the procurement method adopted — or the size and complexity of the project — can have an effect on Tender Action and timing. For example, in management procurement, there will be a tendering procedure to select the management contractor (or construction manager) followed by separate tendering for each Works package. Normally, however, Stage H is when the main contract tenders are invited and evaluated, and advice is given to the client on appointing the contractor.

Tenders may be obtained by following one of these routes:

- Open tendering – open to all and in theory competitive but generally regarded as wasteful, often unreliable, and not in the client's long term interests.
- Selective tendering – open to selected invitees only, competitive and appropriate for all forms of procurement.
- Negotiated tendering – applicable where price is not the main criterion, and not necessarily competitive except perhaps where it forms the second step in a two-stage process.

Tendering will mostly be a single stage activity but where the project is particularly large and complex, or where the procurement method makes it desirable, two-stage tendering can be a more efficient and satisfactory way forward.

Regardless of the route chosen, it is important to ensure that tendering is always on a fair basis. Competition should only be between firms who have the necessary skills, integrity, responsibility and reputation which will enable them to deliver work of the nature and standard required. Competitive tendering should involve only a realistic number of bids, from firms who have been given the same information, and the same realistic period in which to formulate offers.

It is sound practice always to follow current relevant guidance. The CIB *Code of Practice for the Selection of Main Contractors* sets up a clear procedure for selective tendering which is referred to below. The Guidance Notes and Codes of Procedures which were published by the National Joint Consultative Committee for Building (NJCC), are also extremely helpful and were endorsed without reservation in *Constructing the Team*. Tendering in the local or public authority sectors may also be subject to standing orders, and the Public Works Contracts Regulations 1991 and any subsequent legislation. Where such legislation applies it is important that it is followed exactly.

Key obligations which may apply:

	Reference	To do
- from SFA/99: design services		
Contribute to appraisal and report on tenders.	SFA/99/H/1	☐
If instructed, revise Production Information.	SFA/99/H/2	☐
In addition to the above, the architect should note the obligations set out in the SFA/99 Conditions of Engagement 2.1-2.8.		

- from SFA/99: management services

(i.e. architect acting as design leader and lead consultant)

Inviting and appraising a tender or tenders. ☐

Developing and managing change control procedures. ☐

Reporting to the client. ☐

Actions

Stage input

Check that all information necessary during Stage H is available, which might include the following: ☐

- Tender documents, complete and ready for dispatch to invited tenderers.

- Pre-tender Health and Safety Plan.

- Tender list as agreed with client.

- Completed tender documents from nominated or named sub-contractors and suppliers with all sections properly completed.

- Relevant published procedure notes and guidance on selected method of tendering (e.g. CIB).

- Completed particulars for contract, and for Supplements to form of contract.

- Pre-tender cost estimate prepared by QS based on Bills of Quantities/Specification/Schedules of Work.

Preliminary issues – architect

Establish scope, content and context for Stage H activities. ☐
Put it into context, particularly if previous Stages were undertaken by others. If possible, establish whether material produced now is likely to be acted upon by others taking over subsequent Stages.

If coming new to the project at this Stage in the *Plan of Work:* ☐

- Ascertain that Pre-Agreement and earlier Stage checks have been carried out.

- Allow for familiarisation and reviewing of all usable material when agreeing fees and timetable with the client.

- Confirm the role of the architect in relation to the rest of the consultant team.

Check the client's instruction to proceed has been given and confirmed in writing. ☐

Check the client has settled all accounts submitted to date. ☐

Check appointing documents with respect to services and fees. ☐

- If the Services, cost or time targets are different from the Agreement with the client, agree a formal variation by letter or deed, as appropriate.

- If the extent of professional services for Stage H is not yet settled, agree with the client and confirm in writing.

- If the methods and levels of charging for Stage H are not yet settled, agree with the client and confirm in writing.

Assess office resources needed for Stage H and ensure that they are adequate and available. ☐

Carry out checks for compliance with in-house quality management procedures, including updated project quality plan. ☐

Review application of practice procedures to project. ☐

Preliminary issues – client

Check whether the client has confirmed the following: ☐

- Whether tendering for the particular project is subject to legislative control.

- The preferred tendering method, and names to be included on the tender list.

Clarify and confirm any outstanding matters related to the tendering procedure to be followed in writing, including procedures to be followed following receipt of tenders. ☐

Check with the client that the site will be available to the contractor on the date stated in the documents, and that there is nothing likely to prevent possession or commencement. ☐

Preliminary issues – management and team working

Agree timetable and input to the Stage by consultant team members. ☐

Confirm programme and pattern for any further meetings of the consultant team. ☐

Check with consultant team members their input to main contract tender documents to discover inconsistencies or omissions. ☐

Review with consultant team members tenders and accompanying information received from specialist sub-contractors and suppliers and if acceptable, approve them. ☐

Ascertain the extent to which the planning supervisor expects to be involved in tendering procedures. ☐

Sending out for tenders

Make a final check of information for main contract tenders, including: ☐

- that documents sufficiently explain the requirements, that they are accurate, listed and numbered.

- that drawings required under SMM7 Measurement Code are ready to accompany Bills to tenderers.

- that any requirements for a warranty or guarantee bond must be made known to tenderers at the time of invitation.

Design and build Make a final check that Employer's Requirements are complete. **C/CM1**

Make a final check to ascertain if the selected firms have all **H/CM1** completed tendering questionnaire, any non-collusion or other similar certificates required by the client. ☐

Invite tenders for main contract works from contractors on the final **H/CM3** tender list. ☐

Follow the relevant Codes of Procedure for Tendering to ensure fairness and reliable pricing.

Supply all tenderers with identical information. If queries are raised during the tendering period, deal with them promptly and notify all other tenderers in identical terms.

Do not accept late tenders.

Initiate action for second stage tendering if relevant.   **H/CM4**   ☐

Inspections/tests

Arrange for tenderers to have the opportunity to inspect the site and/ or existing buildings during the tender period.   ☐

Arrange for tenderers to have the opportunity to inspect drawings not issued with the tender documents.   ☐

Design and build   Arrange for submission and testing of prototypes designed by contractors or specialist sub-contractors, as required by tender procedure.   ☐

Approvals/consents

Check all necessary statutory and other consents have been obtained, and that Party Wall Awards are in place.   ☐

If any permissions, consents or awards are still under negotiation at this stage this could mean that alterations will be required to the tender negotiations or that start on site will be delayed.

Contract – tender review

Appraise with the QS and planning supervisor tenders received and prepare a report with recommendations for the client: ☐

- Check with the QS for arithmetical errors in the most acceptable tender and if any are found, use the appropriate stated procedures.

- Inspect draft programmes submitted by tenderers, if required.

- Arrange for the planning supervisor to inspect material submitted by tenderers relating to health and safety requirements, and to appraise the construction phase Health and Safety Plan submitted by the most acceptable tenderer.

Be wary of a very low tender. Explain to the client the possible risks in accepting it.

Deal with tender errors, or the need for a reduction, strictly in accordance with recommended procedures.

Review the tender report with the client and discuss recommendations about acceptance. ☐

Discuss with the QS the most appropriate measures for reducing the lowest figure, if this proves necessary, and initiate action. ☐

Assist as necessary with negotiations following consideration by the client of the most acceptable tender. ☐

Continue with appraisal of tenders from specialists. Check that offers are still open for acceptance and that particulars on which they tendered are still correct. ☐

Check that the planning supervisor has certified that the Health and Safety Plan has been developed sufficiently by the firm to be appointed as principal contractor for the construction phase to commence. ☐

Design and build   Assist the client with negotiations following the submission of the **H/CM5** Contractor's Proposals and Contract Sum Analysis, as relevant. This might be equally relevant whether acting for an Employer Client or a Contractor Client. *(Employer Client, Contractor Client)* ☐

Notify unsuccessful tenderers of the result when the contract is signed and provide figures when appropriate. ☐

General procedures

Regularly check progress against the timetable for services. ☐

Continue resource control procedures for job: ☐

- Check expenditure against the office job cost allocation for Stage F;

- Monitor fee income against projected fee income.

Report regularly to the client on fees and expenses incurred, and submit accounts at agreed intervals. ☐

Check that the client settles all accounts promptly. ☐

Stage output

- Check that all the agreed outputs have been produced before the ☐
  conclusion of Stage H, which might include the following:

- Main contract tenders and report with recommendations.

- Tenders received from specialists with appropriate forms (e.g.
  NAM/T, NSC/T) and 'numbered documents' where appropriate.

Design and build Report for client on appraisal of Contractor's Proposals and Contract
Sum Analysis. *(Employer Client)*

Design and build Report for client on appraisal of tenders submitted by specialist sub-
contractors and suppliers. *(Contractor Client)*

Design and build Final material for incorporation into Contractor's Proposals and in
connection with Contract Sum Analysis. *(Contractor Client)*

References and further reading

CIB (1997) *Code of Practice for the selection of Main Contractors*,
London, Thomas Telford Publishing.

JCT (2001) Practice Note 6 (series 2): *Main Contract Tendering*,
London, RIBA Publications.

H/CM1

Selective tendering principals

The CIB *Code of Practice for the Selection of Main Contractors* sets out key principles of good practice to be adopted when appointing contractors:

- clear procedures should be followed that ensure fair and transparent competition in a single round of tendering consisting of one or more stages;
- the tender process should ensure compliant, competitive tenders;
- tender lists should be complied systematically from a number of qualified contractors;
- tender lists should be as short as possible;
- conditions should be the same for all tenderers;
- confidentiality should be respected by all parties;
- sufficient time should be given for the preparation and evaluation of tenders;
- sufficient information should be given for the preparation of tenders;
- tenders should be assessed and accepted on quality as well as price;
- practices that avoid or discourage collusion should be followed;
- tender prices should not change on an unaltered scope of works;
- suites of contracts and standard un-amended forms of contract from recognised bodies should be used where they are available;
- there should be a commitment to teamwork from all parties.

H/CM2

Selective tendering lists

The first stage in the tender process is the compilation of the tender list. Although this may not be finalised until Stage H, some preliminary enquiries can be made as soon as the overall scope, nature and approximate time-scale of the work is known.

The CIB *Code of Practice for the Selection of Main Contractors* defines three steps in the selection of a contractor:

(1) qualification, in which potential contractors are assessed as to their general skills and performance to undertake a given type or range of projects;

(2) compilation of a tender list, in which the field of qualified contractors is refined to a short tender list of comparable, competent contractors who are willing and able to tender for a specific project;

(3) selection of successful tenderer, in which tenders are sought from those on the tender list and assessed to identify the preferred contractor.

During the period of qualification potential contractors will normally be required to provide information about their firms and their track records. Architects will then wish to take up references and make further enquiries about those who seem suitable for inclusion in the final tender list. It is advisable to maintain a file or record of all enquiries to contractors and sub-contractors and their responses.

Lists of potential contractors can be as follows:

List of contractors for larger projects

The preliminary list will be compiled from previous experience and after discussion with the client, the QS and other consultants. If a wider pool is needed enquiries could be made of registering bodies or from Construct On-line.

A questionnaire can then be sent to all those on the preliminary list to ascertain their interest in, and suitability for, the project. The questionnaire might be expected to cover:

- name and details of company;
- business status of company, names of directors, etc;
- financial status, share capital, etc;
- details of quality system and accreditation;
- details of insurers and liability insurance;
- construction turnover and details of contracts completed recently;
- particular skills and experience of relevance to the proposed project;
- the personnel who would be available for the proposed project;
- names of three referees;
- Health and Safety policy and procedures;
- policy on discrimination.

At this initial stage the tenderers should be informed of:

- the job name and location;
- nature, scope and approximate value of the works;
- the proposed dates and duration of the works;
- the procurement method and contract form;
- any contractor responsibility for design or other particular skills or experience sought;

- the selection process and criteria to be used;
- details of the tender procedure to be followed; e.g. whether any particular Code or principles will be followed, the numbers of tenders to be invited, the anticipated dates and period of tendering

The completed questionnaire should be signed by a director of the company. On larger projects the questionnaire might also be followed by an interview. It should then be possible to finalise the tender list. It may be wise to identify one or two contractors as reserves, in the event that nearer the tender date one of the list can no longer tender. Those on the list and reserves should be informed, and any changes to the list notified to them immediately.

List of contractors for small projects

On smaller projects contractors are generally selected by reputation or from previous experience, and after consulting the client, office records, other consultants and other sources. It would still be good practice to write to all potential contractors requesting up to date information about their firm, a reference, and enquiring as to their current availability and anticipated workload. This would help ensure that the tender process runs smoothly and that only suitable contractors are invited.

Approved standing list of contractors

It is often a good idea to develop a 'standing list' of approved contractors that can be drawn on at the preliminary stage of a new project. This may be particularly helpful where the office is often involved in repeat — or very similar — projects. The list could be compiled after responses to a questionnaire sent to potential tenderers. Shortlists of tenderers for future particular projects can then be drawn up as and when required.

The questionnaire might be expected to include the information shown above, with additional entries to indicate the type of work the firm has experience of, and whether they would be interested in tendering for non-traditional procurement contracts.

H/CM3

Selective tendering: Specialist sub-contractors and suppliers

Identify items

During the detail design and Production Information stages, items where a measure of control over choice needs to be exercised should be identified. These might include for example:

*   materials or suppliers named or nominated;
*   acceptable sub-contractors restricted to listed names;
*   sub-contractors named or nominated, as provided for by the contract.

Where sub-contractors or suppliers have been nominated or named under procedures laid down in the particular contract, there is usually a requirement or opportunity to use a standard design warranty in favour of the employer. However, where sub-contractors or suppliers are referred to in items in the Bill or Specification and are intended to be domestic appointments, then the contractor will have no liability for their design input. In such cases the employer's interests might need to be protected by a warranty, should this be available. The client's consent should always be obtained in writing where sub-contractors have a design input which might be regarded as sub-contracting by the architect.

The purpose of tendering should be identified, e.g. whether it is to obtain information necessary to complete detail design, to obtain a realistic basis for a provisional sum, or to facilitate advance ordering, where desirable.

List suitable firms

Compile a list after discussion with other members of the design team and the contractor (if appointed). Refer to office records of previous experience and check out references if necessary.

Make preliminary enquiries

Consult the QS and other consultants to establish a timetable for inviting tenders so as to provide necessary information for inclusion in Bills/Specification/Schedules.

Check that current information is obtained concerning the financial status of firms and that they have adequate resources.

Send a preliminary invitation to tender, or to ascertain willingness for inclusion in a list of sub-contractors or as a named supplier. If approximate dates and figures can be given at this stage, it should be possible to obtain a reliable response. See specimen letter, Fig. H1.

Fig. H1   Specimen letter of preliminary invitation to tender

It may be sufficient to make initial enquiries by telephone but if a letter is preferable, this may be used to approach:

- nominated contractors (JCT 98)
- named sub-contractors (IFC 98).

The text should be adapted to suit the particular circumstances.

We are preparing a list of tenderers for specialist works and items in connection with this project.

(Under JCT 98, clause 35)
Tenders will be invited under JCT forms NSC/T and NSC/W and the standard conditions of sub-contract NSC/C will apply.

(Under IFC 98, clause 3.3)
Tenders will be invited using JCT form NAM/T and the successful tenderer will be required to enter into agreement under form ESA/1 direct with the employer. Standard conditions of sub-contract NAM/SC will apply.

(Under JCT 98, clause 19)
Tenderers who wish their names to be specified or listed as potential domestic sub-contractors are asked to signify that they are able and willing at this stage to undertake the work and that they will cooperate in preparing a suitable description and measured items for inclusion in the main contract documents.

(and)

If you wish to be included in our preliminary list of tenderers, you should reply by 12 noon on (date). You should also supply information about three recent commissions in which you have been involved, giving the names and addresses of the main contractor and architect in each case.

Invite tenders

Use the correct standard forms appropriate to the form of contract (e.g. NSC/T or NAM/T etc) and check that all relevant information is entered before sending.

Check the information to be issued with the tender form, in particular the numbered documents (e.g. drawings, schedules, Bills or Specification) relevant to the sub-contract works. They should adequately define the work to be tendered for. A covering letter may or may not be considered necessary.

If the sub-contract work is such that no particular form or set of procedures is required under the terms of the main contract, then send tender information under a suitable enclosing letter. See specimen letter, Fig. H2.

Fig. H2   Specimen letter of invitation to tender for domestic sub-contract works

In the majority of cases, domestic sub-contract works will be entirely a matter between the main contractor and his selected sub-contractors. The CIB publishes a Code of Practice for the Selection of Sub-contractors for use in this situation. However, if the building contract makes provision for the architect to select sub-contractors, who will nevertheless be domestic and the contract does not require any practitioner form to be used, this letter may be adapted to suit the circumstances.

There may also be situations where the architect wishes to include the name of domestic sub-contractors in main contract tender documents. If the building contract does not preclude this, the specimen letter of invitation might be appropriate.

We note that you wish to tender for the above works. We enclose:

- (three) copies of our Form of Tender
- one copy each of the 'numbered documents' (list them)
- an addressed envelope for the return of the Tender.

Please note that:

1. Drawings and details relating to the main contract may be inspected by arrangement with this office.
2. The site may be inspected by arrangement with (name) at (address).
3. Tendering procedures will follow the spirit of the CIB Code of Practice for the Selection of Sub-contractors.
4. The Form of Tender should be completed fully and properly.
5. You may be required to enter into a design warranty agreement direct with the employer.
6. You should send three completed Forms of Tender in the enclosed envelope to reach this office not later than 12 noon on (date). Priced documents will be required later, if you are selected to execute the sub-contract works, and upon acceptance by the main contractor.
7. Specialist drawings should be submitted to us for general inspection but any failure on our part to detect inconsistencies or errors will not relieve you of responsibility.

Please confirm that you have received this letter and enclosures and that you are able to tender in accordance with these instructions.

Deal with tenders

Tenders should be opened as soon as possible after the date for receipt. Check that everything specified has been included. Note any omissions or added conditions and pass to relevant consultants for comment, and to the QS for cost checking.

Approve the selected tender (NB: only the main contractor can accept the offer) on behalf of the employer after discussion.

Notify unsuccessful tenderers at once but do not give tender figures until a decision to proceed with the successful tenderer has been reached. See specimen letters, Figs. H3, H4.

Where there is a direct sub-contractor/client agreement, and only if considered desirable in the particular circumstances, issue instructions concerning advance ordering of design works, materials, or fabrication. Do not do this before obtaining the client's agreement in writing. See specimen letters, Figs. H5, H6.

After the appointment of the main contractor, follow meticulously the procedures set out in the main contract for instructing the acceptance of the sub-contract tender. Before issuing the instruction, check that the offer is still open for acceptance, and that the particulars on which the tender was based have not changed.

Fig. H3   Specimen letter to unsuccessful tenderers for specialist sub-contract works or supply items

This interim notification is not usually sent until after the successful tenderer has been selected.

We wish to inform you that the tenders were opened on (date) and your price was not the lowest received. We will send you a list of tenderers and prices in due course.

Thank you for tendering. Although your tender was not successful, this will not prejudice your opportunities for future work.

Fig. H4   Specimen letter notifying tendered prices for specialist sub-contract works or supply items

---

Further to our letter of (date) we wish to inform you that (name) have been appointed as specialist sub-contractors (or suppliers) for this work. The tenderers and tendered prices are listed below. There is, of course, no correlation.

Fig. H5   Specimen advance order to named sub-contractor

For use with IFC 98.

On behalf of the employer we have approved your tender of (date) under form NAM/T and will issue an instruction to the contractor to accept this.

In accordance with paragraphs 7.2 and 7.7 of Agreement ESA/1 between you and the employer, we are authorised to issue the following instructions:

(For example)
• Please purchase the following materials:
....
• Please fabricate the following components:
....

and confirm in writing that you have put these matters in hand.

Your rights concerning payment, and the right of the employer to the benefit of your work if the sub-contract is not entered into, are covered in paragraph 7.2 if Agreement ESA/1.

Fig. H6   Specimen advance order to nominated sub-contractor

For use with JCT 98.

On behalf of the employer we have approved your tender of (date) under form NSC/T.

Until the main contractor is appointed we are unable to issue a nomination instruction on form NSC/N. However, under Clause 2.2.1 of NSC/W, which became operative when we approved your tender, we are authorised to issue the following instructions:

(For example)
- Please design/prepare installation drawings in accordance with the programme set out in your tender
- Please order/fabricate the following items

....

and confirm in writing that you have put these matters in hand.

Your rights concerning payment, and the right of the employer to the benefit of your work should nomination not proceed, are covered in Clause 2.2 of Agreement NSC/W.

Fig. H7   Specimen letter of preliminary invitation to tender for main contract works

The purpose of this letter is to establish a list of potential main contractors. The Description of Project attached to it should relate to the form of contract it is intended to use.

We are preparing a list of tenderers for constructing the works (description attached) under the JCT standard form of building contract (e.g. JCT 98 or IFC 98 or MW 98). We draw your attention to the option clauses which will apply. Any amendments will be set out in the tender documents.

If you wish to be invited to tender on this basis you must agree to submit a bona fide tender in accordance with the CIB Code of Practice for the Selection of a Main Contractor, and you must not divulge your tender price to any person or body before the time for submitting tenders. When the contract has been signed, we will send all those who tendered a list of the tenderers and prices.

Please reply to this letter by (date). Your inclusion in our preliminary list does not guarantee that you will receive a formal invitation to tender, nor will your opportunities for tendering for future work be prejudiced if you do not wish to tender this time.

(For JCT 98)

a   Job
b   Employer
c   Architect
d   Quantity Surveyor
e   Consultants
f   Location of site (enclose site plan)
g   General description of the work
h   Approximate cost range £ .... to ....
i   Nominated sub-contractors for major items
j   Form of contract (which edition, amendments, supplements)
k   Fluctuations (if applicable):
    Clause 38, 39, 40
    Percentage addition to clause 39.8 (if applicable)
l   The contract is to be executed as a deed/simple contract
m   Anticipated date for possession is ....
n   Period for completing the works is ....
o   Approximate date for dispatch of tender documents is ....
p   Tender period is .... weeks
q   Tender to remain open for .... weeks
r   Liquidated damages:
    Anticipated value £ .... per ....
s   Details of bond/guarantee requirements
t   Particular conditions applying to this contract

H/CM4

Selective tendering: Main contract — Traditional procurement

Decide whether single- or two-stage tendering is required

The single stage operates on the assumption that full information is available to tenderers at the time of tendering. The tender figure is then the price for which the contractor offers to carry out and complete the works shown on the drawings and described in the contract bills/specification/schedules.

Two-stage procedures allow the selection of the contractor by means of a first stage competitive tender based on 'pricing documents' relating to preliminary design information. There will then follow negotiations when the design is completed, and Bills of Quantities are priced on the basis of pricing provided in the first stage tender. This procedure is only suitable for large complex projects where there could be advantage in collaborating with the contractor during design stages.

Make preliminary enquiries

Send a preliminary invitation to tender, to selected potential contractors (see Fig. H7). This will enable contractors to decide whether they will tender, and allow them to programme tendering staff effort. The letter of invitation should have attached to it a description of the project, relating to the form of contract it is intended to use, together with all information that might be necessary for a contractor to assess whether it is competent and interested in undertaking the project (see H/CM1). It is essential that full details are sent in this preliminary enquiry.

Invite tenders

Send formal letters to tenderers informing them of the date for issuing tender documents and the closing date for submission of tenders. Documents may be dispatched by first class post or made available for collection if the number of documents is considerable.

A standard form of tender should be issued, and all tenderers clearly told that tenders will be submitted on exactly the same basis. Adequate time for tendering will be determined in relation to the size and complexity of the job. See specimen letters and specimen forms of tender, Figs. H8, H9.

Any particular requirements of the client concerning, for example, guarantee bonds or a certificate of non-collusion should be clearly stated in the formal invitation. See specimen certificate, Fig. H10.

Fig. H8   Specimen letter of invitation to tender for main contract works using Bills of Quantities

Suitable for use with JCT 98 and IFC 98 under the *CIB Code of Practice for the Selection of a Main Contractor.*

We note that you wish to tender for these works.

We enclose:
- two copies of the Bill(s) of Quantities
- two copies of the location drawings, component drawings, dimension drawings and information schedules
- an addressed envelope in which to return the tender
- copies of relevant advance orders.

The completed form of tender, sealed in the envelope provided, should reach this office not later than 12 noon on (date).

Please note that:
1. Drawings and details may be inspected at (address).
2. The site may be inspected by arrangement with (name) at this office.
3. Tendering procedures will be in accordance with the CIB Code of Practice for the Selection of a Main Contractor.
4. Any queries should be raised with (name) at this office.
5. The building owner reserves the right to accept any tender from those submitted or to refuse all.

Please confirm that you have received this letter and enclosures and that you are prepared to tender in accordance with these instructions.

Fig. H8 *continued*

Suitable for use with JCT 98, IFC 98, either separately or attached to a letter of invitation.

We have read the conditions of contract and Bills of Quantities delivered to us and have examined the drawings referred to in them.

We offer to execute and complete in accordance with the conditions of contract the whole of the works described for the sum of £........... (and in words) within (number of) weeks from the date of site possession.

This tender remains open for consideration for (number of) days from the date fixed for submitting tenders.

We agree to provide a bond as required by the employer and name the following:

1 ....
2 ....

(assurance/guarantee societies/banks) as sureties, who are willing to be bound jointly and severally by us to the employer in the sum of £........... for the performance of this contract. The amount included in the tender sum to cover the provision of a bond is £...........

Fig. H9 Specimen letter of invitation to tender for main contract works using drawings and specifications/ schedules

Suitable for use with JCT 98, IFC 98 and MW 98 under the CIB Codes of Procedure for Selective Tendering.

We note that you wish to tender for these works.

We enclose
- two copies of the specifications/schedules and drawings and schedules
- two copies of the form of tender
- an addresses envelope in which to return the tender

The completed form of tender, sealed in the envelope provided, should reach this office not later than 12 noon on (date).

Please note that:
1. Drawings and details may be inspected at (address).
2. The site may be inspected by arrangement with (name) at this office.
3. Tendering procedures will be in accordance with the CIB Code of Practice for the Selection of a Main Contractor.
4. Any queries should be raised with (name) at this office.
5. The building owner reserves the right to accept any tender from those submitted or to refuse them all.

Please confirm that you have received this letter and enclosures and that you are prepared to tender in accordance with these instructions.

Fig. H9 *continued*

Suitable for use with JCT 98, IFC 98, MW 98, either separately or attached to letter of invitation.

We have read the conditions of contract and have examined the drawings, specifications and schedules which you have sent us.

We offer to execute and complete in accordance with the conditions of contract the whole of the works described for the sum of £........... (and in words) within (number of) weeks from the date of site possession.

We enclose our schedule of rates (or contract sum analysis) giving a breakdown of our tender figure. This tender remains open for consideration for (number of) days from the date fixed for submitting tenders.

We agree to provide a bond as required by the employer and name the following:

1   ....
2   ....

(assurance/guarantee socleties/banks) as sureties, who are willing to be bound jointly and severally by us to the employer in the sum of £........... for the performance of this contract. The amount included in the tender sum to cover the provision of a bond is £...........

Fig. H10   Specimen certificate of non-collusion

For use as an appendix to any form of tender. The employer may have his own document for this purpose.

Recognising the principle that the essence of selective tendering is that the employer receives bona fide competitive tenders from all firms tendering, we certify that we will submit such tender and that we will not fix or adjust the amount of the tender by or under or in accordance with any agreement or arrangement with any other person. We also certify that we have not done and we will not do at any time before the date for this tender to be submitted, any of the following acts:

1.   Communicate to any person other than the person calling for our tender the amount or approximate amount of the proposed tender.
2.   Enter into any agreement with or arrange for any other person to refrain from tendering, or indicate the amount of any tender to be submitted.
3.   Reward, or promise to reward, any person for performing or causing any of the actions or effects described in 1 and 2 above.

In this certificate, the word 'person' includes any persons, bodies or associations, corporate or incorporate; and 'any agreement or arrangement' includes any such transaction, formal or informal, and whether legally binding or not.

Deal with tenders

Tenders should be opened as soon as possible after the date for receipt, and strictly in accordance with the procedures agreed with the client. Qualified tenders should be rejected if it is considered that the qualification affords an unfair advantage, or the tenderer should be given an opportunity to withdraw the qualification.

The priced Bills of Quantities should be submitted at the same time as the tenders but in separate sealed envelopes clearly marked with the tenderers' names. Bills from unsuccessful tenderers should be returned unopened.

Tenders under consideration should be referred to the planning supervisor to check adequacy of allocated resources in respect of health and safety requirements.

Examination of the priced bills of the lowest tenderer should be undertaken immediately by the QS who should report on arithmetical errors.

Unsuccessful tenderers should be informed as quickly as possible, and once the contract has been let, every tenderer should be sent a list of firms who tendered (in alphabetical order) and a list of tender prices (in ascending order). It should not be possible to cross-reference the lists. See specimen letters, Figs. H11–13.

Fig. H11   Specimen letter to contractor submitting most acceptable tender

Where applicable the construction phase Health and Safety Plan of this tenderer should accompany priced documents and will be examined at the same time by the planning supervisor.

> We are pleased to inform you that your tender for these works was the most acceptable. The priced documents are now being examined by the quantity surveyor. Please send us priced documents as soon as possible.
>
> We will write to you again when the examination has been completed.

Fig. H12   Specimen letter to contractor submitting second most acceptable tender

> The tenders were opened on (date). Yours was the second most acceptable.
>
> If the tender at present more acceptable than yours is found not to be satisfactory, you may be asked to stand by your tender and to submit Bills of Quantities.
>
> We will write to you again as soon as a decision has been reached, and in due course we will send you the full list of tenderers and tendered prices.

Fig. H13   Specimen letter to other unsuccessful tenderers

> We regret to have to inform you that your tender was not successful. In due course we will send you a full list of tenderers and tendered prices.
>
> Thank you for tendering. Although you have been unsuccessful this time, this will not prejudice your opportunities of tendering for our work in the future.

H/CM5

Selective tendering: Main contract — Design and build procurement

Make preliminary enquiries

Send a preliminary invitation to tender, to selected potential contractors. This will enable contractors to decide whether they will tender, and allow them to programme tendering staff effort. The letter of invitation should have attached to it a description of the project, relating to the form of contract it is intended to use, together with all information that might be necessary for the contractor to assess whether it is competent and interested in undertaking the project (see H/CM1). It is essential that full details are sent in this preliminary enquiry.

In particular, for design and build, the letter of invitation should clearly state whether this is a single-stage or two-stage process, and the extent to which the contractor will be expected to design the works and carry professional indemnity insurance.

The letter should have attached to it information relating to planning requirements, e.g. whether the project is within a conservation area, likely to be affected by the Defective Premises Act 1972, etc.

Tenderers will also need to know the basis for awarding the contract, e.g. on price alone, and if not, the extent to which other considerations will be taken into account, such as design quality, maintenance or running costs.

Arrange interviews

It is particularly important to arrange for interviews in the context of design and build. Matters to be raised might include:
- construction forms and methods favoured;
- time considered appropriate for tendering and mobilisation;
- design liability and insurance arrangements;
- professional and technical support available to the contractor;
- design and construction programme envisaged by the contractor.

The interviewing panel should include the client, the planning supervisor, and appropriate professional advisers.

Invite tenders

Send formal letters to selected tenderers either enclosing the tender documents in duplicate or informing them of the date for collection. The extent of these documents will depend on whether the tendering is single or two-stage, but should include everything which is intended to form part of the final agreement (see C/CM1 for checklist of what may be included in Employer's Requirements).

A standard form of tender should be issued. Adequate time for tendering will depend on the size and complexity of the project, and whether this is a single- or two-stage submission.

Deal with tenders

Tenders should be opened as soon as possible after the date for receipt and strictly in accordance with the procedures agreed with the client.

With a single-stage procedure where price is stated to be the sole criterion, supporting design proposals and pricing documents should be submitted at the same time but under separate cover.

With a two-stage procedure the tender will also include an undertaking to enter into second stage negotiations on the basis of the first stage tender sum.

The examination of the Contractor's Proposals and pricing documents will be undertaken by the employer, the planning supervisor and other professional advisers, to establish that the proposals are consistent with the Employer's Requirements.

Unsuccessful tenderers should be informed as quickly as possible, and all documents received should be treated as confidential and returned.

H/CM6

Selective tendering: Main contract — Management procurement

Make preliminary enquiries

Send a preliminary invitation to tender to selected potential contractors. This will enable contractors to decide whether they will tender, and allow them to programme tendering staff effort. The letter of invitation should have attached to it a description of the project, the form of contract it is intended to use, the anticipated duration of the project pre-construction and construction, together with all information that might be necessary for the contractor to assess whether it is competent and interested in undertaking the project (see H/CM1). It is essential that full details are sent in this preliminary enquiry.

With management contracting the emphasis will be on ascertaining the nature and extent of the contractor's managements skills and experience.

Arrange preliminary interviews

Because of the large or complex management nature of projects usually procured by this method, it might be necessary also to hold preliminary interviews at this stage. This will enable the employer to gain a better understanding of the philosophy and management structure offered by some of the potential firms, to an extent not obtainable solely through written enquiries.

Invite tenders

Send formal letters to selected tenderers. Tender documents should contain:
- clear conditions for the submission, so that all tenderers provide the same amount of information;
- proposed timescales pre-construction and construction;
- a clear indication of the assessment and interview procedures which will form part of the overall assessment.

Criteria to be satisfied will normally include:
- management service offered;
- key personnel for the project;
- financial: both in respect of fees and ability to manage costs;
- conditions of engagement;
- programmes;
- method statements.

Deal with tenders

Tenders should be opened as soon as possible after the date for receipt, and strictly in accordance with the procedure agreed with the client.

A detailed evaluation of each submission should be prepared. When the written submissions have undergone preliminary evaluation they can be assessed by the employer. It will then be necessary to interview each tenderer. This will enable them to explain their proposals in detail, clarify any points in the submission which need comment, and allow the employer to meet the key personnel which the tenderer proposes using. Further interviews may be necessary before a decision is reached.

Unsuccessful tenderers should be informed as soon as possible.

J: MOBILISATION

Letting the building contract, appointing the contractor.
Issuing of Production Information to the contractor.
Arranging site hand-over to the contractor (RIBA Outline Plan of Work).

Description

Key obligations from SFA/99

Actions

Stage input
Preliminary issues   architect
                                 client
                                 management and team working
Approvals/consents
Contract
Cost planning
General procedures
Stage output

Core material

J/CM1	Dealing with contract documents
J/CM2	Site inspectorate appointment and briefing
J/CM3	Pre-contract meeting
J/CM4	Insurances check

MOBILISATION

Description

In the strict sense of the term, Mobilisation is likely to be mainly the responsibility of the appointed contractor. However, an architect acting as the lead consultant can do much at this stage to see that the contract is properly set up from the outset.

Contract documents have to be prepared and the agreement should be signed before work on site commences. There will need to be an exchange of information between architect and contractor, and confirmed agreement on procedures to be followed.

The client will enter into the building contract as the employer, and the site given into the possession of the contractor so that work may proceed as programmed. The employer, contractor and relevant consultants will need to be advised on their respective responsibilities under the contract.

The contractor must have reasonable time to mobilise resources. Site inspectorate will need to be appointed and briefed. Arrangements should be made for the formal initial project team meeting, sometimes also referred to as the pre-start or pre-contract meeting.

Key obligations which may apply:

	Reference	To do

- from SFA/99: design services

Provide production information as required for building contract and for construction. SFA/99/J/1 ☐

In addition to the above, the architect should note the obligations set out in the SFA/99 Conditions of Engagement 2.1-2.8.

- from SFA/99: management services

(i.e. architect acting as design leader and lead consultant)
Considering with the client the appointment of a contractor and the responsibilities of the parties and the contract administrator. ☐
Preparing the building contract and arranging for signatures. ☐

Actions

Stage input

Check that all information necessary during Stage J is available, which might include the following: ☐

- Form of contract, with all necessary entries and Supplements, ready for completion by the parties.

- Contract documents, including drawings and Bills of Quantities/ Specification/Schedules of Work, incorporating any necessary adjustments, ready for issue.

- Completed tender documents from the succesful tenderer.

- Written records of any post tender reduction exercise.

- Published reliable commentaries or guides to assist with contract administration. Copies of relevant JCT Practice Notes and CIB Guidance Notes.

- Administration forms published for use in contract administration, suitable for the particular contract to be used.

- Contractor's preliminary programme and required method statements.

Preliminary issues – architect

Establish scope, content and context for Stage J activities. ☐
Put it into context, particularly if previous Stages were undertaken by others. If possible establish whether material produced now is likely to be acted upon by others taking over subsequent Stages.

If coming new to the project at this Stage in the *Plan of Work:* ☐

- Ascertain that Pre-Agreement and earlier Stage checks have been carried out.

- Allow for familiarisation and reviewing of all usable material when agreeing fees and timetable with the client.

- Confirm the role of the architect in relation to the rest of the consultant team.

Check the client's instruction to proceed has been given and con- ☐
firmed in writing.

Check the client has settled all accounts submitted to date. ☐

Check appointing documents with respect to services and fees: ☐

- If the Services, cost or time targets are different from the Agreement with the client, agree a formal variation by letter or deed as appropriate.

- If the extent of professional services for Stage J is not yet settled, agree with the client and confirm in writing.

- If the methods and levels of charging for Stage J are not yet settled, agree with the client and confirm in writing.

Assess office resources needed for Stage J and ensure that they are adequate and available. ☐

Carry out checks for compliance with in-house quality management procedures, including updated project quality plan. ☐

Review application of practice procedures to project. ☐

Preliminary issues – client

Check whether the client has confirmed the appointment of a clerk of works. ☐

Remind the client that any insurances for which the client has **J/CM4** accepted responsibility should have been taken out. Policies should be kept available for inspection by the contractor at all reasonable times. ☐

Discuss with the client the main contractor's master programme. Draw to the client's attention significant dates by which any further decisions or information will be needed, and by which any persons directly employed are programmed to start and finish. ☐

Confirm to the client the responsibilities and obligations under the contract as employer. Confirm the architect's role and duties as agent and contract administrator. ☐

Remind the client of the obligation to honour certificates of payment in full and within the period stated in the contract. ☐

Explain the notices provisions in detail. If any deduction is intended from amounts certified it will be essential to issue notices as required by the contract.

Remind the client that empowered instructions to the contractor can only be issued by way of an architect's instruction. ☐

Design and build Check whether the client has confirmed the appointment of an Employer's Agent. The authority of this person should be clearly stated in writing, and the contractor should be informed. *(Employer Client)* ☐

Preliminary issues – management and team working

Check the scope of professional services agreed with the client for continued presence of consultant team members as members of the project team. ☐

Agree the scope and timetable for any amendments needed to contract documents as a result of post tender negotiations. ☐

Agree with the QS a timetable for the preparation of a Bill of Reductions or similar document setting out agreed adjustments to the tender figure, if relevant. ☐

Brief site inspectorate. **J/CM2** ☐

Site inspectorate who are under the direction of the architect should be thoroughly briefed. Give the clerk of works clear instructions on procedures and reporting.

Confirm dates for construction phase with the client and planning supervisor. ☐

Approvals/consents

Check that any necessary approvals and consents have been obtained and are on file. If any are still outstanding, explain to the client the consequences of starting on site prematurely. ☐

Check that all notices granting planning permission and approval under Building Regulations are to hand. Check that statutory approvals are still valid within time limits. ☐

Check the Health and Safety Executive has been given particulars required by law under the CDM Regulations. ☐

Check with the client that all necessary Party Wall Awards are in place. ☐

Contract

Review post tender situation. In the event of an omission or a substitution necessitating revisions to detail design, take appropriate action if authorised by the client. Alert the client to any additional costs, fees, or alterations to programme. ☐

Post tender cost reduction exercises usually mean additional work. Allow time for this.

Amend Production Information as necessary. Establish whether changes are to be reflected in the contract documents (which will then differ from tender documents) or whether amendments are to be the subject of immediate variations under an architect's instruction issued when the contract has been entered into. ☐

Check the effects of any amendments on specialist sub-contract work and arrange for adjusted tenders if necessary. ☐

Record all amendments. Identify changes clearly on revised documents. Retain and file all original issues. ☐

Confirm dates for commencement and completion. Clarify any queries from the contractor. Establish and inspect contractor's programmes, confirm information schedules. ☐

Call for all the contractor's insurance policies. Pass on to the **J/CM4** employer for checking by his brokers or insurance advisers. ☐

Check original documents carefully for cover and renewal dates. Do not accept assurances.

Check bonds and warranties required from contractor. ☐

These should be obtained before the contract is signed — it may be impossible to obtain them later.

Check that the client's planning supervisor has expressed satisfaction with the contractor's construction phase Health and Safety Plan, and that this is confirmed in writing. ☐

Prepare contract documents for signature. Send by registered/ **G/CM1,** recorded post or deliver by hand. It is customary to send these first **J/CM1** to the contractor and then to the employer. ☐

When preparing contract documents for signature or completion as a deed, check meticulously that entries are correct, and relate to tender documents. If more than one copy, check that they are identical.

Collate approved specialist tender documents for issue to the contractor. ☐

Check that parties have properly signed contract documents and any agreed alterations initialled. ☐

Check that all unsuccessful tenderers have been properly notified. ☐

Check that additional copies of drawings and other documents are handed to the main contractor as required by the contract. Issue identical set to the clerk of works. If an Information Release Schedule does not form part of the contract, agree with contractor a schedule for further necessary information. ☐

Carefully inspect the contractor's preliminary programme, particularly if it indicates dates by which critical information is required. Comment as appropriate but do not approve it. ☐

Check that the contractor has prepared a Health and Safety Plan which is acceptable to the planning supervisor. ☐

Under no circumstances can work start on site without a Health and Safety Plan in place which conforms with the CDM Regulations.

Check quality management proposals and procedures with the contractor. ☐

Check proposed site planning and accommodation with the contractor. ☐

Check arrangements for hoardings, site security, etc with the contractor. ☐

Hold an initial project team meeting with the employer, main contractor, **J/CM3** consultants, QS and clerk of works. Chair the initial project meeting, if appropriate, and issue minutes. ☐

When chairing the initial project team meeting, be fair, firm and pleasant. This is an opportunity to make relevant introductions and establish clear procedures.

Arrange for the handover of site and/or existing buildings, allowing the contractor exclusive possession or to the extent previously agreed. ☐

Cost planning

Check with the quantity surveyor, if appointed, the contractor's Schedule of Rates and the Contract Sum Analysis where relevant. ☐

General procedures

Regularly check progress against the timetable for services. ☐

Continue resource control procedures for job: ☐

- Check expenditure against the office job cost allocation for Stage J;

- Monitor fee income against projected fee income.

Report regularly to the client on fees and expenses incurred, and submit accounts at agreed intervals. ☐

Check that the client settles all accounts promptly. ☐

Set up procedures for ensuring drawings and other information are prepared and provided to contractor as required, or as set out in the contract. ☐

Set up accounts procedures for invoicing the appointed main contractor monthly for the cost of copies of drawings and documents additional to those stated in the contract, whether these involve prints or software. ☐

Compile a directory of all involved at construction stages. ☐

Check stationery stocks for correct and current contract administration forms. ☐

Stage output

Check that all the agreed outputs have been produced before the conclusion of Stage J, which might include the following: ☐

- Bill of Reductions or similar document setting out agreed adjustments to the tender figure, if relevant, to arrive at an acceptable contract figure.

- Contract documents duly signed and initialled as appropriate by employer and contractor as parties to the contract.

- Requisite sets of drawings, schedules and other documents for issue to the main contractor.

- Approved tenders and numbered documents in respect of specialist sub-contractors for issue to main contractor.

- Health and Safety notice as required under CDM Regulations, to be deposited before work commences.

- Construction phase Health and Safety Plan by main contractor under the CDM Regulations.

- Requisite forms and documents for issue to the clerk of works.

References and further reading

CIB (1997) *Code of Practice for the Selection of Main Contractors*, London, Thomas Telford Publishing.

Cox, S. (ed.) (2000) *Architect's Guide to the Contract Administration Forms JCT98*, London, RIBA Publications.

Cox, S. (ed.) (2000) *Architect's Guide to the Contract Administration Forms IFC98*, London, RIBA Publications.

Cox, S. (ed.) (2000) *Architect's Guide to the Contract Administration Forms MW98*, London, RIBA Publications.

JCT (2001) Practice Note 6 (series 2): *Main Contract Tendering*, London, RIBA Publications.

J/CM1

Dealing with contract documents

Notifying all tenderers

A letter should be sent to the selected tenderer confirming the decision to accept the tender. This letter might state that a contract will not exist until the documents have been prepared and signed by the parties. If this is so, it is important to make sure that the signing of the contract takes place before the date agreed for possession to avoid possible allegations of frustration.

As a general rule the formalities of the contract agreement should always be completed before work starts on site. However, where for some good reason there is insufficient time for the documents to be prepared before work has to commence, a letter from the client accepting the selected tender may be sent. Once in the post, such a letter establishes a contractual relationship; it should therefore be sent by recorded delivery. The letter should inform the contractor that the employer is entering into the contract on the terms described in the tender documents, recording clearly any matters agreed post tender, and that formal documents will follow by a specific date. The documents should then be produced as quickly as possible. For a specimen letter, see Fig. J1.

Once the tender has been accepted, a list of compliant tender prices and tenderers should be sent to all tenderers within a reasonable period of time as recommended in the CIB *Code of Practice for the Selection of Main Contractors* and the *NJCC Codes of Procedure for Selective Tendering*. For a specimen letter, see Fig. J2.

If minor matters remain to be negotiated, a 'letter of intent' may need to be used. The letter below could be adapted, but not without taking legal advice. 'Letters of intent' are ambiguous in their effect, and place the employer at some risk.

Under no circumstances should construction work be started before the contractor has prepared a Health and Safety Plan which complies with the CDM Regulations.

Fig. J1 Specimen letter to contractor notifying early start to the main contract works

We are pleased to appoint you as contractor on the basis of your tender dated .... in the sum of £..........., and your submitted Health and Safety Plan.

The contract documents will be sent to you for signing not later than .... Meanwhile, will you please mobilise for site operation to commence on ...., when you will be given possession.

An initial project meeting will be held at .... on .... which will be attended by ourselves, the Architect, planning supervisor, consultants and clerk of works. Please arrange to be represented by your key personnel.

You should immediately ensure that all insurances which are your responsibility under the building contract are effective, and original policy documents should be sent to us to inspect. Please inform all specialist sub-contractors and suppliers of the start date, and check that their insurance obligations have been discharged.

Please confirm in writing that you have put these matters in hand and send us the names of your personnel who will attend the initial project meeting.

Fig. J2   Specimen letter notifying unsuccessful contractors

We refer to our letter dated .... in which we confirmed that your tender was not successful. We promised to send you the full list of tenderers and tender prices, and we now list these below. There is, of course, no correlation.

Tenderers
(in alphabetical order)

....
....
....

Prices
(in descending order)

£ ....
....
....

Completing the contract documents

Both parties should enter into a contract on the basis of a complete set of documents, each of which has been completed as necessary (see G/CM1 for a list of contract documents).

The Agreement between the employer and the contractor should be dated and should reflect the correct titles and addresses of the parties. Normally the addresses will be those to which notices, instructions, certificates, etc are to be sent. If either party wishes to have all contractual communications sent to a different address, this should be recorded in the contract documents.

The Recitals set out the facts on which the Agreement is based, and may start with the customary word 'Whereas'. The description of the intended works may be brief, but it should be clear and adequate. For example, 'constructing a factory and ancillary external works' or 'carrying out alterations to a bank' are clear enough for purposes of identification. The location of the site should also be conveyed precisely in a few words.

Often the name and address of the architect is to be entered in the Recitals and in an Article. This should be the name of the practice rather than an individual. The inclusion of the name in two places takes care of the possibility that the architect appointed under the building contract may not be the same person who was appointed to prepare the design.

The drawings which show the works need to be clearly identified. To avoid any risk of discrepancy, they should be those used for preparing the contract Bills, Specification or Schedules of Work as appropriate. If the number of drawings is greater than can be described within the space available on the contract form, the words 'as in the attached list' may be inserted and a list headed 'Contract Drawings' be fixed securely to the page containing the relevant Recital. Drawings should be identified beyond all doubt by giving the correct number and issue affix (e.g. 261/32e). It might be worth using a rubber stamp to endorse each copy of contract drawings, bills, and any other written material which is to be incorporated as part of the contract. For example, 'This is one of the contract documents referred to in the contract between (employer) and (contractor) and signed hereunder (by both parties)'.

Where alternative contract provisions are to be deleted (an action not now required in the majority of current JCT forms of contract) this should be done clearly in the text of the document and should be initialled by the parties.

Whether or not options clauses are to apply should be clearly indicated in the Appendix.

Alterations to the text are possible, if that is what the parties want. They should be clearly indicated in the text of the document and initialled by the parties. They should have been indicated at the time of tendering.

Conditions should not be amended without considerable care and thought, and never without taking legal advice. The conditions in standard forms of contract are often complex and interrelated. Even apparently innocuous alterations to a clause can affect or call into question other parts of the contract.

Most JCT forms of contract provide that the printed conditions of the contract take precedence over any typed or written words in other documents. Therefore any additional articles, conditions or amendments must not be left to the specification or to the preliminaries section of a Bill of Quantities, but must be properly incorporated in the actual articles or conditions.

Most JCT forms of contract have an Appendix. In the interests of accuracy, entries should be copied direct from the tender documents. Full information concerning matters to be included in the Appendix should be given at the time of tendering.

Signing the contract

The form of building contract containing the Articles of Agreement is normally sent first to the contractor, accompanied by the drawings listed in the Recitals and the other contract documents as appropriate. Pencil in a cross to indicate where the contractor is to sign (usually in the lower set of spaces). Documents returned by the contractor should be examined carefully to see that they have been completed properly, as requested in the covering letter. For a specimen letter, see Fig. J3.

Fig. J3 Specimen covering letter to contractor with contract documents for signature

These documents should be sent as soon as possible after notifying the contractor that his tender has been accepted.

Deliver by hand or send by Recorded Delivery.

Further to our letter of (date), we confirm that the employer wishes to enter into a contract with you and we enclose a set of contract documents. This comprises:

- Articles of Agreement and Conditions of Contract for completing as a simple contract (or as a deed)
- Contract drawings (nos.) and other contract documents (list)
  Bills of Quantities in (number of) volumes
  Specification (or schedules) as appropriate.

Please complete the documents as follows:
- Sign where indicated and witness as necessary
- Initial all the alterations (indicated) in the Conditions to clauses (nos.)
- Sign every contract drawing and other contract drawing in the marked space
- Sign the specification (or schedules or Bills of Quantities) in the marked space.

Please return these documents to us as soon as possible, so that we can send them on to the employer for execution. We will provide you with a certified copy in due course.

The documents should then be passed to the employer with a covering letter asking the employer to date the Articles. Documents returned from the employer should be examined carefully to see that they have been completed properly. For a specimen letter, see Fig. J4.

Fig. J4   Specimen covering letter to employer with contract documents for signature

Deliver by hand or send by Recorded Delivery

The contractor has completed and returned to us the enclosed contract documents, which you should now sign. They comprise:

(List them, and repeat instructions for completion given in Fig. J3.)

Please return the documents to us after signature. We will date them and then send a certified copy to the contractor and return the original set to you.

There are a few points of principle which we would like to bring to your attention at this stage.

1.   Architect's responsibilities

As architects administering the contract we try to deal fairly in respect of the rights and duties of both parties, and we are responsible for issuing empowered instructions to the contractor. If you wish the contractor to be instructed about extra work or variations, please inform us so that we can discuss this with you. We will report to you regularly on progress and on the financial position.

2.   Visits to site

The contractor will appreciate your interest in the progress of the works but please ensure that only your authorised personnel visit the site and that this is arranged with the contractor beforehand. To safeguard your interests and to avoid any misunderstandings, the contractor has been specifically told not to accept instructions from anyone except us.

3.   Payments

Payments will be authorised only on presentation of an architect's certificate. The amounts certified must be paid in full and within .... days from the date issued. Prompt payment is essential to enable the contractor to discharge obligations to sub-contractors and suppliers and to complete on time.

If you would like any fuller explanations, please let us know.

Signing confirmed

Instead of signing separately, the parties may agree to meet at some convenient place and complete the execution of the contract in each other's presence.

If the contract is to be executed as a simple contract, only the signatures of both parties are necessary. The signatures of witnesses – desirable, although not a legal necessity – confirm the existence of the agreement.

If the contract is to be executed as a deed, then appropriate wording should be used for the attestation clause. Special wording may be required depending on the Memorandum or Standing Orders of an authority or corporate body.

The manner of execution of the main contract does not necessarily mean that sub-contracts or collateral agreements have to be similarly executed. However, thought should be given to this matter so as to avoid confusion and unnecessary complications and costs.

It is sometimes stated in the contract conditions who is to have custody of the original contract documents – usually the employer. The documents should be kept in a secure fireproof place. Copies of the contract documents should be suitably endorsed, for example, 'This is a certified copy of the Agreement dated . . . between . . . and . . .' and signed by the architect. A set is given to the contractor and the architect would be wise to keep another complete set safe in the office.

J/CM2

Site inspectorate appointment and briefing

On large works full time resident consultants (e.g. architects, engineers) might be needed to ensure conformity of materials, construction and quality, and also to liaise on the many activities upon which the full standards of the building's performance will depend. If such services are required, this must be clearly stated at tender stage.

On most large contracts a clerk of works is a full time and valuable presence. The clerk of works must appreciate the extent of his or her powers and duties which are generally to observe, inspect, check and report. These will be defined in the particular building contract, which may allow for the clerk of works to be given considerable power by the project manager or employer's agent. Large schemes may justify specialist clerks of works, for example, for structural work or for services installations.

With JCT contracts the clerk of works operates under the direction of the architect and must be thoroughly conversant with the form of contract.

Clerk of works appointment

There are advantages in appointing a clerk of works before work commences on site. This arrangement may prove more difficult in the private sector but the clerk of works can often comment from experience on construction matters and make a significant contribution to production information. Two weeks spent in the architect's office before going on site will allow a clerk of works to get to know the personnel and procedures associated with the project.

The appointment of a clerk of works for a particular project requires thoughtful preparation. It must be clearly established who is to be directly responsible for his or her appointment and payment, and ultimately for his or her performance. The clerk of works' duties will need to be carefully prescribed. Suitable candidates selected from a shortlist, or chosen on the basis of previous experience or personal recommendation, should be interviewed. A report can then be made to the client, and an appointment confirmed by letter, see Fig. J5.

The Clerk of Works Manual is a useful source of information. It sets out standard terms of appointment, defines duties and responsibilities, lists the documents which the clerk of works should maintain and offers a range of forms which might assist both the clerk of works and the architect.

Fig. J5   Specimen letter to newly appointed clerk of works

We are pleased to tell you that our client, (name), has confirmed your appointment on the terms agreed. These are itemised on the attached sheet/in the enclosed formal agreement.

Your duties will commence on (date), and you should report to the project architect, (name), with whom you will liaise throughout the project. He will supply you with project report forms, a daily diary, and a pad of Directions.
Will you please be sure to attend the initial project meeting on .... An agenda is attached.
You will see that Clerk of Works' matters are included as item 4.

So that you can familiarise yourself with the project, we enclose a set of drawings, bills and specifications as issued to the contractor, and a copy of the construction phase Health and Safety Plan.

We hope that you will enjoy working on this project. If you have any queries, please let us know.

Clerk of works briefing

The architect may decide to hold a special meeting to brief the site inspectorate. The architect should describe the project fully, the methods of construction to be used, and the programme of work. More particularly for the clerk of works, the architect should:

- explain routines and procedures to be followed;
- stress the need for work to conform with drawings and instructions, and that materials and workmanship must meet the required standards;
- stress the need to ensure that the latest editions of the relevant British Standards and Codes of Practice are available for reference on site.

As part of the briefing process, the clerk of works might expect to be supplied with the following:

- form of building contract, incorporating any supplements or amendments;
- contract Bills of Quantities (unpriced) and/or specification;
- contract drawings and schedules;
- 'numbered documents' or other information relating to specialist sub-contracts;
- the employer's health and safety policy requirements and the construction phase Health and Safety Plan;
- site diary;
- reports forms;
- quality management plan, contractor's method statement, quality control checklists, verification forms, etc.

The clerk of works should also be briefed about his or her responsibilities and extent of authority in connection with:

- hours of working and notification of additional hours;
- daily labour returns and method of submitting them;
- method of recording time lost in site working;
- signing of authorised daywork vouchers;
- samples of materials;
- testing of samples;
- storage of materials;
- notification of work to be covered up after inspection;
- general procedures for inspection and recording.

Clerk of works reporting

The duties of a clerk of works are to observe, inspect, check and report. A site diary is for recording day-to-day events. There is also a need to provide the architect with periodic reports to record progress on site, usually on a weekly basis. Printed forms will be provided for the clerk of works to complete and sign. The Institute of Clerks of Works publishes a *Project Report Form* which will be suitable for most situations, see Fig. J6

References and further reading

The Clerks of Work Manual (3rd edn.) (1994) London, RIBA Publications.

Fig. J6   Specimen form: Clerk of Works Project Report

Clerk of Works **Project Report**

Report no: _____

Project: _____
Address: _____
_____

Ref. No: _____
Week ending: _____

Institute of
Clerks of Works

Architect/CA: _____
Main Contractor: _____
Clerk of Works: _____
Tel: _____ Fax: _____

Contract start date: _____
Contract completion date: _____
Progress against programme: _____

TRADES (Man days)	Person in charge	Mon	Tue	Wed	Thu	Fri	Sat	Sun
	Scaffolders							
Note	Groundworkers							
Main Contractor's Labour	Drivers and plant operators							
Return may be substituted	Steel fixers and concreters							
	Bricklayers and masons							
	Roofers: Finishes							
	Carpenters and joiners							
	Steel erectors							
	Window fixers							
	Plumbers							
	H & V engineers							
	Electricians							
	Lift engineers							
	Plasterers and screeders							
	Tilers: Wall and floor							
	Ceiling fixers							
	Floor finishers							
	Glaziers							
	Painters							
	Drainlayers							
	Statutory undertakers							
	Road pavers, Tarmac workers							
	Total man days							

WEATHER REPORT	Day	AM	°C	PM	°C	Man hours lost
	Monday					
	Tuesday					
	Wednesday					
	Thursday					
	Friday					
	Saturday					
	Sunday					
	Total man hours lost in week					
	TOTAL TO DATE					

Visitors to site (including statutory inspectors)	Name	Date
	_____	_____
	_____	_____
	_____	_____

GENERAL COMMENTS
_____
_____
_____
_____

Fig. J6 *continued*

Site directions issued	No.	Item			Date	

Delays

Defective work

Drawings/Information received on site

Drawings/Information requested on site

Plant/Materials delivered to site or removed

Health and safety matters

Working conditions on site

PROGRESS TO DATE

T = % Target
C = % Completed

	T	C		T	C		T	C
Preliminaries			Cladding/Curtain wall			Ceiling grid/Tiles		
Excavation			Windows – glazing			Decoration		
Shutter/Reinf			Joinery 1st fix			External works		
Concrete structure			Plastering			Hard/soft landscape		
Steel erection			Drylining/Partitions			Roadworks		
Main drainage m/h			Floor screeds			Mains: Gas		
Floor construction			Plumbing 1st fix			Mains: Electrical		
Floors suspended			Electrical 1st fix			Mains: Water		
Roof structure			H & V 1st fix			Mains: Telecoms		
Roof coverings			Wall/Floor tiles			Lifts		
Drainage fw. sw.			Plumbing 2nd fix			Alarm/Comp systems		
Brickwork external			Electrical 2nd fix			Defects/Handover		
Blockwork internal			H & V 2nd fix					

GENERAL REPORT Summary of work proceeding

Signed   (Clerk of Works)   Date

Complete as appropriate

Enclosures
- ☐ Main Contractor's Labour Return
- ☐ Site Directions
- ☐ Reports

Distribution
- ☐ Architect/CA ☐
- ☐ ☐
- ☐ ☐

Office action

J/CM3

Pre-contract meeting

This meeting, sometimes referred to as the pre-start meeting, is crucial.

The site inspectorate may have already been briefed at separate meetings, or the briefing could form part of the initial project team meeting. At the meeting, all personnel will be introduced and lines of communication can be unequivocally identified and defined. This is the first opportunity for all the project team to meet and for effective working arrangements to be established.

It is essential for the person identified as the contract administrator to know the full range of contractual requirements of the project, and to be alert to potentially difficult areas. As chairman of the meeting, this person must establish mutual confidence and see that different viewpoints are aired and accommodated before the project gets under way.

The business of the meeting is likely to cover a wide range of topics, and it is important to start with a clear agenda and stick to it. For a specimen agenda, see Fig. J7

Fig. J7   Specimen agenda for pre-contract meeting

---

1   **Introductions**
    Appointments, personnel
    Roles and responsibilities
    Project description

2   **Contract**
    Priorities
    Handover of Production Information
    Commencement and completion dates
    Insurances
    Bonds (if applicable)
    Standards and quality

3   **Contractor's matters**
    Possession
    Programme
    Health and Safety File and Plan
    Site organisations, facilities and planning
    Security and protection
    Site restrictions
    Contractor's quality control policy and procedures
    Sub-contractors and suppliers
    Statutory undertakers
    Overhead and underground services
    Temporary services
    Signboards

---

4 Clerk of works' matters
Roles and duties
Facilities
Liaison
Dayworks

5 Consultants' matters
Structural
Mechanical
Electrical
Others

6 Quantity surveyor's matters
Adjustments to tender figures
Valuation procedures
Remeasurement
VAT

7 Communications and procedures
Information requirements
Distribution of information
Valid instructions
Lines of communication
Dealing with queries
Building Control notices
Notices to adjoining owners/occupiers

8 Meetings
Pattern and proceedings
Status of minutes
Distribution of minutes

Agenda items at pre-contract meeting

Introductions

- Introduce the representatives who will regularly attend progress meetings and clarify their roles and responsibilities. The client, contractor and consultants may wish to introduce themselves.
- Briefly describe the project and its priorities and objectives, and any separate contract which may be relevant (preliminary, client's own contractors, etc).
- Indicate any specialists appointed by the client, e.g. for quality control, commissioning, for this contract.

Contract

- Describe the present position with regard to preparation and signature of documents.

- Hand over any outstanding Production Information, including nomination instructions, variation instructions. Review situation for issuing other important information.
- Request that insurance documents be available for inspection immediately; remind the contractor to check specialist sub-contractors' indemnities. Check if further instructions are needed for special cover.
- Confirm the existence, status and use of the Information Release Schedule, if used. Establish procedure for agreeing adjustments to the Schedule should they be necessary.

Contractor's matters

- Check that the contractor's master programme is in the form required and that it satisfactorily accommodates the specialist sub-contractors. It must:
  - contain adequate separate work elements to measure their progress and integration with services installations;
  - allocate specific dates for specialist sub-contract works, including supply of information, site operations, testing and commissioning;
  - accommodate public utilities, etc.
- Agree a procedure for the contractor to inform the architect of information required in addition to any shown on the Information Release Schedule. This is likely to involve a contractor's schedule of information required, which must relate to his works programme and must be kept up to date and regularly reviewed. It should include information, data, drawings, etc to be supplied by the contractor/specialist sub-contractors to the architect/consultants.
- Review in detail the particular provisions in the contract concerning site access, organisation, facilities, restrictions, services, etc to ensure that no queries remain outstanding.
- Quality control is the contractor's responsibility. Remind the contractor of the contractual duties to supervise, of your duties to inspect, and the clerk of works'/site inspectorate's duties in connection with the works. Clarify what standards, quality of work and management are required during the execution of the works.
- Numerous other matters may need special coverage, e.g.:
  - check whether immediate action may be needed by the contractor over specialist sub-contractors and suppliers;
  - emphasise that drawings, data, etc received from contractor or specialist sub-contractors will be inspected by architect/consultants (not approved), and will remain the responsibility of the originator;
  - review outstanding requirements for information to or from the contractor in connection with specialist works;
  - clarify that the contractor is responsible for coordinating performance of specialist works and for their workmanship and materials, for providing specialists with working facilities, and for coordinating site dimensions and tolerances.
- The contractor must also provide for competent testing and commissioning of services as set out in the contract documents, and should be reminded that the time allocated for commissioning is not a contingency period for the main contract works.
- The contractor must obtain the architect's written consent before subletting any work.

Clerk of works' matters

- Clarify that architect's inspections are periodic visits to meet the contractor's supervisory staff, plus spot visits.
- Explain the supportive nature of the clerk of works' role and the need for cooperation to enable him to carry out his duties.
- Remind the contractor that the clerk of works must be provided with adequate facilities and access, together with information about site staff, equipment, and operations for the clerk of works' weekly reports to the architect.
- Confirm procedures for checking quality control, e.g. through:
  - certificates, vouchers, etc as required;
  - sample material to be submitted;
  - samples of workmanship to be submitted prior to work commencing;

- test procedures set out in the Bills of Quantities;
- adequate protection and storage;
- visits to suppliers'/manufacturers' works.

Consultants' matters

- Emphasise that consultants will liaise with specialist sub-contractors only through the contractor. Instructions are to be issued only by the architect. The contractor is responsible for managing and coordinating specialist sub-contractors.
- Establish working arrangements for specialists' drawings and data for evaluation (especially services) to suitable timetables. Aim to agree procedures which will speed up the process; this sector of work frequently causes serious delay or disruption.

Quantity surveyor's matters

- Agree procedures for valuations; these may have to meet particular dates set by the client to ensure that certificates can be honoured.
- Clarify:
  - that dayworks will only be accepted on written instructions;
  - that daywork sheets are required within a stated number of days of work being carried out;
  - tax procedures concerning VAT and 'contractor' status;
  - that the contractor should only order from drawings and specifications, not from the Bills of Quantities.

Communications and procedures

- The supply and flow of information will depend upon programmes being established at the start and will proceed smoothly if:
  - there is regular monitoring of the information schedules;
  - requests for further information are made specifically in writing, not by telephone;
  - the architect responds quickly to queries;
  - technical queries are raised with the clerk of works (if appointed) in the first instance;
  - policy queries are directed to the architect;
  - discrepancies are referred to the architect for resolution, not the clerk of works or contractor.
- On receiving instructions, check for discrepancies with existing documents; check that documents being used are current.
- Information to or from specialist sub-contractors or suppliers must be via the contractor.
- All information issued by the architect is to be via the appropriate forms, certificates, notifications, etc. The contractor should be encouraged to use standard formats and classifications.
- All forms must show the distribution intended; agree numbers of copies of drawings and instructions required by all recipients.
- Clarify that no instructions from the client or consultants can be accepted by the contractor or any sub-contractor; only empowered written instructions by the architect are valid and all oral instructions must be confirmed in writing. Explain the relevant procedures under the contract. The contractor should promptly notify the architect of any written confirmations outstanding.
- Procedures for notices, applications or claims of any kind are to be strictly in accordance with the terms of the contract; all such events should be raised immediately the relevant conditions occur or become evident.

Meetings

- Always issue an agenda beforehand for all architect's meetings and circulate minutes promptly. Agree with the contractor and consultants that:
  - minutes are to be taken as directions for action only where specifically stated and agreed;
  - any dissent is to be notified with 7 days;
  - all persons attending will have authority to act.
- Agree copies and distribution required.
- See also Stage K–L for a summary of the various types of meeting for project administration, and the specimen agenda for the progress meetings, Fig. K–L2. See Stage K–L for advice about site inspections.

J/CM4

Insurances check

Insurance in the context of building construction is a highly specialised area but one of great importance for the contract administrator. Certain insurance obligations arise from legislation but the building contract will usually contain specific requirements concerning insurance cover against injury or damage caused during the works.

These requirements will have been discussed with the client, and the implications fully explained, prior to tender stage. The cost of insurance premiums will have been taken into account by the tenderers. Responsibility for the required cover, whether taken out by the contractor or the employer, will have been established.

Whereas the checking of policy wording is a matter for insurance experts advising either the contractor or the employer as relevant, it is for the contract administrator to check that the obligations to take out cover have been complied with.

An insurances check is necessary before any work on site is commenced. Although most contractors carry an annual policy, endorsements and some cover can take time to arrange. It may be that in some circumstances it proves impossible to obtain the cover stated, in which case it will be for the parties to the contract to decide the arrangements to apply.

Specialist sub-contractors are sometimes mainly responsible for damage which occurs and such an eventuality must be properly covered. The employer pays the cost of insurance in the end and it is important to avoid the risk of double insurance. Cover must be adequate and any figures entered in the building contract should be realistic after taking expert advice on the particular circumstances. The mere repetition of some previously quoted sum is a recipe for disaster.

At mobilisation stage it is vital to ensure that the required insurances are in place before work commences.

For a schedule listing the insurance options included in commonly used JCT contracts (MW 98, IFC 98, JCT 98), see Fig. J8

Fig. J8   Schedule of insurance responsibilies under JCT standard forms

MW 98	IFC 98	JCT 98	Cover	Action
			Insurance against injury to persons and damage to property	
6·1 6·2	6·1·1 6·1·2	21·1·1	Insurance to cover the liability of the contractor or subcontractor against injury to persons and property due to the extent of the contractor's negligence. Cover for any one occurrence or series of occurrences arising out of one event, for not less than the sum stated (either in the relevant clause or the Appendix to the contract).	*Employer* None needed. *Contractor* Arrange immediately for adequate cover. (Figure in contract is only the *minimum* required.) Send documentary evidence to architect for inspection by employer.
			Special insurance against damage to property other than the works	
NA	6·2·4	21·2·1	Insurance in respect of expense, liability, loss, claim or proceedings which the employer may incur by reason of damage to property other than the works and not due to negligence by the contractor or a subcontractor. The Appendix shows that it may be required. Cover in the amount shown in the Appendix for any one occurrence or series of occurrences arising out of any one event.	*Employer* Instruct contractor through architect. Approve insurance. *Contractor* Arrange immediately on receipt of architect's instructions the joint names cover required (usually necessary right from start of site operations). Send documentary evidence to architect for inspection by employer.
			Insurance of the works by contractor against all risks (new buildings)	
NA	6·3A	22A	All risks insurance of the works etc, in joint names, for full reinstatement value (to include professional fees).	*Employer* Approve insurers. *Contractor* Arrange immediately for adequate cover. Supply annual renewal date if applicable. Send documentary evidence to architect for inspection by employer.
			Insurance of the works by contractor against fire etc (new works)	
6·3A	NA	NA	Insurance of the works in joint names against loss and damage by fire etc for full reinstatement value (to include professional fees).	*Employer* None needed. *Contractor* Arrange immediately for adequate cover. Produce documentary evidence as required by employer.

Fig. J8   *continued*

MW 98	IFC 98	JCT 98	Cover	Action
			Insurance of the works by employer against all risks (new buildings)	
NA	6·3B	22B	All risks insurance of the works in joint names, for full reinstatement value (to include professional fees).	*Employer* Arrange immediately for adequate cover. (Note that cost of reinstatement is deemed a variation and is to be valued as such. Employer will bear excess and shortfall.) Produce documentary evidence as required by contractor. *Contractor* None needed.
			Insurance of the works against specified perils (existing structures)	
NA	6·3C	22C	Insurance of existing structures and contents in joint names against specified perils for full cost of reinstatement, repair or replacement.	*Employer* Arrange immediately for adequate cover (see previous action note). *Contractor* None needed.
			Insurance of the works against fire etc (existing structures)	
6·3B	NA	NA	Insurance in joint names against loss and damage by fire etc of existing structures and contents, and new works.	*Employer* Arrange immediately for adequate cover (see previous action note). *Contractor* None needed.
			Insurance against employer's loss of liquidated damages	
NA	6·3D	22D	Insurance to cover employer's loss of liquidated damages, where Appendix shows that it may be required.	*Employer* Instruct contractor through architect to obtain a quotation. Instruct on acceptance of quotation. *Contractor* When instructed by architect, obtain quotations. Arrange cover immediately if instructed to accept quotation. Send documentary evidence to architect for deposit with employer.

K CONSTRUCTION TO PRACTICAL COMPLETION
L: AFTER PRACTICAL COMPLETION

Administration of building contract up to and including Practical Completion.
Provision of further information to the contractor as and when reasonably required.
Administration of the building contract After Practical Completion.
Making final inspections and settling the final account
(RIBA Outline Plan of Work).

Description

Key obligations from SFA/99

Actions

Stage input
Preliminary issues   architect
                             client
                             management and team working
Inspections/tests
Contract
Cost planning
General procedures
Stage output

Core material

K-L/CM1	Keeping the client informed
K-L/CM2	Site meetings
K-L/CM3	Site inspections
K-L/CM4	Issuing instructions
K-L/CM5	Dealing with claims
K-L/CM6	Issuing certificates
K-L/CM7	Preparing for handover

CONSTRUCTION TO PRACTICAL COMPLETION AND AFTER PRACTICAL COMPLETION

Description

The extent of the architect's involvement as the person nominated to administer the building contract will depend on both the terms of the contract for professional services and the wording of the building contract.

The terms of the building contract bind only the parties themselves, i.e. the employer and the contractor. They do not place contractual obligations on the architect. Nevertheless, should the architect fail in the procedural duties set out, for example not issuing a certificate as required, this could constitute a breach of contract on the part of the employer against whom the contractor may be able to claim losses. It is therefore important that the architect's contract for professional services reflects accurately his or her role under the construction contract.

With traditional procurement, the contractor normally undertakes to carry out and complete the works in accordance with the contract, to proceed regularly and diligently, to complete by the agreed completion date and to comply with instructions empowered by the contract.

The client or employer normally undertakes to give the contractor possession in order to carry out the work; ensure all necessary information is made available to the contractor; appoint a contract administrator and pay all amounts properly certified or due under the contract.

With traditional procurement, the role of the contract administrator will vary considerably depending on the particular form used but the administrator would normally issue necessary information to the contractor, issue instructions empowered or required by the contract, issue certificates as required by the contract, and would be required to act in a fair and reasonable manner where impartial judgement is required by the contract.

There is normally no role for an impartial contract administrator with design and build procurement. The architect will therefore have no direct involvement in contract administration. Where acting for an employer client, consultancy advice might be needed, or an architect might be appointed as the employer's agent. Where acting for a contractor client, any involvement will not go beyond giving consultancy advice.

With management procurement there is usually the need for an independent contract administrator whose duties will normally include the issue of necessary information and instructions, and the issue of certificates. The obligations of the contractor will differ from those under traditional procurement and will be fully described in the contract.

Key obligations which may apply:

	Reference	To do
- from SFA/99: design services		
Make visits to the Works in connection with the architect's design.	SFA/99/K/1	☐
Provide further information reasonably required for construction.	SFA/99/K/2	☐
Review design information from contractor and specialists.	SFA/99/K/3	☐
Provide drawings for the Health and Safety File.	SFA/99/K/4	☐
Give general advice on operation and maintenance of the building.	SFA/99/K/5	☐

In addition to the above, the architect should note the obligations set out in the SFA/99 Conditions of Engagement 2.1-2.8.

- from SFA/99: management services

(i.e. architect acting as design leader and lead consultant)

Administer the terms of the building contract. ☐

Coordinate and monitor the work of consultants and site inspectors ☐
to the extent required for the administration of the building contract.

Report to the client as appropriate. ☐

Actions

Stage input

Check that all information necessary during Stage K–L is available, ☐
which might include the following:

- Coordinated Production Information: drawings, drawn schedules, priced Bills of Quantities/Specification/Schedules of Work.

- Contractor's Rates or Contract Sum Analysis if appropriate, and/ or priced Bills of Quantities/Specification/Schedules of Work.

- Specialists' tenders and 'numbered documents' ready for nomination instruction to be issued.

- Contractor's Master Programme.

- Copies of the construction phase Health and Safety Plan developed by the contractor and certified by the planning supervisor.

- Copies of method statements prepared by the contractor as required in the contract conditions.

- Information Release Schedule, or

- Schedule agreed with contractor indicating what further information is needed from the architect and by when, or

- Verification by the contractor, if applicable, that all necessary information has been supplied, and accepting that any further drawings will be his own responsibility.

- Sets of administration forms appropriate for the form of contract being used.

Preliminary issues – architect

Establish scope, content and context for Stage K–L activities. ☐
Put it into context, particularly if previous Stages were undertaken by others. If possible establish whether material produced now is likely to be acted upon by others taking over subsequent Stages.

If coming new to the project at this Stage in the *Plan of Work:* ☐

- Ascertain that the relevant Pre-Agreement and earlier Stage checks have been carried out.

- Allow for familiarisation and reviewing of all usable material when agreeing fees and timetable with the client.

- Confirm the role of the architect in relation to the rest of the consultant team.

Check the client's written instruction to proceed. ☐

Check the client has settled all accounts submitted to date. ☐

Check appointing documents with respect to services and fees. ☐

- If the services, cost or time targets are different from the Agreement with the client, agree a formal variation by letter or deed, as appropriate.

- If the extent of professional services for Stage K–L is not yet settled, agree with the client and confirm in writing.

Remember that the agreed services must reflect the role of architect under the form of building contract selected. Inform the client in advance if more frequent visits are required than those allowed for in the Agreement and which would incur additional expenditure.

Assess office resources needed for Stage K–L and ensure that they are adequate and available. ☐

Carry out checks for compliance with in-house quality management procedures, including updating project quality plan. ☐

Review the application of practice procedures to the project. ☐

Preliminary issues – client

Check with the client that the contract documents have been completed and signed as a simple contract or a deed as applicable. ☐

Check that the site or existing buildings have been given into the possession of the appointed contractor for the duration of the works. ☐

Remind the client of relevant statutory obligations under the CDM Regulations relating to the role of the planning supervisor and the competence of the principal contractor and other contractors' performance in health and safety matters. ☐

Advise the client of the employer's obligations under the building contract and of the role and duties of the architect in administering the building contract. ☐

Remind the client that all instructions to the main contractor must be channelled through the architect. ☐

Remind the client of the obligation to honour monetary certificates within the periods stated in the contract and of the procedure, should any deduction be anticipated, for example in respect of liquidated damages. ☐

Explain to the client the implications of Practical Completion. Advise the client, should partial possession be desired, about the contractual implications and procedures. ☐

Discuss with the client the need to appoint maintenance staff in time to attend the commissioning of the project, and to enter into maintenance agreements if relevant. ☐

Discuss with the client requirements for 'as built' information and maintenance manuals. ☐

Remind the client of the requirement for a Health and Safety File to be deposited in a safe place at the completion of the project. ☐

Preliminary issues – management and team working

Convene and chair site progress meetings or attend progress meetings chaired by the contractor. K-L/CM2 ☐

Keep accurate minutes of meetings and record discussions methodically. In assessing subsequent claims or allegations, these records may prove invaluable and more than justify the effort needed to maintain them.

Confirm that all instructions concerning specialist sub-contractors or suppliers are to be channeled through the architect. If acceptable, they will be included under an architect's instruction issued to the main contractor. ☐

Confirm that consultants are to supply relevant information for the preparation of operating instructions, maintenance manuals, record drawings of installation, etc. ☐

Check the designers' cooperation with the planning supervisor. ☐

Confirm that consultants are to pass relevant information to the planning supervisor for inclusion in the Health and Safety File. ☐

Confirm that consultants are to carry out detailed inspection of specialist work and report to the architect. If authorised, they should also attend commissioning, testing and witnessing, and report. ☐

Confirm with the client and QS procedures for valuation and certification. ☐

Confirm arrangements for reporting regularly to the client, and for providing regular financial reports. ☐

Inspections/tests

Confirm programme and procedures for the architect's site visits. **K-L/CM3** ☐

Brief site inspection staff, including the clerk of works if appointed, about their duties and the procedures to be followed. ☐

Visit the site as provided for in the Agreement with the client, whether for periodic checks, predictive checks or spot checks, to observe and comment on the contractor's site supervision and examples of work. ☐

Prepare an inspection plan which identifies when visits should be made, and when checks can be made on tests which the contractor is obliged to make under the contract. ☐

Keep methodical records of all site visits and results of all tests **Fig. K-L3**   ☐
witnessed or reported.

Allow adequate time on site to carry out checks properly. Make care-
ful notes and compile a systematic record of visits. It helps to pre-
pare checklists relating to the stage of the work.

Check that work is being executed generally in accordance with the   ☐
provisions of the building contract, in a proper and workmanlike manner and in accordance with the Health and Safety Plan. Inspect the
contractor's progress measured against the master programme, and
generally inspect goods and materials delivered to the site.

Check the contractor's quality management performance measured   ☐
against the plan submitted in the contractor's method statement.

Contract

Provide the contractor with copies of contract documents as required   ☐
under the contract.

Meet the contractor on site to note setting out, including boundaries,   ☐
fencing and hoardings, site huts, amenities and welfare arrangements, protective measures, spoil heaps, etc to establish compliance
with contractor's method statements and contract requirements.

Administer the contract in accordance with the procedural rules and
the conditions, acting fairly and impartially between the parties.

It is essential to acquire a good knowledge and understanding of all
the contract documents. Keep a copy to hand at all times.

Issue architect's instructions, discretionary or obligatory as empow-   ☐
ered under the contract, and in accordance with the contract provisions:

- All instructions to the contractor should be in writing. It is good
  practice to issue them on an architect's instruction form (not via
  correspondence or site meeting minutes).

- Only empowered instructions should be issued. Keep the wording
  concise and unambiguous.

- Confirm oral instructions as soon as necessary to avoid
  difficulties and to ensure that cost appraisals are realistic.

Provide information as set out on the Information Release Schedule, or provide additional necessary information to the contractor as required under the contract provisions.

☐

It is important to ensure that there is no reasonably necessary information outstanding, general or specific. Watch the contractor's programme and progress for indicated dates and signs.

Deal with claims as empowered under the terms of the contract. **K-L/CM5**

☐

Variations should be pre-priced if possible; otherwise the likely full **K-L/CM5** *implications should be estimated and agreed before action is taken. It may be that negotiation is the best way forward, but do not exceed your authority. Do not be overawed by the volume of documents sometimes presented by claims consultants — quantity does not equate with the validity of a case.*

Be careful of claims regarding matters not dealt with under the express terms of the contract. The architect has no power to settle these, which must be dealt with between the parties.

Issue instructions with respect to provisional sums, and appointment **K-L/CM4** of specialist sub-contractors, etc.

☐

If possible, nominated or named sub-contractors should be appointed at the commencement of the contract, always strictly in accordance with stipulated procedures. Note the sub-contract dates for compatibility with the main contractor's programme.

Issue certificates as empowered and required in accordance with the **K-L/CM6** contract procedures. Request vouchers from the contractor as empowered under the contract.

☐

Be punctilious about valuations and certificates for payment. Notify the QS in writing of any work not properly carried out, so that such work is not included in any valuation. Alert the client to any rights to make a deduction from the amount certified, and the procedures involved.

Review Health and Safety File information at regular intervals.

☐

Maintain 'as built' records or drawings, as required under the contract provisions and pass relevant information to the planning supervisor for possible incorporation in the Health and Safety File.

☐

Check that the clerk of works and consultants maintain adequate records and pass relevant information to the planning supervisor for possible incorporation in the Health and Safety File. ☐

Obtain contractor's forecast date for Practical Completion and advise **K-L/CM7** the client of the procedures. ☐

Remind the client of his responsibility for the building in terms of insurance, security and maintenance in good time. ☐

Initiate pre-completion checks on the works with the clerk of works and make records of outstanding items. ☐

Any lists are for the benefit of the design team and the client, and not normally for issue to the contractor. Under JCT traditional forms quality control on site, snagging, etc, is entirely the responsibility of the contractor.

When completion is near, make sure that the contractor is fully aware that commissioning must be completed and operating manuals available before the building is handed over. ☐

Check that commissioning, testing and witnessing of engineering services is carried out according to the provisions of the contract. ☐

Check that information relating to the Health and Safety File, maintenance manuals and operating instructions, is complete and ready for handing over to the planning supervisor. ☐

Make sure that operating manuals have been properly checked and are ready by the time of handover.

Cooperate with the planning supervisor, who will want to make sure that the Health and Safety File has been compiled and is ready at the time of handover.

Issue certificate of practical completion in accordance with the provisions of the contract. ☐

Certify Practical Completion only when, in your opinion, this state has been attained. Be very wary of pressure from the contractor or client to certify Practical Completion early – the consequences can be serious for all concerned.

Hold a formal handover meeting, if terms of appointment or contract require it. ☐

Prepare a list or schedule of defects to be made good at the end of the defects liability period, in accordance with the provisions of the contract. Issue to the contractor within the period stated in the contract. ☐

Check for application of CDM Regulations to remedial works and report ☐

Check with the planning supervisor that an updated Health and Safety File is given to the client. ☐

Carry out final inspection of the works and issue a certificate of making good defects. ☐

Issue the final certificate but only when all the requirements of the contract provisions have been satisfied. ☐

Do not certify completion of the making good of defects or issue a final certificate until you are sure that there are no matters still outstanding.

Cost planning

Liaise with the QS to monitor costs arising from architect's instructions, and for forecasting monthly reports. ☐

Provide the client with estimates of costs arising from architect's instructions, including variations. ☐

Notify the QS of any work against which monies must be withheld or where 'an appropriate deduction' is to be made from the contract sum. ☐

Liaise generally with the QS over remeasurement, valuations and the issue of monetary certificates, and applications for direct loss and/or expense. ☐

Deal with applications for reimbursement of direct loss and/or expense fairly and promptly. ☐

Report to the client on cost matters at agreed intervals. ☐

General procedures

Regularly check progress against the timetable for services. ☐

Continue resource control procedures for job: ☐

- Check expenditure against the office job cost allocation for Stage K.

- Monitor fee income against projected fee income.

- Report regularly to the client on fees and expenses incurred, and submit accounts at agreed intervals.

Check that the client settles all accounts promptly. ☐

Maintain accounts procedures for invoicing the contractor for copies of additional drawings and documents. ☐

Set up procedures to issue certificates and fee accounts regularly. Issue final certificate and final fee account only when all obligations are complete. ☐

Stage output

Tangible results/material produced before the conclusion of Stage K–L might include the following: ☐

- Information (drawn and written), decisions and instructions (obligatory or discretionary), as necessary for the contractor to perform his obligations under the contract, issued during the progress of the works.

- Valuations (on minor works) and certificates (monetary and otherwise), issued in accordance with the contract, during the progress of the works.

- Records of all correspondence, instructions and certificates, and 'state of the art' documents, whether from manufacturers or other sources, which should be retained in case there are later disputes.

- 'As built' drawings, manuals or other maintenance information required under the contract.

- Health and Safety File information, as required under the CDM Regulations.

- Final certificate, to be issued only when all outstanding contractual obligations are performed.

- Programmes for maintenance, if required.

References and further reading

Cox, S. (ed.) (2000) *Architect's Guide to the Contract Administration Forms JCT98*, London, RIBA Publications.

Cox, S. (ed.) (2000) *Architect's Guide to the Contract Administration Forms IFC98*, London, RIBA Publications.

Cox, S. (ed.) (2000) *Architect's Guide to the Contract Administration Forms MW98*, London, RIBA Publications.

Lupton, S. (1999) *Guide to JCT98*, London, RIBA Publications.

Lupton, S. (1999) *Guide to MW98*, London, RIBA Publications.

Lupton, S. (2001) *Guide to IFC98*, London, RIBA Publications.

K-L/CM1

Keeping the client informed

The client will expect to be kept informed about the progress of work and given a regular report on the financial situation. Any material changes in design or construction will need prior approval.

How this is best handled will depend on the size of the job, the client's own organisation and the stipulated procedures for the project team. A few clients might prefer to leave matters almost entirely in the hands of the architect but the majority will expect formal reports at regular intervals. Some clients will expect to be directly represented at site progress meetings. Matters to be kept in mind include the following:

Time

The client will need to be kept informed about programme and progress. This information will be available through minutes of site progress meetings (issued by the architect), copies of correspondence relating to notices of delay, and the award of any extensions of time. It is particularly important that the client is kept informed about any anticipated change to the completion date, as this will have managerial and financial implications for the client.

Quality

The client will need to be kept informed about any problems concerning materials and workmanship where it becomes necessary to issue architect's instructions. The client should also be advised in good time about such matters as regular maintenance and the need to appoint or instruct staff about installation requirements, control and maintenance of systems. It might also be necessary for the client to take out maintenance contracts for certain installations.

Cost

The client should receive detailed statements of expenditure at regular intervals, with an appraisal of the current position and a forecast of total costs. The client must agree any extra expenditure in advance, whether this is for unavoidable adjustments in design or modifications requested by the client or an adjustment because of provisional sums expenditure. Where possible, it is good policy to have variations costed before the instruction is implemented. Cost reports will normally be prepared by the QS, but where no QS has been appointed (e.g. on minor works) then these might have to be prepared by the architect. For a typical financial report to client, see Fig. K-L1

Fig. K-L1   Specimen financial report to client

Job no: Job title:

Financial report to client

To end of (month)	(year)	Savings £	Extras £	£
Financial approvals	Contract sum as adjusted			
	Additional approvals to date of last report			
	Total approvals to date of last report			
Adjustments	Contract sum as adjusted including contingencies			
	Cost adjustment on PC sums ordered			
	Cost adjustment on provisional sums			
	Value of AIs issued to date			
	Changes of work anticipated			
Contingencies	Original contingencies sum £			
	Estimated proportion £ absorbed to date			
	Estimated remainder £			
Cost of works	Estimated cost of works £ including contingencies sum			
Reconciliation	Variations instructed by the employer since last report			
	(a) [addition] estimated cost			
	(b) [omission] estimated saving			
	Additional approvals to last report			
Final estimate	Estimated final expenditure on present information			
	Not included in assessments: VAT, fees, other works (eg piling, landscape, advance orders)			

K-L/CM2

Site meetings

The usual procedure is for the architect to arrange and chair site progress meetings, and for the contractor to arrange and chair production meetings. In addition, the architect will call and chair special meetings including additional consultant team meetings for as long as the project requires this. There are also site inspections by the architect, which may or may not be formal and which may take place the same day as the site progress meeting.

As a general rule meetings should only be called for a clear purpose and should only involve those persons necessary for the successful conduct of the business. All meetings should be properly convened with a precise agenda issued in advance and be chaired in a firm and fair manner. All decisions should be clearly minuted.

Architect's site progress meetings

These are essentially policy meetings and should take place at regular intervals (e.g. the first Tuesday in the month). It is sometimes helpful if they are immediately preceded by site visits but the two should be kept distinct as they serve an entirely different purpose. The main business of the meetings will be to receive reports and to agree action necessary as a result. They are not the place to answer routine queries or provide general information. All the people who attend these meetings should have the authority to act.

A standard agenda of items should be maintained, and it is useful to include an 'Action' column. Minutes are normally issued by the architect — although this is sometimes done by the contractor, the architect should be alert to the fact that instructions contained in minutes prepared by the contractor or other person may not carry the same legal effect. Minutes should be issued soon after the meeting to all those named on the agreed distribution list. It is sensible to require that any dissent from the minutes is made in writing with seven days of issue. For a specimen agenda, see Fig. K-L2.

Meetings for special purposes

Even with meetings called ad hoc for some special purpose there should still be an agenda and a formal minute of decisions taken. Meetings might be needed for various reasons, for example, with representatives of adjoining owners, or statutory bodies. It might also be necessary to convene further consultant team meetings during work on site and as long as they are needed a consistent agenda and format should be maintained. Such business should not be merged with the architect's site progress meetings.

Contractor's production meetings

These are technical meetings with the sub-contractors and are arranged by the contractor to take place before the architect's progress meetings. The architect may be asked to attend; if so, he or she should make a note of any decisions and act appropriately. The contractor should prepare and distribute the minutes.

Site inspections

These are visits by the architect to observe and comment on the contractor's site supervision and examples of work at intervals appropriate to the stage of construction. This is periodic inspection, which should be carried out to the extent determined by the nature of the work, and as agreed with the client in the appointing document. If more frequent visits or constant inspection are required, then the client should be recommended to appoint a clerk of works or other resident site inspector.

Fig. K-L2   Specimen agenda for architect's site progress meeting

	ACTION
1 Minutes of last meeting	
2 Contractor's report	
• General report	
• Sub-contractor's meeting report	
• Progress and programme	
• Causes of delay	
• Health and Safety matters	
• Information received since last meeting	
• Information and drawings required	
• Architect's instructions required	
3 Clerk of works' report	
• Site matters	
• Quality control monitoring	
• Lost time	
• Tests observed and verified	
4 Consultants' reports	
• Structural works	
• Mechanical works	
• Electrical works	
5 Quantity surveyor's report	
6 Communications and procedures	
7 Contract completion date	
• Likely delays and their effect	
• Review of factors from previous meeting	
• Factors for review at next meeting	
• Revision to completion date	
• Revisions required to programme	
8 Any other business	
9 Date of next meeting	

K-L/CM3

Site inspections

The purpose of these visits, whether to the site of the works or to places off site where work is being prepared, is simply to observe and comment. It should not be termed or thought of as 'supervision', because this suggests the authority to issue instructions to operatives, which clearly an architect does not possess.

Visits may be on a periodic basis (e.g. at fortnightly intervals) or on a predictive basis (e.g. programmed to match certain stages or operations on site) or as spot checks made without prior warning. It will be for the architect to decide the most appropriate course to adopt, subject to the arrangement with the client.

Visits should have a specific purpose and they require preparation beforehand. This might mean devising a plan after studying the most recent reports and minutes of meetings. The architect will then visit the site with the purpose of observing particular parts or items and of checking that specified tests are being carried out and verified. Checks of a general nature might include:

- whether quality complies generally with the provisions of the contract;
- whether progress accords with the contractor's master programme;
- whether essential parts of the design have been/are being carried out in accordance with the contract provisions.

Such visits should be carried out carefully, and comments systematically noted. Where certificates refer to work, etc 'properly executed', it is helpful to have a record of notes made at the time of a visit. Queries are often raised during site visits, and it may be prudent to reserve answers until returning to the office. Any decisions made or information given while on site should be confirmed in writing as soon as possible.

Reports of site visits should be prepared to a consistent format as soon after the visit as possible. Record photographs (dated), notes and sketches should be attached and carefully filed. These should be retained strictly for in-house use. Fig. K-L3 is a specimen site visit report form.

Fig. K-L3   Specimen report form for predictive site visits

Job no: _____

Job title: _____

Site visit report

Date _____

No. of visits scheduled _____

Visit by _____

Visit no. _____

Purpose

_____

_____

_____

_____

_____

_____

_____

_____

_____

Observed

_____

_____

_____

_____

_____

_____

_____

_____

_____

_____

_____

_____

_____

_____

_____

_____

Checked

Samples _____

Verification of tests _____

Vouchers _____

Records _____

Recorded

Photos _____

_____

Video _____

Other _____

Summary

☐ Work properly executed

☐ Materials properly stored and protected

☐ Proceeding in workmanlike manner

☐ Progress to programme

K-L/CM4

Issuing instructions

Under most building contracts the only person authorised to issue instructions to the contractor will be the contract administrator. It is sensible to establish at the start of the job what constitutes an 'architect's instruction', and it is suggested that only written instructions issued on a standard form should be regarded as valid. The giving of oral instructions, using contractors' site instruction books, or taking the minutes of site meetings as instructions should all be avoided.

The particular form of contract used will state what powers are given to the contract administrator with regard to instructions, and only empowered instructions will bind the contractor. When issuing an instruction it is advisable to check the following:

- that it is empowered under the contract, and the relevant clause number can be cited;
- that the identifying details are entered on the form (e.g. name of project, contractor, date of instruction, serial number, etc);
- that the instructions are precisely worded and their meaning unambiguous;
- that the instruction is signed by the authorised person.

A file copy will be retained, and it is also good practice to keep a record of AIs issued for the project. See Figs. K-L4 and 5 for specimen forms.

Fig. K-L4   Specimen record form of architect's instructions issued

Job no: _____   Job title: _____

Architect's Instructions issued

Date	AI no.		Item	Subject (including relevant item/drawing no.)	Estimated +/- cost (£)
	1		Gas main	Quotation ref 8438/63	+ 150
	2		Cills	Revised detail drwg. L.51/03	− 75
	3		Opening	First floor. revised. drwg. L.51/12	+ 100
	4	(1)	Hip tiles	omit Farcand / add Red Bank	+ 142
		(2)	Hip irons	omit / add finials	

1. Use an AI for all instructions and notifications to the contractor.
2. List all individual items in any AI.
3. Make sure all instructions are clearly worded and unambiguous.
4. Do not reserve numbers for future issue; do not miss out any numbers. If any error in numbering is found, immediately notify everyone on the distribution list.

Fig. K-L5   Specimen record form of site delays observed

Job no: _____   Job title: _____

Record of site delays observed

Date	Delay	Item	Reason	Observed by
6.1.95	1 week	Site clearance	Plant hire equipment late	C of W
17.1.95	1 week	Weather	Heavy snow	C of W
23.2.95	3 days	Foundations	Excavations waterlogged	C of W
10.4.95	2 days	Steelwork	Erectors arrived. Problem with crane jib. Left site.	HRJ

1. Record observations in sequence of work element/location, conditions or situation and note the source of information where relevant.
2. Liaise closely with clerk of works and consultants.
3. Check against and coordinate with your site inspection reports.

K-L/CM5

Dealing with claims

Although the word is frequently used, 'claim' is something of a misnomer as far as contract administration is concerned. The architect has the authority to act where the contract conditions expressly provide for entitlement in certain events, particularly concerning extensions of time and reimbursement of loss and expense.

Claims not expressly within the contract provisions or where, for various reasons, a contractor has elected not to follow the procedures or is unable to conform to the express terms, would be 'ex-contractual' claims to be pursued in arbitration or litigation.

Extensions of time

Most construction contracts include a mechanism for dealing in a convenient way with events which might affect progress, which are beyond the control of the contractor, and which were not foreseeable at the time of tender. For this to be operable there must be a clearly stated date for possession or commencement, and a date for completion. There is usually an extension of time provision and a separate provision for dealing with additional costs which might arise.

Extensions of time provisions benefit the contractor in that he or she is relieved of paying liquidated damages for failure to complete because of stated reasons. The express terms are also very much in the client's interests by keeping alive the right to liquidated damages even though the contract period is extended because of the client's intervention. It is, of course, essential that such intervention is included as an event covered in the contract conditions, and that the architect operates the extensions of time provisions strictly in accordance with the contract requirements.

When dealing with extensions of time, remember the following:

- Respond to each and every proper notice of delay from the contractor — at least it is evidence that the claim has been considered.
- When awarding extensions of time, do so only for the causes specified in the contract. State the causes but do not apportion. Keep full records in case the award is contested.
- Comply strictly with the procedural rules. For example, if the contract requires it, notify every nominated sub-contractor of a decision.
- Observe the timescale if one is stated in the contract. If none is stated, act within a reasonable time.
- Form an opinion which is fair and reasonable in the light of the information available at the time.

Loss and/or expense applications

Monetary claims arising in the context of building contracts are usually made as a result of loss due to regular progress being affected or because of additional costs due to a prolongation of the time on site. The wording in the contract usually identifies events or matters which are recognised as causes. There may be procedures to be followed which exist for the convenience of both parties. It is only these types of claims which the architect administering the contract has the authority to settle.

For an application to be valid:

- the loss and/or expense must be a direct actual loss;
- the works (or a part) must be materially affected;
- interference or disturbance to regular planned progress must have occurred;
- reimbursement must not be possible under any other contractual provision.

The architect has a duty to decide whether the claim is valid and, if information supplied is not adequate, additional reasonably necessary information must be requested.

Ascertainment of the amount claimed can rest with the architect but normally the contract allows specifically for this function to be referred to the QS.

When dealing with applications for reimbursement, remember the following:

- The object of these provisions is to put the contractor back into the position he or she would have been but for the disruption. It is not an opportunity to profit.
- The contractor must make written application at the proper time.
- The architect must form an opinion about whether direct loss and/or expense has been incurred or is likely to be incurred, and that regular progress has been materially affected.
- The burden of proof rests with the contractor. If the notice is not sufficient, more information must be requested.
- Ascertainment is a matter of certainty and not approximation. Particularisation of claims, i.e. 'actual' figures relating to specific items, should be expected.

The importance of keeping good records cannot be emphasised enough.

It is recommended that a record should be kept of site delays observed or noted from reports; defective work observed which might relate to subsequent applications when instructions are issued; a schedule of 'claims' submitted by the contractor which need to be noted and acted upon. For specimen record forms, see Figs. K-L5, K-L6, and K-L7. Fig. K-L8 is a specimen letter in reply to a contractor 'claiming' loss and expense without following the contract procedures.

Fig. K-L6   Specimen record form of defective work

Job no: Job title:

Record of defective work

Date	Item	Contractor notified	Value if deducted	Cleared
		Date	£	Date
1.8.95	Priming to some steelwork unsatisfactory	2.8.95		2.9.95
16.9.95	Nosing to boiler house steps not satisfactory. Shuttering poor	16.9.95		12.10.95

1. Describe the work in sequence of work element/location: condition as rejected: rectification required.
2. Check and update this record regularly with clerk of works and consultants.
3. Notify QS of any values deducted against valuations made and when items are cleared.
4. Check against and coordinate with your site inspection reports.

Fig. K-L7   Specimen record form of claims by contractor

Job no: Job title:

Schedule of claims by contractor

Date received	Clause no.	Subject of claim	Time/amount: Req'std	Allowed	Date for decision	Date awarded
25.2.95	25	Weather - notice of delay inadequate - more detailed information requested				
		AI No. 1				
	25	Gas main	4 days	2 days		
	26	Consequential loss/expense				

1. Check that contractor uses procedures laid down in the contract.
2. Inform QS, consultants, clerk of works immediately any claim is notified.
3. List adequate description and if necessary open a sub-file to collate the correspondence etc about each claim.
4. Check that your action complies with the time limits stated in the contract.

Fig. K-L8   Specimen letter in reply to a contractor's unsubstantiated claim

Thank you for your notification that the regular progress of the work has been materially affected and that this may give rise to an application for the reimbursement of direct loss and expense under Clause 26 of JCT 98.

Would you please state which of the list of matters you consider apply in this instance, and forward such information that you consider will reasonably enable us to form an opinion, including your reasons as to why you cannot recover the cost under any other condition.

Should we be of the opinion that the delay is covered by Clause 26 you will, of course, be required to provide [the quantity surveyor with] such details as are reasonably necessary to ascertain the direct loss and/or expense.

K-L/CM6

Issuing certificates

Contracts generally provide for the issue of certificates by the contract administrator. The issue will normally be an obligation, always subject to certain conditions being satisfied. A certificate is simply a statement of fact and although a letter might constitute a certificate, it is advisable to establish at the beginning of the job that valid certificates will be those issued on a standard form.

Certificates commonly provided for in a contract may include the following:

Interim certificate

This is for payment to the contractor of an instalment of the contract sum. It might be on a monthly valuation (although the architect when certifying must use skill and care, and not blindly follow the QS's valuation), on a stage or milestone basis as agreed by the parties and in accordance with the contract conditions.

Certificate of non-completion

A factual statement, upon which much may depend, e.g. the deduction of liquidated damages by the employer, or the right to deduct damages by a main contractor against a nominated sub-contractor, etc.

Certificate of practical completion

A statement which expresses that the works have reached practical completion. The contractor is relieved from various obligations henceforth.

Certificate of making good defects

Issued only when those defects listed at the close of the defects liability period have been remedied.

Final certificate

Issue of the final certificate brings the authority of the contract administrator, under the terms of the building contract, to a close. The contractor's liability continues, of course, until the end of the limitation period.

There might, in addition or alternatively, be contract provisions which refer to Statements issued by the contract administrator or by the employer (e.g. in the case of design and build contracts). These should be regarded as requiring the same care and consideration before being issued as certificates. Recent case law has confirmed that there is no immunity from negligence in certifying.

K-L/CM7

Preparing for handover

Although not usually referred to in building contracts, the process of completion and handing over the building should nevertheless be subject to careful planning and procedures. It is suggested that these should comprise:
* final commissioning, testing and witnessing of services installations;
* pre-completion checks by the contract administrator;
* preparation for the formal handing over;
* issue of the practical completion certificate;
* the formal handover meeting.

Normally the contract administrator can expect to be advised by the contractor when the works are approaching Practical Completion. Sometimes this indication is premature. Sometimes the client will pressure the contract administrator to certify prematurely. The contract administrator should act strictly in accordance with the conditions of the contract. The parties are free to agree an expedient arrangement outside the contract terms if they so wish.

Final commissioning, testing and witnessing of services installation

Commissioning is the process whereby static completion of an installation is brought to the state of full working order for proving. Testing is a matter of checking a commissioned installation and evaluating its performance measured against specified requirements. Commissioning and testing are operations which, on a sophisticated project, might need to be carried out by specialists, will need to be effectively managed, and should be subject to a commissioning specification and system for commissioning. They might also need to be phased, and although the installations will need to be commissioned before handover, some adjustment and testing might not be possible until after installations have been in use for a certain period.

Almost every project includes a services installation, and proper thought is needed at the outset concerning design, installation, inspection and arrangements for commissioning and testing. Many larger client bodies expect particular codes to be observed and stated procedures to be followed. The Chartered Institution of Building Services Engineers publishes a series of Commissioning Codes which clearly itemise the checks necessary for various installations. The Building Services Research and Information Association publishes a guide to operating and maintenance manuals for building services installations. Reference to appropriate documents such as these will normally be made when specifying methods of commissioning.

Tender documents should clearly state the level of commissioning and testing which will be required, both before handover and additionally, perhaps, with a defects liability period of appropriate duration. Thought should also be given to the need for incorporating special conditions of contract because most standard forms do not make specific reference to such matters.

Where services installations are of a complex nature, it is likely that consultants and specialist firms will be involved, and expert commissioning engineers might need to be brought in. Nevertheless, the main contractor still has the responsibility for overall programming, and for ensuring that the works are finished by the contract completion date. This will usually necessitate commissioning, testing, and the preparation of operating or maintenance manuals before handover. Sometimes difficulties arise where these latter operations are not allocated sufficient time, or where the costs entailed have not been fully covered in the contract sum.

A common difficulty is the precise definition of responsibilities. Architects will obviously have a responsibility to see that requirements are properly included for and stated at the outset.

Manufacturers will also have a responsibility, particularly where use of particular components is specified. Inspection of services installations as work proceeds may be largely in the hands of consultants and sub-contractors, although the main contractor will ultimately remain responsible for all matters of workmanship and materials. Whilst architects will have a duty to see what appropriate arrangements are made for commissioning and testing, responsibility for carrying out such operations should clearly lie with others.

The following checklist is based on guidance published in *RIBA Practice*, issue 78, September 1991.

Pre-completion checks by the contract administrator

Pre-completion checks
- Warn the contractor to make sure that the building is ready for inspection well before the date of practical completion.
- Instruct the clerk of works to maintain systematic preliminary inspections and to keep the architect informed of progress and any difficulties likely to arise as well as defects discovered.
- Consolidate a schedule of outstanding items from:
  - the architect's progress meeting minutes
  - the consultants' reports
  - the clerk of works' reports
  - the architect's instructions
  - site visit notes.

Note: these lists are for communication between the consultants and for the architect's own records. They should not be issued to the contractor as quality control is the contractor's responsibility and the architect should not be drawn in to taking on this role.

- If necessary, inform the contractor that the works are not complete according to the contract, and indicate general areas of concern.
- Remind contractor to complete record drawings, etc according to the agreed programme.

Inspection and commissioning
- In collaboration with consultants, advise the contractor and all sub-contractors to coordinate a programme of checks.
- Instruct the clerk of works accordingly and ensure he or she checks that defective work has been replaced and reports any delays anticipated, where relevant asking the client's staff to attend inspections and checks.
- Ask the consultants to make detailed inspections and to report back.
- Check that the associated contractors' works are completed.
- Remind sub-contractors to complete record drawings, etc and to prepare maintenance instructions as agreed.
- Make formal arrangements with the client for handover inspections.

Preparation for the formal handover

Before the meeting
- Remind the client of the reasonable standards which are appropriate to the class of work specified. It is the architect's responsibility to certify.
- Inform the client's representative of the basis of the contract (if he has not been personally involved from the start).
- Write to the contractor and all those who are to attend the meeting to let them know the time, date and venue.

Inspecting the buildings and site
- Hold meeting(s) for inspection and handover.
- Check that the following are ready to hand over as required:
  - building owner's operating manual
  - keys
  - as built drawings
  - details of maintenance arrangements
  - Health and Safety File.
- Outline the client's and contractor's responsibilities during the defects liability period.
- Outline arrangements for dealing with any future defects.
- Agree any additional works required by the client.

Additional works (if necessary)
- Liaise with the QS and contractor to negotiate the basis for pricing.
- Prepare drawings and instructions and obtain the client's approval of these and the related costs.
- Instruct the contractor to proceed (by means of an extension of the contract, or a separate agreed instruction).
- Check that these are covered by the construction phase Health and Safety Plan.

Issue of the practical completion certificate

There may be a number of 'completion certificates' which the contract administrator is obliged to issue. For example:
- Statement of partial possession (where practical completion is deemed to have occurred).
- Practical completion for sectional completion.
- Practical completion for nominated subcontract works.
- Practical completion of 'the Works'.

It is the latter which triggers off a sequence of events, namely:
- the contractor's liability for damage to the completed works is ended;
- the contractor's liability for any further liquidated damages is ended;
- the contractor's liability for insurance of the works is ended;
- the contractor's liability for damage to the works as a result of frost is ended;
- half the retention money is usually released to the contractor.

The practical completion certificate is issued only when in the opinion of the contract administrator (or other person referred to expressly in the contract) the works have reached a state of practical completion.

The formal handover meeting

The arrangements listed will be relevant in nearly all cases, including where there is sectional completion or partial possession.

Record attendance, date, etc.

Define purpose of meeting:
- Explain that inspections of building and site are to establish agreement that work is ready to hand over to the client for occupation.
- Note defects due to faulty workmanship or materials and issue instructions to the contractor to rectify them, immediately if appropriate.
- Ensure that all the contractor's plant and property have been removed from site.

Tour of inspection
- Inspect building(s) and site.

Handover of building
The client accepts the building and site from the contractor, and the contractor hands over the keys.
- Ensure that meters have been read and fuel stocks noted.

Maintenance manuals, servicing contracts, etc.
- Confirm with the planning supervisor the contents of the Health and Safety File, and arrangements for delivering it to the client.
- Hand over any further building maintenance information as relevant, including:
  - directory
  - servicing contracts
  - maintenance of plant
  - maintenance of building
  - attention to landscape and planting
  - routine replacement schedules
  - record or as built drawings as applicable.

Post completion

Defects liability
Once Practical Completion is reached, the defects liability period starts to run. Under this convenient contractual arrangement the employer may give the contractor an opportunity to rectify certain defects which have arisen, at the contractor's own cost. Defects will not include damage inflicted during this period, nor should defects liability be confused with maintenance.

On Practical Completion the architect should:
- fix the date for the defects liability inspection;
- advise the employer to list any defects as they become apparent, and notify immediately those defects which should receive attention during the defects liability period;
- prepare a draft schedule of defects (see Fig. K-L9) as a checklist for the defects liability inspection;
- carry out an inspection at the end of the defects liability period accompanied by the employer, contractor and clerk of works, if available;
- complete a schedule of defects and deliver it to the contractor within 14 days of the expiry of the defects liability period;
- arrange for a programme of remedial work, with the agreement of the employer and contractor;
- determine whether remedial work is subject to compliance with CDM Regulations and advise the contractor accordingly;
- carry out a final inspection after defects have been remedied;
- issue a certificate that defects have been made good when satisfied.

Fig. K-L9   Specimen record form of defects reported after practical completion

Job no: _____   Job title: _____

Defects reported after practical completion

Date reported	Location of defect	Description	Health and Safety implications

The final account

Final adjustments to the contract sum should be made in accordance with the conditions of the contract, and to the timescale and procedures stated. Deductions and additions as necessary will result in the sum for the final account. Where the sum is agreed with the contractor, subject to any provisos expressed in the contract, preparations can be made to issue the final certificate. Where the sum is not agreed by the contractor, if the architect and QS are in agreement over the figure, it may, nonetheless, be necessary to inform the employer and proceed with the issue of the final certificate.

The architect should:
- review the progress of the final account each month with the QS, checking on outstanding items;
- estimate the date for completing the final account after consulting the QS and consultants;
- obtain from the QS a statement of outstanding claims from the contractor and sub-contractors and their financial implications, if necessary calling a meeting with the QS and contractor to resolve them;
- resolve specialists' outstanding claims at a meeting with consultants if necessary;
- keep the client informed of the progress of the final account and any significant cost adjustments arising from claims;
- report the value of the final account to the client when the QS sends it to the contractor for final agreement;
- start procedures for issuing the final certificate when it is agreed;
- if necessary, and only if authorised by the client, arrange for separate accounts for works ordered After Practical Completion.

The final certificate

The final certificate effectively terminates the opportunity for any further discussion and brings the authority and power of the contract administrator under the contract to an end.

Either party will be able to challenge the certificate to the extent and subject to the timescale expressed in the contract conditions.

The contractor's obligations under the contract are at an end, although the contractor will still be liable for the duration of the limitation period applicable.

The architect should:
- check that the final inspection with consultants has been carried out, that all defects have been made good to the architect's satisfaction, and that a certificate of making good has been issued;
- arrange for the release of the remainder of the retention monies, where relevant;
- write to the contractor to return drawings and other documents, where relevant;
- receive the final account and final valuation from the QS, referring it to the local authority or other official or auditor, as required;
- issue the final certificate in accordance with the contract conditions;
- agree with the client which documents he or she wishes to retain.

M: FEEDBACK

Description

Actions

General procedures
Preliminary issues   client
Stage output

Core material

M/CM1	Keeping office records
M/CM2	In-house appraisal
M/CM3	Debriefing
M/CM4	Post-project evaluation

FEEDBACK

Description

A Stage M Feedback was shown in the RIBA's *Plan of Work* as printed in the 1967 issue of *the Handbook of Architectural Practice and Management*. It is not now listed in *the Architect's Plan of Work*, nor is it referred to in current standard appointing documents.

On completion of a project there will always be the need to assemble documents for retention, and to compile records. This is an activity appropriate to nearly all projects. A study of such material could lead to an updating of the office systems to take account of lessons learned. There are then three levels at which further post-completion studies may be carried out.

First, there can be an investigation or appraisal restricted to an in-house operation. Second, there may be a debriefing exercise which could involve other people concerned with the project, and this could commence shortly after completion. Third, there could be a full post-project evaluation but this is unlikely to be possible until several years after completion.

Both in-house appraisals and debriefing are exercises not normally listed in the services provided by the architect and are unlikely to be funded by the client. However, they can provide useful lessons for the members of both the design and the construction teams.

A full feedback study can be costly and if the client wishes this to be undertaken, it will probably have to be the subject of a separate commission. With partnering arrangements it is likely to be an essential part of assessing whatever targets have been met. The CIB report *Briefing the Team* points out that full post-project evaluations can be particularly useful to clients who construct more than once, in order to improve the briefing they provide for future projects. However, it is a sensitive area and confrontation should be avoided at all costs. It will not therefore be a productive exercise in all cases and great care needs to be taken in deciding whether or not it will be worthwhile for a particular project. The architect's professional indemnity insurers should be informed before a full feedback study is undertaken for the client.

Actions

	Reference	To do
General procedures		
Collate all documents issued to contractor and store.	**M/CM1**	☐
Collate 'state of the art' trade information, etc and store.		☐
Note: preparation of 'as built' drawings and maintenance manuals are included already under Stage K–L.		
Conduct in-house appraisal of office performance on project.	**M/CM2**	☐
Revise/update office quality plan, manual and procedures.		☐
Consider desirability of a debriefing exercise.	**M/CM3**	☐

Debriefing and feedback are management exercises. If it is agreed to extend the commission to include these, establish the scope and content of Stage M.

Do not allow an exercise to be undertaken if it seems likely that it might result in recriminations – and even arbitration or litigation. Always inform your professional indemnity insurers before embarking on any feedback study.

Check if the design and production teams would cooperate in debriefing. ☐

Check if the client would cooperate in debriefing. ☐

In-house appraisal is a healthy operation for nearly all projects but participants must feel able to exchange views freely. Debriefing can become a sensitive matter and will only succeed with the full cooperation of all involved.

Preliminary issues – client

Explain to the client the purpose of a de-briefing exercise or post-project evaluation debriefing or feedback might be an essential part of this activity. ☐

Discuss with the client to what extent key persons in the organisation could be expected to contribute opinions at a meeting chaired by the architect. ☐

Agree with the client body who from its organisation should be consulted, and with what objectives in mind. ☐

Discuss with the client to what extent the managers and users of the project could be expected to cooperate in completing a questionnaire. ☐

Discuss with the client whether authorised photographers would be allowed access after final completion, for feedback purposes. ☐

Discuss with the client whether it would be permissible for the architect to carry out a survey of the building in use some time after completion. ☐

If a full feedback study is planned, agree with the client what access will be available, what the timescale should be, and in what form the findings should be presented. ☐

The de-briefing exercise

Raise with all consultants the desirability of engaging in a systematic **M/CM3** analysis of the management, construction and performance of the project. ☐

Arrange a series of debriefing meetings. ☐

Convene debriefing meetings upon completion to evaluate technical matters, to involve all design team members, the main contractor and possibly the client. ☐

At debriefing meetings, watch out for partisan or defensive attitudes. Honest and objective discussion should not be allowed to degenerate into acrimony.

Record discussions. ☐

Formulate overall conclusions from debriefing. ☐

Circulate findings of debriefing as appropriate. ☐

Consider desirability of a full feedback study or post-project evaluation. **M/CM4** ☐

Stage output

Tangible results/material produced before the conclusion of Stage M might include the following as relevant: ☐

- Record of conclusions reached at debriefing meetings, distributed only to participants.

- Results of full feedback study conducted with client or user client, or everyday users of the building, perhaps several years post-completion.

It is essential that the benefits and lessons learned from appraisals are passed to all members of staff. The office quality plan, manuals and procedures might need amendment or revision as a result.

M/CM1

Keeping office records

Once a job is complete, a decision has to be made about which drawings and documents should be kept. No office has the space to keep all project records indefinitely.

A set of project records, properly maintained and completed, should be a useful condensed history of the project – a point of reference for quick comparison of working methods, timescales and costs. Photographs of the work in progress and as completed, presentation drawings and models should also be kept available for prospective clients and for general publicity purposes. However, it is essential to keep proper records of the kind of information that will be required in the event of disputes, in particular:

- the client brief and related correspondence;
- the contract documents;
- architect's instructions;
- minutes of project meetings;
- certificates issued;
- notes of inspections, surveys;
- any crucial state-of-the-art information (manufacturers' key information, current BSs, Codes, etc);
- progress charts, etc;
- selected working drawings.

It is important to remember that the personnel involved with the project may not be available to give evidence if litigation occurs some years later.

M/CM2

In-house appraisal

Appraise the project under the headings given in the following checklist:

1. Office costs
    Relate office costs to reserve and profit targets.

2. Performance of design team, site inspectorate in terms of:
    *   communications with client;
    *   communications between design team members;
    *   communications with planning supervisor;
    *   communications with contractor;
    *   design team programming;
    *   quality of drawings, specifications;
    *   cost planning, final costs against budget;
    *   quality control;
    *   energy effectiveness;
    *   meeting completion date(s), etc.

3. Contractor's performance in terms of:
    *   project management, quality of staff;
    *   site management, quality of staff;
    *   health and safety compliance;
    *   continuity of personnel;
    *   quality of work;
    *   effectiveness of programming;
    *   cooperation in settling claims;
    *   cooperation over material for Health and Safety File.

4. Working arrangements between design team and contractor in terms of:
    *   architect's progress meetings, actions on minutes;
    *   quality control;
    *   early identification of problems relating to progress, information and quality;
    *   potential disputes;
    *   financial arrangements, certificates, dayworks and measurement evaluation.

5. Completed works in terms of:
    *   resolution of the brief;
    *   relation to site and surroundings;
    *   quality of building, functional and abstract;
    *   incorporation of M & E services into structure;
    *   energy efficiency;
    *   wear and tear, maintenance.

6. Prepare reports:
    Include proposals for long term reviews; distribute, file as appropriate.

7. Complete project records:
    - collect all relevant project records and information;
    - collate material and keep available for quick reference and comparison with that of other completed jobs;
    - arrange photographs for record and/or promotional purposes.

M/CM3

Debriefing

Obtaining valuable lessons with the benefit of hindsight is unlikely to be an activity commissioned by most clients. For a few this might be a worthwhile exercise and for a truly objective report, impartial 'auditors' could be engaged.

Debriefing after completion is something which should happen in all major projects to some extent. A series of meetings convened by the architect who acted as lead consultant could achieve this, as follows:

* meetings between the architect and planning supervisor to evaluate matters related to compliance with the CDM Regulations;
* meetings between key design team members and the contractor to evaluate design and technical aspects of the project;
* meetings between the architect and contractor to evaluate the management of the construction of the project.

A frank exchange of views might be expected at meetings and the success of the operation will depend very much on the cooperation of all parties involved. Opinions on, for example, the overall timescale, the effectiveness of cost control, whether AIs including variations could have been avoided, whether drawings production and issue could have been improved, whether site reporting and quality control were effective, etc, might provide valuable lessons for future projects. Obviously the time spent on this kind of operation and the cost of meetings has to be weighed against the fact that the project is usually a 'once only' occurrence, and the particular team might never again be assembled.

M/CM4

Post-project evaluation

The more intensive investigations for Feedback, which might not be practicable until several years after completion of the project, could include structured interviews with the client's staff or with users, access to the buildings, access to information and records held by various team members.

Neither of these kinds of activities should be attempted if there is a risk of inviting acrimony and dispute.

The purpose of a post-project evaluation is to analyse the management, construction and performance of a project. This could entail:
- an analysis of the project records;
- an inspection of the fabric of the completed building;
- studies of the building in use;
- meetings and workshops with the client, consultants and users.

The CIB document *Briefing the Team* suggests that a post-project evaluation should cover:
- the purpose of the study;
- the description of the need;
- performance against cost, quality and timescale targets;
- client satisfaction with the project and the facility;
- user satisfaction with the facility;
- performance and communications between project participants
    - project sponsor
    - client project manager
    - where relevant, client advisor
    - project team;
- overview and recommendations
    - lessons learned
    - major points of action
    - costs;
- technical appendices
    - user survey data
    - monitoring data.

Further Reading

CIB (1997) *Briefing the Team,* London, HMSO.

INDEX

ARCHITECT'S JOB BOOK